Tina Miller has written one of '' read! There is not one of us who <crisis. Now there is a book that chr ____God" interventions that gives us hop ____d our self in. I highly recommend this ____who needs his or her hope strengthened, or knows so. ____who needs to get their hopes up! This book is a great resource for devotions, life groups, bible studies, sermons and studies on God's character and attributes. My prayer is that this book will ignite an unquenchable fire to get to know the Lord, our Bridegroom, and his calling and destiny for your life!

Dave Collins
Executive Administrator of Wagner Leadership Institute
Community Pastor at Cucamonga Christian Fellowship

Tina Miller has written a wonderful book that is biblically sound and a needed reminder of the greatness and goodness of our Father in heaven and His Son who knows everything about us and loves us unconditionally. May we demonstrate that same unconditional love to Him and to those around us with a confidence and faith that our Lord promises to meet all of our needs and will never leave us nor forsake us.

Dr. Richard Booker
Bible Teacher, Author of *The Miracle of the Scarlet Thread*

The **But God** Devotional is an amazing collection of experiences, testimonies, and wisdom purposefully gathered together to introduce you to the character of God and provides you with hope and healing when things around you are falling apart. I highly recommend you grab your Bible and discover God's love for you as you uncover His character in this *life-giving* devotional.

RJ Jackson, The Courage Giver
Speaker, Personal Wellness Coach,
Author of *His Grace- Amazing, Redeeming, Sufficient*

"But God." Two small words that are absolutely loaded with meaning. In this comprehensive study on the "But Gods" of the Bible, Tina Miller takes readers on an incredible journey into better understanding the transforming and redemptive nature of God. You'll love digging into this treasure chest that is overflowing with wisdom and encouragement from God's Word. Whatever situation you are facing, you can be sure there is a "But God" that will bring perspective and hope!

Cindy Powell
Blogger, Author of *The Key to His Heart*

Wow!!! The Holy Spirit has truly given Tina insight to the Characteristics of God, in BUT GOD devotional bible study . . . I love what Tina wrote, "Right now, we are in a time of engagement with Jesus. He wants us to engage with Him as we make ourselves ready for our wedding day." In this study the Holy Spirit will help you understand your Bridegroom better and make yourself ready for him. We read in Revelation 19:7, "Let us be glad and rejoice and give Him glory, for the marriage of the Lamb has come, and His wife has made herself ready." You will be blessed as you devote time to your bridegroom in this study!!!!

Dr. Patricia Venegas,
Founder/CEO Without Spot or Wrinkle Ministries

The powerful little phrase "But God" has long been one of my favorite concepts to linger over in Scripture. Just two little words bursting with huge spiritual impact. So you can image how excited I was when I saw the title of Tina's devotional study . . . "But God"! Trust me you will be blessed as you join Tina on an enlightening journey through Old Testament "But God" verses. Tina exquisitely weaves powerful "But God" moments together with the beautiful marriage imagery of Scripture to help us discover or perhaps rediscover the God of the Bible and His marvelous plan for an eternal love relationship with His beloved.

Martha Lawley
Speaker and Author of *Attending the Bride of Christ: Preparing for His Return*

But God

Getting to Know Your Bridegroom in the Old Testament

Tina Miller

WestBow
PRESS
A DIVISION OF THOMAS NELSON

Copyright © 2013 Tina Miller.

All rights reserved. No part of this book may be used or reproduced by any means, graphic, electronic, or mechanical, including photocopying, recording, taping or by any information storage retrieval system without the written permission of the publisher except in the case of brief quotations embodied in critical articles and reviews.

Edited by Nicole Miller
and Next Step Editing

Scripture quotations marked MSG are taken from The Message. Copyright © 1993, 1994, 1995, 1996, 2000, 2001, 2002. Used by permission of NavPress Publishing Group.

Scripture quotations marked NLT are taken from the Holy Bible: New Living Translation, copyright © 1996. Used by permission of Tyndale House Publishers, Inc., Wheaton, Illinois 60189. All rights reserved.

Scripture quotations marked NIV are taken from the Holy Bible, New International Version®. Copyright © 1973, 1978, 1984, 2011 by Biblica, Inc.™ Used by permission. All rights reserved worldwide.

Scripture quotations marked AMP are taken from The Amplified Bible Copyright © 1954, 1958, 1964, 1965, 1987 by The Lockman Foundation. All rights reserved. Used by permission.

Scripture quotations marked NKJV are taken from the New King James Version. Copyright © 1982, by Thomas Nelson, Inc. Used by permission. All rights reserved.

Scripture quotations marked KJV are taken from King James Version of the Bible.

WestBow Press books may be ordered through booksellers or by contacting:
WestBow Press
A Division of Thomas Nelson
1663 Liberty Drive
Bloomington, IN 47403
www.westbowpress.com
1-(866) 928-1240

Because of the dynamic nature of the Internet, any web addresses or links contained in this book may have changed since publication and may no longer be valid. The views expressed in this work are solely those of the author and do not necessarily reflect the views of the publisher, and the publisher hereby disclaims any responsibility for them.

ISBN: 978-1-4908-0587-0 (sc)
ISBN: 978-1-4908-0586-3 (hc)
ISBN: 978-1-4908-0588-7 (e)

Printed in the United States of America.

Library of Congress Control Number: 2013915116

WestBow Press rev. date: 9/26/2013

Table of Contents
BUT GOD ...

Acknowledgements

First and foremost, thanks to Jesus, to Him be all the glory! He made sure my ears were wide open to hear when people would say things that went exactly with the BUT GOD verse I happened to be working on. I must also thank my amazing husband Aaron and my babies, Nicole, Natalie, and Elijah. Aaron, thanks for your help and patience. Thank you for giving me the time I needed to finish this study and loving me unconditionally. I love listening to your wisdom and perspective. Natalie, thank you for double-checking my references, and Nicole, thank you for making my sentences flow together and making me sound smarter than I am. Elijah, thank you for your late night back rubs and checking in on me while I typed! Thanks to my parents, Dick and Sandy Modzeleski, who taught me the goodness of God and support me endlessly. To my awesome brother, Adam, I dedicate #92 to you- GO! GO! GO! Thanks for helping me set up the website (www.ButGodBibleStudy. com). I love you all more than words can describe.

I would like to give special acknowledgement to my initial proof reader and first draft editor, Deena Page. You are a constant source of encouragement and an amazing best friend. Your insight is scattered throughout the pages and this book is better because of you. Christine and Alyssa Annunziato, Sheila Haber, Arlene Cole, Toni Belko, Dava Santos, Sheila Sayegh, Leslie Schultz, RJ Jackson, Dave and Becky Collins, Cindy Powell, Dr. Patricia Venegas, Martha Lawley, and Dr. Booker thank you all for investing your time to read this book before it was released and give me feedback. Without your editing, proofing, thoughtful suggestions, friendship, and prayer, this book would have been less than it is. To my pastor and his wife, Dan and Gale Carroll (www.wateroflifecc.org), thank you! In this study I do not always indicate where I have learned things from you because, after sitting under your teaching for ten plus years, it is too much to mark, but it is mixed in here.

To my family and friends in the Bay Area, my Bible study groups, my friends in Rancho and all over—you all are amazing! It is so unbelievably hard not to list every single one of your names here and tell you exactly what you mean to me! Many of you have walked and talked things out with me as I have written this study and made it better. Thank you for letting me include your stories and persuading me to finish so you could read it. I love you all!

Thank you to Leanna Annunziato (www.portraitsbyleanna. com) for using your fancy camera to take my picture. Lastly, thank you Janet Hyun, my book cover artist. The creations you make during worship not only glorify the Lord, but they facilitate a new way to navigate into His beauty. Who would have ever known that the artist who painted the picture I wanted in 2011, the day after I had written about Jesus being the Lion of Judah (#99), would be willing to let me display her work on the cover of my book? No one BUT GOD!

About the Book Cover Artist

Janet Hyun studied fine arts at the Art Institute of Chicago and graduated from Art Center College of Design in Pasadena, CA, in 1998. She is one of the leading prophetic artists who want to impact this generation in a Christ-based culture. Her works are world renowned, from being made into New York billboards to calendars and various products in Korea and the USA. She has painted at many Christian gatherings and conferences. Her paintings are displayed in New York, Texas, California, and Taiwan. She has been featured in newspaper and magazine articles for her work and testimony. Janet lives in Southern California with her husband and three children. www.Janethyun.com

Contact the Author

Let's study the Word together, I would love to hear from you.
Email:
ButGodBibleStudy@yahoo.com

Website:
www.ButGodBibleStudy.com
www.ButGodBibleStudy.weebly.com

Facebook:
www.facebook.com/ButGodBibleStudy.com

Blog:
www.ButGodBibleStudy.wordpress.com

I look forward to hearing from you! I plan to put up special videos and study questions to go with this book. I pray Jesus pulls you in close as you read this. Use this study to help you understand our Bridegroom better. He wants you to pursue Him. He wants you to get to know Him better. He desires that you seek Him with all your might and crave His company. He is chasing after you to spend time with Him, and once He catches you, He will never want to let you go. He desires that you would never want to let Him go. He intends for you to be His bride so that you can spend eternity together.

-Tina Miller

Introduction

Have you ever heard someone exclaim, "BUT GOD!" and then wonder what he meant? There are hidden treasures God has been waiting for *you* to uncover from this simple phrase. In this study, you will read through the Bible in a unique way as all the Old Testament BUT GOD verses are highlighted. You will see how these verses reveal significant characteristics of God. The thrilling part of the study begins when you discover how God has implanted His strategies and plans for His people, along with the message of the gospel, within the BUT GOD verses. God unveils it in each new verse leading up to the last BUT GOD phrase in the Bible. This full treasure would be missed if you studied only a few verses. I am constantly amazed when He shows me something new in His Word that has been there all along. I do not know all the answers, BUT GOD does! I did not know why people made such a big deal about the phrase "BUT GOD," but now I do, and soon you will too! After reading this study, you will hear a Bible story and immediately recall if it was a story containing a BUT GOD verse. I know, because it now happens to me all the time!

The bride of Christ is a collection of Christian believers who have asked Jesus to be the Lord over every aspect of their lives in accordance with God's Biblical truths. As a Christian believer, we are preparing for the day when Jesus will come to collect His bride. Right now, we are in a time of engagement with Jesus. He wants us to engage with Him as we make ourselves ready for our wedding day (Rev 19:7). It is a wedding of the heart, an intimacy that is not physical, but spiritual. There are many references in the Bible symbolizing God's relationship with His people as being likened to the relationship between a husband and wife. Since we are promised to one husband, who is Christ, that makes Him our Bridegroom (Mark 2:19-20, 2 Cor 11:1-3, Eph 5:22-33). This is why I have subtitled this book *Getting to Know our Bridegroom,* because as we read His Word, we get to know Him more!

God created us and knows us well. This study will encourage you to pursue knowing Him. It will push you into His living waters as you dive deeper into understanding God's thoughts. What makes Him happy or sad, who is He watching, and what are His plans? Believers are handed a blueprint of His ways in the Bible and many are found in the BUT GODs. Jesus demonstrated God's character for us to model, which helps the bride make herself pure and holy. Christians will learn about Jesus being their Bridegroom as they discover His characteristics in a special way. During your reading, you will catch glimpses of what was fulfilled, as well as what is to be fulfilled upon His second coming. Jesus is the Lion of Judah; He has all authority and all power. He is capable of taking down strongholds with His might. Our Bridegroom encases the fury of a lion, yet is gentle enough to lay down His life for His sheep. Jesus is the Lamb who was slain, but also the eternal Lamb. He desires for you to take advantage of the pathway leading to God the Father that He has reestablished for you. Seek the Lord while He may be found (Isaiah 55:6), learn of His beautiful ways during this time of engagement, and join together with the rest of the bride of Christ as we celebrate all that He is.

If you are a new Christian, or seeking God and seeking answers, this BUT GOD devotional study will give you a quick overview of who He is and what His plans are for those who love Him. Many of the patriarchs of the Bible had "BUT GOD" moments, so you will be reacquainted with several main stories in the Bible. Seasoned Christians will also benefit as you discover new revelations from stories you thought you knew so well. You will learn why people will exclaim, "BUT GOD!" and you may find you have a few BUT GOD moments yourself. You will be able to examine your situations further to see what God was trying to teach you about who He is. You will see how the verses connect to each other even though they are chapters, or full books, apart. You will learn about Jesus in a whole new way.

Leave it to God to use a word so small to lead us to huge revelations. "But" is a word that, when heard, usually means you are not going to get the answer you were looking for. Instead, you will most likely get an excuse (i.e.: "I wanted to, *but* . . ." "it was a good idea, *but* . . ." "I like you, *but* . . ."). It is a word that does not usually invoke a smile when it is heard—*except* when it is followed by His name. God consistently uses His Word to correct our misconceptions. In this case, we have to wrap our minds around the fact that when He uses the phrase "BUT GOD" in His Word, we need to assume something good will happen for those who love Him. The BUT GODs help you focus on the promises of God and not life's problems. The BUT GODs show our Bridegroom's flawless and righteous character and His tender heart. The BUT GODs are found in the stories that prove it. Get ready to be amazed as we mine for some treasures from this little phrase! (Prov 2:1-13, Matt 13:44)

How It Started

"Don't forget about the 'BUT GOD' verses in the Bible," Cindy Powell said in a Bible study on the life of David in March, 2008. I had never heard that before, so I wrote down "look up BUT GOD" to see what she meant. l looked them up on the BibleGateway website in five different translations: NLT, NIV, MSG, AMP, and KJV. I was shocked when almost two hundred verses on the phrase popped up. So, I printed them all out.

About a month passed as I slowly hashed through the pile of verses. My husband, Aaron, and my friend, Sheila, were the only two people who knew I was reading them. Sheila and I were headed to a Beth Moore conference in San Diego in April, 2008. I brought the pile along just in case I had some extra time to look at them. As we were driving on the highway, I noticed a big white truck was about to pass me on the right. He pulled ahead in the lane and my eyes did a double take. On his rear tinted black window in big, bright, white bold lettering were the words "BUT GOD." I would not have believed it if Sheila were not sitting next to me in the car. I said, "Did you see that?" Just as stunned as me she said, "I did!" I was glad I had brought the stack of verses and was wondering what God was going to show me that weekend. Beth taught on Psalm 139 and, at the time, I had no clue what that had to do with the BUT GOD verses, but I would soon find out.

In May 2008, I went to a women's retreat, where again I brought the verses with me. The speaker devoted part of her time the first night talking about how Jesus is our Bridegroom. I kept hearing the Holy Spirit tell me this teaching was a piece of the puzzle. Instead of socializing with my friends that night, I spent some time alone in my room. With my Bible opened to Psalm 139, the stack of BUT GOD verses, and the notes from that evening spread out all over the bed, I began praying for revelation because I could not see how the puzzle fit together. Then, He opened my eyes!

Psalm 139 says it all. God knows everything about us. He knows our character, what we are thinking, and what we are doing. He knows when we sit and when we stand. He knows the words we will speak before they are on our tongues. He also knows where we live, when we travel, and when we rest. Always. We are His tabernacle, His chosen people, His church. Of course He knows every little detail about us—why wouldn't He? We are His bride, He created us and loves us! What the Lord revealed was this: Can we say we know our Bridegroom just as well? Do we take the time to notice the details of His character—what He is thinking or what He is doing? Always? Do we notice when He is moving, when He is speaking, what He is revealing, or how He is feeling? Always? As His bride, shouldn't we? I believe the answer is YES! Because this is our time of engagement with the Lord, and this is the time we are supposed to get to know our Bridegroom and our heavenly Father.

Armed with this new revelation, I began rereading all the BUT GODs and saw how they exposed the quality of His nature. I began writing out all Jesus' characteristics as each BUT GOD seemed to portray something new. It did not take long before I became overwhelmed with all the information and I had to put it aside. After all, what was I going to do with all these stacks of papers?

As months went by, I felt the Holy Spirit pushing me to keep studying them. Even my pastor, unknowingly, would say in his sermons, "BUT GOD" or, "the BUT GODs are important in the Bible." I remember looking around to see if anyone else thought it was interesting that he had said that, but no one acted like it was a big deal. I knew it was though—to me! So, one night, I asked Jesus this question, "What am I to do with all these BUT GODs?" He directed me to Psalm 119. If you are familiar with the Bible then you know that it is the longest Psalm ever! I laughed at His sense of humor. I read through it and then He told me we were going to make a devotional poem out of that. "Funny," I told Him, "That has almost as many verses as the BUT GODs!" That, apparently, was precisely His point. Within forty-five minutes the poem was done and I was amazed! I knew He was showing me the amount of verses was not as intimidating as it seemed. I pulled the stack off the shelf and began to review the BUT GOD verses again.*

I knew He had a plan for me to do something specific with them, but I did not know what it was. I devoted lots of time processing the verses. I looked for any information I could find that was relevant to the BUT GOD verses on the Internet, but nothing fit. I tried to sort the verses into reoccurring themes, thinking I should study them that way, but I could not seem to get them to match up. I tried to put them into a poem, but that was not right either. After praying one evening, near the end of 2010, God finally told me to start writing about the very first verse.

I obeyed and got a pen and paper out. To my surprise, the words started flowing as God shared with me His heart about the situation in the Garden of Eden. I felt as if I connected with Him in a whole new way, and my emotions soared as I delighted in the high of that moment. I immediately wanted to write about the next verse and relive that feeling again. That night was amazing as I embarked on this new devotion time just He and I were going to share. My husband was excited for me and said it sounded like I was writing a book, but I dismissed that thought immediately. As I continued writing throughout that month, I considered skipping some of the verses, but the Holy Spirit nudged me to do them all *and* consecutively as they appeared in the Bible. I am so glad I listened to Him as I would have missed the blessing of being reminded that God loves order. I began to accumulate a lot of information and started to share some of it with friends who also encouraged me to put it in a book. So, now my pursuit of knowing my Bridegroom has become something I never intended it to be, but nevertheless, it is my gift to Him and hopefully the Lord will use this to bless you.

I believe the children of Yahweh and the bride of the Son are one. I do not believe the church has replaced Israel, but that together, Jews and Gentiles will be united as one new man (Eph

2:14-16). We have salvation through the redemptive work of Jesus Christ and we are sanctified by the washing of His Word, learning and obeying His commands. I want this work to edify the bride of Christ and to honor the truth of the testimony of Jesus in this unique time of history. My hope is that this study acts as a reminder for you to pursue knowing your Bridegroom as much as He has pursued knowing you.

* Just in case you were curious, I included the Psalm 119 poem in the back of this study.

How You Can Use This Study

This BUT GOD book is a study and devotional mixed together. For each BUT GOD verse I tried to write some context so you would know what was happening. You will get the most out of this study if you read it in order and look up the verses I referenced in each section. The verses are summarized in chronological order as they appear in the Bible. God's characteristic is listed above each BUT GOD verse and then the devotional summary follows. It may include a personal story or poem to further illustrate the point. Some may contain ideas for personal application in facilitating conversations that tell of God's goodness. Others may pose a question or ask you to listen to a song to help you spend some time in worship. Some verses have longer discussions than others depending on the context of the subject. When you see a # symbol, it is referring to that particular BUT GOD as seen in Table of Contents. Many of the BUT GODs seemed to go with the previous one, to further illustrate His faithfulness or be another example of a characteristic that complimented others. I found myself pointing them out as I wrote, but see if you can pick some out yourself as you read them. Jesus may open your eyes to see a completely different characteristic than the one I wrote, if that is the case, write it down, and don't forget to share it with me!

We find God's characteristics scattered all throughout the Bible. Many verses will exclaim how powerful He is, how faithful He is, or how compassionate He is, such as the example below. Next to each of God's amazing attributes is a number. As I said before, the # symbol corresponds with the Table of Contents where you can read a BUT GOD verse that shows an example of God displaying that particular characteristic. You will not find all of

God's traits in the BUT GOD verses, but there are a good handful of them!

> "Then the LORD came down in the cloud and stood there with him and proclaimed his name, the LORD. And he passed in front of Moses, proclaiming, 'The LORD, the LORD (#95, #104), the compassionate and gracious God (#54), slow to anger (#119), abounding in love (#47) and faithfulness (#86), maintaining love to thousands, and forgiving wickedness (#16), rebellion and sin (#16). Yet he does not leave the guilty unpunished (#79, #81, #83, #94); He punishes the children and their children for the sin of the parents to the third and fourth generation (#26).'"
> **(Exodus 34:5-7 numbers added NIV).**

BUT GOD
Old Testament

As we pursue learning about the Old Testament BUT GODs, I want to teach you a quick lesson about the TaNaK. The "T" stands for *Torah* which includes the first five books of the Bible that Moses wrote. The "N" stands for *Nevi'im* which are the books of the prophets like Isaiah, Joshua, Samuel, and so on. Lastly, the "K" stands for *Ketuvim*, the writings such as the Psalms and Proverbs.

One of the main reasons Christians should still read "the front of the book" is that it points to Jesus—He said so Himself. Luke's gospel proclaims, "Then He said to them, 'This is what I told you while I was still with you: everything which is written concerning Me in the *Law of Moses* and the *Prophets* and the *Psalms* must be fulfilled'" (Luke 24:44-45 AMP, emphasis added).

Isaiah prophesied of Messiah's coming and gave a clue as to what His name would be. He says in Isaiah 59:16 that God saw there was no man, no intercessor, so His arm brought salvation to him.[1] The word "salvation" (#3467 in *Strong's Concordance*) comes from the root Yod-Sheen-Ayin. Jesus' name *Yeshua* also comes from this same root.[2] Isaiah 53:1 says the arm of the Lord is revealed, and the rest of the chapter goes on to describe the Messiah. Unfortunately, not all believed Jesus was God's Son as recorded in John 12:37-43. Jesus reinforced who He is and how to receive eternal life when He spoke with His disciples and said, "I am the Way, the Truth, and the Life. No one comes to the Father except through Me . . . If you had known Me, you would have known My Father . . . He who has seen Me has seen the Father . . . The words that I speak to you I do not speak on My own authority; but the Father who dwells in Me does the works" (John 14:6-11 NKJV).

Tina Miller

God is our heavenly Father, and Jesus, His Son, is our Bridegroom. Remember, Jesus said, "I assure you, most solemnly I tell you, the Son is able to do nothing of Himself (of His own accord); but He is able to do only what He sees the Father doing, for whatever the Father does is what the Son does in the same way [in His turn]" (John 5:19 AMP). So, Jesus' characteristics can be found in God Himself—though they are separate, they, along with the Spirit, are One.

Okay, here we go . . .

1. Protects

"*but God* did say, 'You must not eat fruit from the tree that is in the middle of the garden, and you must not touch it, or you will die'" (Genesis 3:3 NIV, emphasis added).

The very first BUT GOD in the Bible appears in the beginning in the Garden of Eden. God created humanity in His own image for His pleasure and chose to cultivate a relationship with the first man and woman. God said that all He created was good and allowed Adam and Eve to live in His goodness. Shortly after that, Satan showed up and the BUT GOD verses commence. We read how Adam and Eve's story turned as Satan challenged God's relationship with them. God wanted to protect His relationship with His people, which is why He put rules in place for them to follow.

God does not *need* a relationship with us—He *wants* one. We can choose to know Him, be obedient to Him, and reap the rewards (James 1:12), or we can make our own decisions, step out against His will, and render His rewards void. He will never force us to choose Him, but He rewards us when we do. God gives us the opportunity to have a choice, but He wants to protect us from making a bad decision.

In this first BUT GOD, Eve answered the serpent's questions. God gave Adam and Eve permission to eat in the Garden of Eden, but they were to withhold themselves from one tree, the Tree of Knowledge of Good and Evil (Gen 2:17). Eve knew God's warning was to protect them from death, but, unfortunately, she and Adam chose not to listen to His instruction. When the serpent spun words around and poisoned the truth, they did what he said and disobeyed God's rules. The devil deceived Eve by saying they really would not die, but they would be ". . . like God, knowing good and evil" (Gen 3:4-5 NIV). Adam and Eve ate from the tree, and they surely discovered evil, just as the enemy said. Even though they did not physically die that day, physical deterioration toward death came upon Adam and Eve. Their sin brought death into the world (Rom 5:12). They felt a spiritual death as they recognized the depth of their separation from God's presence in the garden. Even though they were to receive death, they immediately received exile. God protected them from eternally living in sin by exiling them from the garden before they could eat of the Tree of Life. That exile was the beginning of a journey that would lead humanity back to life through the resurrection of Jesus into the Promised Land.

How interesting! The first BUT GOD shows God trying to give protection from death, just as Eve is talking to the very one from whom the Lord wants to protect us—the one who brings sin and death. Even today, the enemy wants to trick us. He wants to get us to believe God did not mean what He said. He wants to deceive humanity, turning us from believing God's rules are good for us. He wants to come after the ones who are "purely and undividedly devoted to Christ," just like Eve was (2 Cor. 11:3 NLT). Satan constantly twists things around to make us second-guess God and justify our actions. When we feel an attack, we can call on God and stand on His Word, because we know He desires to protect us. We need to stand firm and turn away from the one who speaks lies. This is what Jesus did in the desert (Matt 4:1-11). The Bible affirms that everyone who calls upon the Lord's name will be saved (Joel 2:32, Acts 2:21, and Rom 10:13).

Notice there were no BUT GODs when God created the world. They begin after humanity came onto the scene and the serpent showed up. BUT GOD had a plan to continue to protect us even after He drove Adam and Eve from the Garden of Eden. The Holy Trinity had already decided, before the foundation of the world, that Jesus would come (1 Peter 1:18-21); we were destined to be adopted by Him (Eph 1:4-5). Remember, Christ Jesus our Lord laid down His life for us so that we might live. Jesus says, "I am the Good Shepherd. The Good Shepherd lays down His life for the sheep" (John 10:11 NIV). Revelation 13:8 calls Jesus the Lamb who was slain *before* the foundation of the world. All along, God had planned that Jesus would redeem us to restore our souls, spirits, and physical bodies at the resurrection.

Romans 5:12-21 tells us that one man let sin into the world, and that sin let in death, which resulted in condemnation for all humanity. Fortunately for us, we have a victorious God. Through the righteous act of one man—Jesus Christ—the gift of grace came to us all, resulting in justification of life. Adam's disobedience made us all sinners, but Christ's obedience gave redemption. Though death entered the world through Adam and Eve's sin, the Lord God Almighty will protect us forever. In the end, our Bridegroom has the final say, and He will destroy death (1 Cor 15:26, Rev 20:14). We will eat from His garden and the Tree of Life again. The risen and reigning Christ says, "He who has an ear, let him hear what the Spirit says to the churches. To him who overcomes I will give to eat from the tree of life, which is in the midst of the Paradise of God" (Rev 2:7 NKJV).

2.   Remembers Us and His Promises

"*But God* remembered Noah and all the wild animals and the livestock that were with him in the ark, and he sent a wind over the earth, and the waters receded" (Genesis 8:1 NIV, emphasis added). *Also found in the NLT.

People began to populate the earth, but most did not live in relationship with God. The human race had become very wicked and evil thoughts were rampant in their hearts. In Genesis 6:6, we are told humanity's sin grieved God's heart. Our heavenly Father opened His heart to us when He made us. In a way, He made Himself vulnerable, as we can affect His emotions, causing Him to smile with happiness or to feel sadness. Noah walked with God and because of this, they had a relationship. God decided to flood the earth and start anew when He saw how prevalent sin was, BUT GOD spared Noah and his family. God told Noah how to build an ark to house his family and the animals during the forty days of rain that were to come. Afterward, God remembered Noah floating around in that ark. This leads us to our BUT GOD verse.

How much do we like to be remembered? Birthdays, anniversaries, graduations, or just being picked up at the airport are all good examples. God is not far away from our circumstances; He is not just watching us from a distance. In 2005, Hurricane Katrina brought many deaths, and in the fall of 2012, Hurricane Sandy left quite a mess. The floodwaters destroyed hundreds of lives, but many people heeded warnings and escaped. Sometimes storms in our life will cause damage. In those times will we trust that God will remember us? We may be on a tiny planet in the universe with billions of galaxies, BUT GOD knows our addresses and exactly where we are; He intervenes in our circumstances. Just like us, Noah was definitely in need of some intervention!

God not only remembers us, BUT GOD also remembers His promises. After Noah departed from the ark, he gave thanks by building God an altar and offering Him sacrifices on it. God was pleased and made a decision (Gen 8:20-22). Even though humans have the tendency to be evil, God promised to never again flood the earth. He placed the rainbow in the sky as a sign of this promise between Him and all living creatures of every kind on the earth. It would be for all generations (Gen 9:11-17). The Bible says God promised that every time the rainbow appeared, He would remember that covenant. Don't we want our Bridegroom to always remember these things? How nice that He does!

In the New Testament, we see many examples which demonstrate how significant it is that our Bridegroom remembers. One of the criminals hanging next to Jesus on the cross asked Jesus to remember him when He came into His kingdom. Jesus responded positively and said he would be with Jesus in paradise that day (Luke 23:42-43). *In our death and His own, He remembers us!* After Jesus' resurrection, He told His disciples to wait in Jerusalem for the gift His Father promised, the Holy Spirit. He told them they would receive power when the Holy Spirit came. Ten days after Jesus ascended into the clouds, on the day of Pentecost, the Holy Spirit did come and they were filled with power (Acts 1-2). *He remembered what He had promised in His Word and the blessings He wants to give!* Later, in Acts 10, we read God sent an angel to Cornelius to tell him his deeds had been remembered in the sight of God. *God remembers what we pray and sees when we do works in His name!* Psalm 139 reminds us how well the Lord knows us because He remembers the instant we were formed in the womb and every moment thereafter. He records every second of our lives and hopes we walk in His will to receive all the rewards He has destined for us. This is why David exclaimed that God's thoughts toward us are precious (Ps 139:17-18)!

During the summer of 2013, I went to a conference alone in Pasadena. While driving, I asked Jesus to be my date. I asked that He would lead me to a parking spot close by the door, bring me some water (I forgot my bottle), help me find a seat at the church, and make sure I was safe getting back to my car. I remember telling Him that, as my date, I thought those would be nice things He could do for me. I spent the next 45 minutes in the car singing, forgetting my requests. Wouldn't you know, I pulled my car right up to a front row spot! As I walked to the front door of the church, I was offered a nice cold bottle of water to take in with me. While I looked for a seat, a friend called my name, and I suddenly had a seat in the second row! It wasn't until after I took a sip of water that I heard Jesus say to me, "Three out of four!" I realized He was answering my requests from earlier. I couldn't stop smiling, but kept it all to myself. The conference ended at 10:15 PM, and I said goodbye to my friends. I walked out quietly wondering how Jesus was going to fulfill my last request. I was all alone, or so I thought, when suddenly my friend, Rolo, walked out beside me. As we talked, he asked where I was parked, not knowing Jesus was my date and fulfilling my last request to get me to the car safely. Jesus used my brothers and sisters in Christ to be His hands and feet that evening. Jesus did everything I asked because He remembers, even when we ourselves forget!

Many of us would agree we have done a few things that we would like to forget. Thankfully, God does not mind erasing some of our bad decisions if we repent and ask for forgiveness. David tells us in Psalm 103:12 that God will cast our sin as far as the east is from the west. The distance between east and west is infinite. This would not be true if the directions of north and south were given. Meaning, if you walk north, eventually you will hit the North Pole and then have to walk south if you continued your journey. God's Word is very precise about His mercy; He will remove our sins from us if we ask and will remember them no more. Everything else, though, He remembers and He has books in heaven full of all the details. I tend to forget things as time goes on, so it is nice to know that God is having someone journal about my life for me. I'm looking forward to watching the expressions on Jesus' face as we read together some of my better moments. Which memories of yours are you looking forward to talking over with your Bridegroom?

3. Cares and Intervenes When We Make Bad Decisions

"Because of her, Abram got along very well: he accumulated sheep and cattle, male and female donkeys, men and women servants, and camels. *But God* hit Pharaoh hard because of Abram's wife Sarai; everybody in the palace got seriously sick" (Genesis 12:16-17 MSG, emphasis added).

Abraham is known as the father of our faith because he believed God (Gen 15:6 and Heb 11). In his book *The Lamb and the Seven Sealed Scrolls*, Dr. Richard Booker called Abraham the natural father of Israel and the spiritual father of believers.[3] Believers in Christ, who are doers of the Word, have not replaced Israel, but they get to join in Israel's inheritance (Rom 11). He goes on to say that, symbolically speaking, Jewish people are not grafted into the Christians' Christmas tree, but Christians have been grafted into their olive tree.

God told Abraham to leave his country and travel to a land God would show him. God had made a covenant with Abraham and said He would make a nation from him (Gen 12:1-3, 7). We know that nation to be Israel.

In this BUT GOD verse, Abraham went to Egypt because of a famine. He feared he would be killed because of his wife's beauty, so he asked Sarah to tell them he was her brother when they got there. Technically, she was his half-sister (Gen 20:12) and it was customary in those days to marry family, but Abraham did not want the whole truth exposed. This lie carried repercussions. When they arrived, she was taken away to Pharaoh's house by the Egyptians because of her beauty.[4] Abraham flourished because of Sarah; however, everyone in the palace suffered.

We are to show the way to God. We cannot reflect His true character if our testimonies are sprinkled with lies instead of truth. What if Abraham had not lied, not tried to spare his *own* life. I wonder how God would have intervened then. God cares about us. He allowed Abraham to prosper despite him deceiving Pharaoh, but He would not tolerate Sarah's separation from Abraham any longer. We learned in BUT GOD #1 that the enemy is the very one God wants to protect us from. If we believe God for the promises, then we need to believe Him for the protection. Honor Jesus by displaying integrity, especially when dealing with unsure situations. We do not want to cause others to stumble and pay the price for our dishonesty. Our Bridegroom represents truth and so should His bride. We can be assured that our Bridegroom would never offer up His bride to His enemy in trying to spare His own life. In fact, Romans 8:32 proves this point as it says, "He who did not spare His own Son, but gave Him up for us all . . ." (NIV). Thank you Jesus!

4.   Communicates and Articulates Clearly

"*But God* replied, 'No—Sarah, your wife, will give birth to a son for you. You will name him Isaac, and I will confirm my covenant with him and his descendants as an everlasting covenant'" (Genesis 17:19 NLT, emphasis added). *Also found in the AMP and MSG.

Have you ever said to someone, "That's not what I heard"? Some of us need things repeated to us, especially important things, until we hear exactly what is being said. God is great at using many different methods until we get it. He might communicate through dreams, prophecy, music, Bible verses, symbols, TV shows, situations, or even an audible voice. The Holy Spirit could also just simply speak in your heart. Let us make sure we understand exactly what our God is saying to us. Communication is key to a good earthly marriage, so why would it be any different with our heavenly Bridegroom?

God was going to make a great nation through Abraham's future son. God explained clearly that Sarah would have a son they were to name Isaac, and he would bring about God's blessing. Since Abraham and Sarah were very old, Abraham thought it would be better if God would use his thirteen year old son, Ishmael, born from Hagar, Sarah's servant. God repeated His will with great clarity in this BUT GOD verse to Abraham to make sure He is understood. Sometimes He does this with us as we can be slow to understand His ways. God basically said, "No, that is not what I mean" and then proceeded again with His promise. God also had to correct Sarah who laughed at the idea and made a sarcastic remark when she heard she was going to have a son at her age. God called her out on her disbelief and said nothing was too hard for Him to accomplish (Gen 18:10-15).

God made a covenant with Abraham (Gen 15), which was reconfirmed with his descendants. God changed Abraham and Sarah's names by adding the Hebrew letter *he* (Gen 17). The following is taught by Perry Stone on his program, *Manna Fest,* entitled, "The Fullness Factor—God's Sign of the End."[5] The letter *he* is also found in God's Hebrew name and is pronounced "YOD HE VAV HE." *He* is the fifth letter in the Hebrew alphabet and also stands for the word "grace." When *he* is connected to another letter, it means the word "life." So, when God inserted this letter onto their names, He breathed *life* into them. A year later, we see that a new *life* was born! Abraham was one hundred and Sarah was ninety years old when they welcomed Isaac into the world. Just like this BUT GOD verse states, we read in later verses that God reconfirmed His covenant with Isaac (Gen 26:3-5), and then later with his son, Jacob (Gen 28:10-20). In Genesis 32:22-31, Jacob's name was changed to Israel and "Israelites" became the name of his descendents.

There are different theories among Christians about the covenants. Since we believe God's promises are true, we can learn how some of the very first ones were established. We already discussed in BUT GOD #2 the covenant God made with all living things. God's next promise was for Abraham and his descendants. Abraham believed God's word to him, but asked God how he would know for sure that God would do it. This is when God made a covenant with him (Gen 15). I took a Bible study class through Fruits of Zion Ministry (www.ffoz.org) called *HaYesod,* and I liked how they explained it.[6]

When God made a covenant with the Israelites at Mt. Sinai, it was based on their *agreement* to obey the Torah. The Torah itself was not the covenant (Ex 19:5-6, Deut 28:1-2, 15). I think this is where many people get confused about the old covenant, thinking the Torah is done away with. The Torah is God's loving instructions for us. That is why Jesus spent much of His ministry teaching the people about it and how to obey God's commands. He was instructing them on the true meaning of the law. He said that He came to fulfill the law, not abolish it (Matt 5:17). We do not throw it out; we just do not use it as a way to be justified. No one could obey the whole Torah, only Jesus could. We cannot be righteous by following rules; we are made righteous by faith, led by the Spirit (Rom 3:28, Gal 5:16-18). This is why we are justified by faith through Jesus (Gal 2:16).

The Israelites had difficulty obeying the Torah. They broke the promises to God that they made in their covenant agreement on Mt. Sinai. Abraham's covenant with God was so important because the Israelites still needed to be able to stand on a promise from God when they failed. It was Israel's safety net, the covenant God would fall back on every time the Israelites broke it. As shown to us in Leviticus 26:40-45, God *remembers* His previous covenants and takes them seriously (#2)!

We are living in the new covenant now and Jesus is the Mediator (Heb 12:24). Jeremiah 31:31-34 says God was going to make a new covenant with Israel. This is also repeated in the New Testament in Hebrews 8:10. The promises of the new covenant are also found in Ezekiel 36:24-28. Gentiles (everyone who is not Jewish) are included in the "covenants of promise" (Eph 2:12-13) by being grafted in through Jesus (Rom 11). The New Testament explains how the new covenant is brought about with the Holy Spirit as a pledge (the covenantal sign) of our inheritance (2 Corinthians 1:22, 2 Corinthians 5:5, and Ephesians 1:13-14). The new covenant is unconditional and based on the sincerity of people's hearts.

Hopefully, I have communicated and articulated clearly what covenants are and why they are important to us. God will stand by His covenant with Israel, and Jesus will stand by His covenant with His bride and His Jewish brethren. Our Bridegroom will continue to communicate with us because He loves us and desires a relationship with us. Even though *He* knows our every thought, we also need to spend time talking to Him so *we* can know His as well. God communicates His love toward us in the Bible, but it is up to us to read it. God will talk to our hearts, but we need to spend time quietly in His presence to hear it.

5. Listens and Responds

"*But God* had listened to Abraham's request and kept Lot safe, removing him from the disaster that engulfed the cities on the plain" (Genesis 19:29 NLT, emphasis added).

God was about to destroy the cities of Sodom and Gomorrah because of their perverse and wicked sin. They had prideful attitudes and lacked in helping the poor and needy (Gen 18 and 19:4-5, Ezekiel 16:49). Abraham asked the Lord not to kill the righteous with the wicked and to spare the city if He found a certain number of righteous people in the land. The Lord listened to Abraham's request and responded by saying yes, even after Abraham kept lowering the number. Sadly, there were not even ten righteous people there. The whole place was corrupt, BUT GOD allowed for some of Lot's family to be taken out and saved before the cities were completely destroyed (Gen 19:12-25).

One time, I had lost my sunglasses and asked the Lord to tell me where they were. He told me immediately, but I knew I had not put them where He said, so I doubted that idea came from Him. I searched the entire house for at least thirty minutes, until finally I came to the room He had initially told me. It was the only place I had not looked. I was so frustrated by that time, and late to where I was supposed to be, so I figured I would give it a try. Wouldn't you know, they were in the exact spot He told me to look in that room. All I could do was laugh and repent for not listening to Him when He had actually responded to my request.

In the previous BUT GOD, we noted that communication is key to a good marriage. The counterpart to that is listening. How brilliant that God puts these two qualities next to each other here in our BUT GOD study. Talking does no good if your groom does not listen. It is especially nice when he not only listens, but responds. This BUT GOD verse shows God listened and deemed Abraham's request reasonable and responded by doing what he asked. Just because we know He is listening does not always mean He will respond the way we want. When He does respond, we should listen—as I learned from my sunglasses example. Since we do not always know His plans, our requests may not always be aligned with His will for us or others, but it never hurts to ask. Now if He would just take out the garbage for me . . .

6.   Stands Up for Us

"*But God* came to Abimelek in a dream one night and said to him, 'You are as good as dead because of the woman you have taken; she is a married woman'" (Genesis 20:3 NIV, emphasis added). *Also found in KJV, AMP, and MSG in Genesis 20:2-3.

How often do we dream and then forget what it was about? I doubt dreams like we see in this BUT GOD verse would be easily forgotten! Dreams and visions are often used by God to forewarn us or shed light on a subject that we need help with. So many dreams have symbolism that can be hard to interpret. It is important to write them down and list as many details as you can, because as time goes by it is harder to remember. When you read them back, you might be able to see what the symbols mean or have a better understanding of the interpretation. I had a dream once that my friend's husband had died and we were at his funeral. I told my friend the next day, and she confided that she was worried for him and asked for prayer because he had been making some unwise decisions. There was no way we would have expected that within a week my dream would become reality. It did, though, and he died. It was horrible! God still speaks to people in dreams, some more than others.

Not all of us hear God while we are awake and as clearly as Abraham, but the Lord still knows how to get our attention.

Clearly, Abraham feared for his safety and hid behind his wife, so to speak, allowing the king of Gerar to take her into his home. Abraham wanted Sarah to show kindness to him by doing this favor (verse 13), but how kind was he being to her? Abraham's fear caused him to lie, and though he was the father of our faith, he was far from perfect. We should remember that many of the patriarchs in the Bible struggled with issues we all face. Sin will rob us of our spiritual confidence. When we discount what God can do for us, we relinquish the opportunities for rewards He has awaiting us. As a result, this may cause unwelcomed consequences. The good news is that, even with their imperfections, God still stood up for them. This means that even in our failures, if God is our friend, then He will stand up for us, too. Whether we have sinned, or been the recipient of someone else's bad decision, He will not abandon us.

Let's take a moment to consider Sarah. Her husband continued to give her up to men she did not trust, and did not even know, because he was scared for his own life (See #3). Some wives sacrifice much for their husbands, but this was a little too extreme and it displeased God. Since Abraham would not risk standing up for his own wife, God stepped in. God enabled the king not to violate Sarah even though he did not realize it (Gen 20:6). It was time to rescue Sarah and return her to Abraham. Like a romance scene out of a movie when the hero comes to save the damsel in distress, here comes our Bridegroom. Threatening the very life of the king did not matter to our Lord as He said to Abimelek, "You are a dead man." My hero! Of course, the king took that threat very seriously and returned Sarah to Abraham immediately, thanks to God. God will always stand up for us. Our Bridegroom knows who belongs to whom.

7. Soothes and Reassures

"But God said to him, 'Do not be so distressed about the boy and your slave woman. Listen to whatever Sarah tells you, because it is through Isaac that your offspring will be reckoned. I will make the son of the slave into a nation also, because he is your offspring'" (Genesis 21:12-13

NIV, emphasis added). *Also found in NLT and MSG in Genesis 21:11-13.

This BUT GOD shows us the prophetic fulfillment of BUT GOD #4. We see that Isaac has indeed been born, and God is again stating Isaac is the one God will use in Abraham's lineage. Earlier in the story, Sarah had seen Ishmael scoffing at Isaac and it offended her, so she wanted Ishmael sent away. Obviously, Abraham was worried about Ishmael's well being, wondering how he could send Ishmael and his mother alone into the desert. God told Abraham to listen to Sarah because He had a plan for Isaac, and Ishmael's departure was not going to change that plan. He had already told Abraham that He would make Ishmael into a nation (Gen 17:20), but reaffirmed it again in this BUT GOD verse so Abraham knew that he would be okay. God may have been trying to help bring peace in his household. After all, everyone knows, "A happy wife, a happy life."[7]

Our Lord is keenly aware of when we are upset over something—especially family. Like a good Bridegroom, He consoles us and lets us know everything will be alright. He will not sugar coat things to make us feel better. He will only tell us the truth. God tells Abraham in verse 13 that because Ishmael is his son, he will be taken care of. Abraham trusts God and sends them on their way.

Interesting to note, had Sarah been patient in waiting for the prophecy, she would have never given her maidservant to Abraham to "help" fulfill God's promise of a future son. Ishmael would have never been an issue. God does not need our help and He has His own timeline. With Ishmael being born, the devil had a foothold to cause dissension in Abraham's household and took full advantage of the opportunity (Gen 16). The enemy still does so today as the Muslim/Islam religion believe Ishmael was the promised son to Abraham, not Isaac.

Though the conflict with the Muslims goes beyond disagreeing on this one story, it points to how long the enemy can use one lie to create havoc. The Muslims believe in a Mahdi (their messiah) who will come and rule over the world. Side by side comparison of the characteristics of the Mahdi coincides exactly with the antichrist described in Revelation.[8] So, from a religion who bases their belief in a lie comes a counterfeit messiah. Both Sunni and Shia Muslims agree the Mahdi will arrive first, and after him, Jesus. This would not be our Bridegroom Jesus, it would be someone falsely announcing to be Jesus who will proclaim that the true leader is the Mahdi. This was who Iran's previous leader, Mahmoud Ahmadinejad, constantly referred to in his past speeches (he was replaced in 2013). In *The Rise of Nuclear Iran*, former Israeli ambassador to the UN, Dore Gold, writes, "Mahdi Khaliji, an Iranian Shi'ite scholar . . . has noted that there are apocalyptic hadiths [received Shi'ite traditions] that the Mahdi will not return unless one-third of the world population is killed and another third die. But Ahmadinejad and his followers believe man can actively create the conditions for the Mahdi's arrival in the here and now . . ."[9] Bible believers also have a prophecy about one-third of the population dying (Revelation 8-9). It is interesting that many religions take information from the Bible to try and authenticate their beliefs, but then twist its words around to suit their agenda.

Hinduism is looking for their "savior" in the tenth avatar, *kalki*, who will liberate the world from suffering and enlighten man. Buddhism believes in a maitreya appearing who will also enlighten mankind and be a world ruler. There is already great deception with the New Age movement as well. They try to bring about their leader, what we would call an antichrist spirit, by giving their energy to it. It would be all the gods rolled up into one.[10] Secret societies, such as the Masons, encourage a new world order where all religions would mesh together.

The Masonic religion and many others could send you on a huge rabbit trail, but that is not our focus here. We don't want to get sidetracked, so we will focus on what God's Word says is true. Remember, bride, we are *reassured* by our Bridegroom throughout the Bible (our book of promises) that, as long as we remain in Him and are not deceived, He will protect us and give us eternal life with Him. Our God does not require our energy to appear, nor does He require that we sacrifice our lives to obtain salvation. We do not have to participate in rituals or keep secrets in order to prove our loyalty. Do not be deceived when other religions say their God is the same as ours. There are many beliefs that do not line up with the Word of God. You will always know a false religion when it claims Jesus is anything different than what the Bible says. Christianity is not a religion, but a relationship. Through Jesus' relationship with you, He will reassure you of your place with Him.

8.   Hears

"*But God* heard the boy crying, and the angel of God called to Hagar from heaven, 'Hagar, what's wrong? Do not be afraid! God has heard the boy crying as he lies there'" (Genesis 21:17 NLT, emphasis added).

Isn't God good? In this very next BUT GOD, we have the example of God following through with His Word. He means what He says, just like this example shows. God told Abraham Ishmael would survive and become a nation; God is faithful, even if we are not around to see it (Gen 25:12-18). Abraham did not know the Lord would meet Hagar and Ishmael in the desert, but He did and He helped them. Abraham did not know *how* they were going to be alright, he just knew God told him they would be and by faith believed.

God did not ignore the boy's cry; He addressed it. He hears our "noises." God hears when we cry out—He hears people of all ages. God is a Father to the fatherless if we allow Him to be (Ps 68:5). Isn't it good to know our Lord not only shows Himself to be a good Bridegroom, but also a good Father as well? He instructed Ishmael's mother as to what to do so she could care for him. He directed her to a well of water. I love that Ishmael was thirsty and God provided him water—that is His specialty! Revelation 22:17 says, "The Spirit and the bride say, 'Come!' And let the one who hears say, 'Come!' Let the one who is thirsty come; and let the one who wishes take the free gift of the water of life" (NIV).

God can hear because He has ears, like we do. Since we are made in God's image (Gen 1:27), we can see how we have some similar features. He is not just spirit, but He has a face (Gen 32:30), eyes and ears (Ps 34:15), and a mouth to speak (Prov 2:6). God has a mind (Rom 11:34) and a heart that feels emotions (Gen 6:6). He has outstretched arms (Jer 32:17), a hand (Job 19:21), a finger (Ex 31:18), and feet (Ex 24:10). He has hair on His head, is clothed in white, and sits on a throne (Dan 7:9). Knowing God's characteristics includes how He looks. Jesus said God is Spirit and does not have flesh and bones (John 4:24), but Jesus does (Luke 24:39-40).

When Jesus was born of a woman, He did not empty Himself of His deity, but added on our human qualities. He is fully man, yet fully God (Gal 4:4). My friend Caitlyn wrote an excellent essay on this to which she said I could quote. "As human, Jesus experienced every weakness and emotion that all humans do. He was hungry (Mark 11:12), thirsty (John 4:7), and tired (John 4:6). He felt joy (Luke 10:21) and sorrow (John 11:35). He experienced loneliness (Matt 26:38) as well as the need to be alone (Matt 14:13). However, in all this time, Jesus did not sin. Jesus performed acts that no human could. He forgave sins, and then validated His authority by demonstrating His power to heal (Matt 9:1-8). He demonstrated His authority over the natural elements (Matt 8:23-27), demons (Mark 5:15-20), and death (Luke 7:1-10, John 11:38-44). He also received worship (Luke 24:51-53, John 9:35-38)."

My daughter shared with me that she may not always see her sister's face in the crowds at high school when they are changing classes, but she recognizes the back of her head and knows it is her by the way she moves. Do we recognize God's movements? God knows how *you* move, and He knows how *you* look. The bride of Christ should recognize her Bridegroom from afar. Just as we put our loved ones in picture frames to see their faces and study their features, we can close our eyes and meditate on God's features as if He were in a picture frame. Seek to know Jesus' face and all His characteristics. The time has come for the bride of Christ to be serious about her Bridegroom! Know His personality and know His features. He wants you to! Ask Him to show you glimpses of Himself; He will hear you.

9. Gives Favor / Is a Righteous Judge / Stays the Same

"So Jacob sent word for Rachel and Leah to meet him out in the field where his flocks were. He said, 'I notice that your father has changed toward me; he doesn't treat me the same as before. But the God of my father hasn't changed; he's still with me. You know how hard I've worked for your father. Still, your father has cheated me over and over, changing my wages time and again. *But God* never let him really hurt me. If he said, "Your wages will consist of speckled animals" the whole flock would start having speckled lambs and kids. And if he said, "From now on your wages will be streaked animals" the whole flock would have streaked ones. Over and over God used your father's livestock to reward me'" (Genesis 31:4-9 MSG, emphasis added). *Also found in Gen 31:7 KJV, AMP, and NLT.

To catch you up . . . Isaac had grown up, gotten married to Rebekah (Laban's sister), and had two sons, one of whom was Jacob. Jacob grew up and fell in love with Rachel and worked for her father, Laban, for seven years to marry her. He was tricked into marrying Rachel's older sister, Leah, and so worked another seven years to also marry Rachel. Then he stayed and continued to work for his father-in-law. It was common to have more than one wife in those days. It was also common to wait for and get the father's approval, unlike today when people often do what they want, in disregard of the family's values, customs, or traditions.

Laban did not appreciate the hard work his son-in-law had done for him to help the family business prosper. Laban kept changing the rules to try and prevent Jacob from succeeding, BUT GOD would not concur. Our Bridegroom is a great business partner and He has our backs. He wants us to succeed when we are positioning ourselves within His will. Even when someone is trying to swindle us or cheat us out of what is legally ours, He will bless us for doing what is right. It might not be immediate, BUT GOD's Word says His favor surrounds the righteous (Psalm 5:12) and He will reward the righteous. Psalm 58:11 says, "So that a man shall say, 'Verily there is a reward for the righteous: verily He is a God that judgeth in the earth'" (KJV). Jacob was in a position where he could have easily become bitter, but he did not stay or harbor resentment. He took what was his and made a decision to leave. God judges fairly and saw Jacob's situation and rewarded Jacob for his attitude.

Have you ever been in a situation before similar to Jacob? My husband and I have. Aaron had been working for two and a half years for a boss that pulled shenanigans all the time. Aaron got approval for two weeks paid vacation when Nicole was born. When he returned to work and the paycheck came, it was short the two weeks' pay. When it was brought to his boss' attention, his boss told Aaron he did not have to compensate him. Aaron had to quit immediately because he could not trust that the boss would pay him for the future work he would do. We had to file a claim to take him to court. I obviously was not working since I was on maternity leave, so I could not help financially. There was a lot of stress with a new baby and now no income, BUT GOD never let this hurt us. Aaron immediately found a temporary job that paid for all our expenses along with a regular paycheck for three months until he found a permanent job. When the court date came, the mediator sided with Aaron and the boss wrote him a check that day. Though it was a trial, we knew God had our back through the whole ordeal.

There is a hidden BUT GOD in this verse (it has the word "the" in it). Jacob mentions to Leah and Rachel their father has changed, "BUT the GOD of his father has not." Remember, God is the same yesterday, today, and forever (Heb 13:8). Just because these are stories from long ago does not mean they cannot have meaning for us now. They are still talking about the same God we love today. This is how we know our Bridegroom will stay true: if He says it, He means it. Situations in the world change, people change, and societies change, but that does not mean He will change. Malachi 3:6 proves His faithfulness with the words, "I the LORD do not change. So you, the descendants of Jacob, are not destroyed" (NIV). He still remains as mighty and powerful as before. His commands still apply, as do His judgments, love, and grace through Christ Jesus. God may change His mind, but He will always remain true to His character.[11]

10. Warns

"*But God* came to Laban the Syrian [Aramean] in a dream by night and said to him, Be careful that you do not speak from good to bad to Jacob [peaceably, then violently]" (Genesis 31:24 AMP, emphasis added).

Again speaking in a dream (#6), God this time speaks to Laban. Laban was pursuing Jacob because Jacob left secretly and Laban claimed he did not get to say a proper good-bye. God warned Laban to "watch it" and to "stay in line" when speaking to Jacob. God will speak up when He sees hostility headed our way. Perhaps Laban was considering an attempt to sabotage Jacob somehow as the verse states "peaceably, then violently." God may allow others to have their say and speak their mind, but He does not want us to be physically or verbally threatened in the process. Our Bridegroom listens to how others speak to us and knows what is in their hearts. Since God has our backs, He will hold those who are going after us accountable. He may warn them to back off. God is making sure Laban understands that if he is not careful with his words to Jacob, He may have to deal with God later.

Family dynamics can be tricky. You may think you can talk however you want to your family members, but that is not always wise. Emotions can run high and feelings can get hurt easily, especially when there are opposite personalities or values at play. This can cause breaks in relationships supposed to be the strongest. Jacob was trying to do his job, but there comes a time when enough is enough and parting ways may be best for everyone involved.

Ephesians 4:26-32 tells us how we are to talk with one another. We are not to let our anger cause us to sin. Sin gives the devil a foothold. We are not to have any unwholesome talk come from our mouths, only what is helpful in building others up. We are to get rid of bitterness and rage and instead be forgiving of one another. We are to be compassionate to each other, following Jesus' example. We do not have to be a doormat to people we do not get along with, but we still need to be kind. This is a good lesson for us to apply from this day forward when speaking to other believers.

Have you ever had a situation where another believer, family member, or friend spoke rudely to you or took advantage of your close relationship? Did you harbor bitterness? What steps did you take to resolve it? If you have been affected negatively by something like this, take a moment to repent and ask God to forgive you for holding onto it. Try to remember if someone rubs you the wrong way, not to let a sour attitude or anger cause you to say something rash *to* them or *about* them; you might regret it. Give room for the Lord to correct them. Pray first, and then let them know you would like to talk with them, if need be. Come gently after assessing the situation and speak your mind in peace. Humbling yourself to move on, and giving them grace and forgiveness is a step of maturity in your walk with God. Even if they do not know how hard it is for you, or you do not think they deserve it, God commands that we love one another (John 13:34-35). I know it is hard, believe me, I KNOW, but remember, we are brothers and sisters in Christ. Move on, let go, and let God deal with it.

11. Sees Our Hardship and Our Hard Work

"In the twenty years I've worked for you, ewes and she-goats never miscarried. I never feasted on the rams from your flock. I never brought you a torn carcass killed by wild animals but that I paid for it out of my own pocket—actually, you made me pay whether it was my fault or not. I was out in all kinds of weather, from torrid heat to freezing cold, putting in many a sleepless night. For twenty years I've done this: I slaved away fourteen years for your two daughters and another six years for your flock and you changed my wages ten times. If the God of my father, the God of Abraham and the Fear of Isaac, had not stuck with me, you would have sent me off penniless. *But God* saw the fix I was in and how hard I had worked and last night rendered his verdict" (Genesis 31:38-42 MSG, emphasis added).

It does not matter how much we plead our side of the story to the other party, sometimes they just do not care. Laban was Jacob's father-in-law, uncle, and boss. Jacob was being taken advantage of at work and at home. Jacob never received validation for his work from Laban. Laban showed his appreciation by cheating Jacob in changing his wages over and over, BUT GOD preserved Jacob by providing for him when he was being ripped off.

Aaron and I know firsthand about being preserved by God. We have lived in our current home for over ten years. We have always made our house payment on time. We refinanced a few times to use the equity in our house to help with other things. Unfortunately, the economy went bad, the stock market crashed, and home values all went upside down. Our loan was okay for a while, but we knew the payment was going to go up, so we tried to work with the bank honestly and tell them we needed to resolve the issue before we were unable to pay. We were denied the ability to refinance several times because, basically, they did not care. Since we were making our monthly payments, we were told they did not need to help us. Well, the day arrived when the loan terms changed (the company wanted three times the amount we had been paying) and we could not afford it, so we had to stop making payments. They finally decided to look at our situation to see if they would help. We prayed to God that He would see our hardship and how we had tried to do our part honestly, because the system did not seem to honor our efforts. We knew God would, though, because our Bridegroom notices! We were in a fix, and He rendered a verdict that was in our favor. We did not make payments for five months, and our loan was modified to an affordable amount! I know God answered our prayers and will again when the time comes. Whether we stay in this house or have to move, He will keep a roof over our heads.

Our Lord makes sure we get what is rightfully ours. If we work hard for something, we will reap what we sow. He will not stand silently by and watch someone else gather our reward or steal from us. In fact, He will reprimand those in due time who have wronged us, whether we see it or not, He will defend our rights. Of course, we live in an unjust world and thieves are among us, but we will not know on this side of heaven how often He has protected and defended us until we are face to face with our Bridegroom and He tells us. Jesus never said things in this life would be fair, He just said that we need to live honestly and be a light in the darkness. We cannot expect people who do not know Him to treat us as if they are following the same set of rules. They are not, and therefore, we may see injustice. We will be a stark contrast to those who do not know God and it *will* be noticed, especially by our Bridegroom. You may work in an environment where your wages are changing and where your employer does not treat you fairly, BUT GOD will take care of you. Remind God that you need Him to provide for you just like He did for Jacob.

12. Sees Abuse / Defends

"In fact, if the God of my father had not been on my side— the God of Abraham and the fearsome God of Isaac—you would have sent me away empty-handed. *But God* has seen your abuse and my hard work. That is why he appeared to you last night and rebuked you!" (Genesis 31:42 NLT, emphasis added). *Also found in the NIV.

Jacob is continuing to tell Laban how God defended him. Since BUT GOD #9, all the BUT GODs have to do with this same story. I have included them all because I wonder if God is trying to get our attention to show that He sees how unjust and unfair things seem towards the righteous, He is not letting it go unnoticed.

When I read this BUT GOD verse, my mind immediately began processing all the people who have been denied justice at one time or another. I think of the slaves who were mistreated in this country and not treated as equal human beings. I think of the Native American Indians who were overtaken and who were unjustly compensated. I mostly think of the children, mistreated through child labor, human trafficking, physical and/or sexual abuse. I have even seen videos, mostly from the Middle East, where the children have been brainwashed to hate Israel and America and have machine guns with intent to murder, not protect. Matthew 18:6-7 says, "But whoever causes one of these little ones who believe in and acknowledge and cleave to Me to stumble and sin [that is, who entices him or hinders him in right conduct or thought], it would be better (more expedient and profitable or advantageous) for him to have a great millstone fastened around his neck and to be sunk in the depth of the sea. Woe to the world for such temptations to sin and influences to do wrong! It is necessary that temptations come, but woe to the person on whose account or by whom the temptation comes!" (AMP).

Our Bridegroom sees if we have been abused, have worked hard, or have been taken advantage of. Do not think for a second He does not keep that in mind when dealing with the one who is oppressing us. Jacob may have been an adult when this happened to him, but he lived with it for years before he said something, just as children do. Jacob was able to speak his mind and was set free. Children do not have that luxury; they need an advocate. God lets us see here that He will be our advocate because He is just and will defend. We, as the bride, need to partner with Him by praying to release and break the demonic strongholds that prey on children. We can ask God to remember this story and be our Defender when we cannot. We need Him to be the big brother who steps in and says, "You mess with her, then you have me to deal with." It is a fact that He will stand up for us (#6).

13. Has the Answers and Gives Understanding

"It is beyond my power to do this," Joseph replied. "*But God* can tell you what it means and set you at ease" (Genesis 41:16 NLT, emphasis added). *Also found in the NIV and MSG.

Again, to catch you up . . . Jacob had twelve sons who formed the twelve tribes of Israel. Joseph was Jacob's favorite (Rachel's firstborn son) and was despised by his older brothers, so they got rid of him by throwing him in a pit and then later selling him as a slave. Joseph found favor in Egypt no matter what his situation and learned to rely on God alone.

Pharaoh had a dream. When Pharaoh heard Joseph could interpret dreams, he sent for Joseph. God had the answers to

Pharaoh's dreams and Joseph was very clear about giving credit where credit was due. God helped establish Joseph's position by allowing Joseph to share what the dream meant. He gave Joseph wisdom to share how to prepare for the upcoming famine.

When a company has employed people who are children of the Most High God, the company will be blessed by them. Pharaoh was blessed because he had Joseph; Nebuchadnezzar and a couple other kings were blessed because they had Daniel. Daniel also interpreted a dream for a king. When no one could interpret King Nebuchadnezzar's dream, he ordered all the wise men to be killed, including Daniel. In Daniel 2:19, we see that God revealed the dream to him, and in Daniel 2:28 we read that Daniel actually stated that no one could make known these secrets BUT GOD. Daniel told the king the dream had to do with future empires and, indeed, the Lord has fulfilled this dream precisely as Daniel said. Always remember to point to God and give Him the glory for everything, even when He allows us (His bride) to give the answers.

Aaron and I are both therapists and have specialties in different areas. Sometimes I am asked a therapy question I cannot answer, so I will ask him. He has access to resources I do not. It is because of this relationship I have with my husband that I can come back to my patient later and respond with a great answer.

I think it is interesting that the very ones who may give you a hard time about your faith are usually the first ones to come ask for prayer when they need it. Since I have a relationship with Jesus, I have access to the One who can help and I can ask Him whatever questions I want. I know He has all the answers! How good it is that our Lord positions us, His bride, to be in places where people can ask us questions that will lead to answers from Jesus. In the process, we can point to Him and be a blessing to those we serve.

14. Provides and Sends

"Come closer to me," Joseph said to his brothers. They came closer. "I am Joseph your brother whom you sold into Egypt. But don't feel badly, don't blame yourselves for selling me. God was behind it. God sent me here ahead of you to save lives. There has been a famine in the land now for two years; the famine will continue for five more years—neither plowing nor harvesting. God sent me on ahead to pave the way and make sure there was a remnant in the land, to save your lives in an amazing act of deliverance. So you see, it wasn't you who sent me here *but God*. He set me in place as a father to Pharaoh, put me in charge of his personal affairs, and made me ruler of all Egypt" (Genesis 45:4-8 MSG, emphasis added). *Also found in Genesis 45:7-8 NIV and Genesis 45:8 KJV and AMP.

Joseph was a Messianic figure (someone who was a shadow type of the Messiah, Jesus). Many of his stories reflect pieces of Jesus' life. The idea was for the Jewish people to know these stories of the Old Testament so well that when Jesus came, they would be able to see similarities and relate to what He was doing. There were thematic equivalences to facilitate these connections. Many Israelites missed Jesus the first time because the TaNaK also contained mysterious prophecies, though, now obvious. Two different pictures of the Messiah had been foretold; one as the servant and one as the King. The Israelites did not understand this and did not see that He was going to come twice—once to redeem the sinners (1 Tim 1:15), and again to reign in righteousness (Rom 5:17, Rev 19-22). Here are a few of the similarities between Joseph and Jesus I learned while listening to "The Sign of the Messiah" teaching by Tony Robinson (www.restorationoftorah.org).[12]

Joseph lived with his brother and had His father's favor (Gen 37:3)	Jesus dwelt with His Jewish brethren and had great favor from His Father in Heaven (Matt 3:17)
Joseph was one of twelve brothers (Gen 35:23-26). There are 12 tribes of Israel. (Levi was a tribe unto the Lord and Joseph's two children took Joseph's spot)	Jesus had 12 disciples (Mark 3:16-19)
Joseph was sold by his brother for silver and taken away (Gen 37:28)	Jesus was sold by his disciple, Judas, for silver and taken away (Matt 26:14-15, John 18:2)
Joseph was falsely accused (Gen 39:7-20)	Jesus was falsely accused (Matt 26:1-5)
Joseph was imprisoned with a cup bearer and a baker (Gen 40:5)	Jesus' blood was the wine (cup-bearer) and His body the bread (baker) (1 Cor 11:23-26)
Joseph said to the cup bearer, "And please remember me and do me a favor when things go well for you . . ." (Gen 40:14 NLT)	The man next to Jesus on the cross said similar words, "Jesus, remember me when you come into your kingdom." (Luke 23:42 NIV)
Joseph forgave his brothers as we see here in the BUT GOD verse	Then said Jesus, "Father, forgive them; for they do not know what they do . . ." (Luke 23:34 KJV)

It was not because of the Jews that Jesus died, it was FOR the Jews and all of us that He died. That is WHY God sent Him (John 3:16). Jesus was sent to "save lives" in "an amazing act of deliverance." Now, He is in heaven preparing a place for us. Just like this BUT GOD verse states, Joseph was sent ahead to "save lives" in "an amazing act of deliverance" and to prepare for what was to come. God provided a way for the Israelites to survive in the famine by sending Joseph ahead. God always will provide for us.

When I first read this BUT GOD verse, I could not help but immediately think of Romans 8:28, "And we know that in all things God works for the good of those who love him, who have been called according to his purpose" (NIV). If we are working with the Lord, He will make sure we are at our destinations at the right time to be part of the solution. He puts us in places of influence and power to guide others to salvation. He sends us ahead to where we need to be, even though it may be uncomfortable, unfair, lonely, and inconvenient, to make a way for others. Nothing is by luck or chance. Our Bridegroom guides our steps and circumstances even when it seems the enemy tries to trap us in a pit. Remember, Joseph's brothers literally threw him into one (Gen 37:23-24). We do not always know our mission ahead of time until we have completed it, but our Bridegroom knows, and has a divine purpose for our lives. We can successfully fulfill those purposes as long as we continue to look to Him for direction and give Him the glory along the way.

15. Is With Us

"Then Jacob said to Joseph, 'Look, I am about to die, *but God* will be with you and will take you back to Canaan, the land of your ancestors'" (Genesis 48:21 NLT, emphasis added). *Also found in the KJV, NIV, and AMP.

Jacob is about to die, but reminded Joseph God lives. When you feel the Lord's presence in someone's life, it is hard to say goodbye because you like the feeling you get when you are around them. It is peaceful, comforting, and easy. If that person also happens to be someone from your family, it makes it more difficult. Joseph's father, Jacob, is reminding his son that God will continue to be with Joseph even though Jacob's presence will be absent. God's presence is everlasting and is strong and evident in many people's lives; He will never die. Our Bridegroom wants to be with us all the time. Imagine that! A Bridegroom who enjoys being around you and with you. Jacob told Joseph that God would take him back to Canaan which was the Promised Land. God wants to bring you back to the land where you belong—the Promised Land! Did you catch that?

I have not really lost anyone that was very close to me. I do not want to even think about how sad that day will be. I jokingly tell my parents they will have to live forever. I know many people have lost close loved ones, though, and hopefully you will see them again in heaven. The only way I can relate to this verse right now is by remembering a time when I was saying goodbye to an old life and hello to a new life—literally! God was the only One who could really be with me as I struggled to deal with the unknowns of labor and delivery, along with everything else in parenting that was to follow.

The night before I was supposed to see the doctor to induce labor, I was so nervous. I hate needles and pain and did not want to do this part at all. I was twenty-six years old and had never been a patient in the hospital before, only an employee in one. I did not know how to be a mom. I had been married for five years to Aaron and I liked the freedom we had because it was just the two of us. I knew everything would be different the following day and I was not mentally prepared. Thankfully, the Lord had me in His Word (Matt 25-28) and guided me to keep reading until I reached the points in the story that He would use to comfort me. As I read, He interjected how He knew exactly what I was feeling by showing me where He felt the same way. He suffered much more than I ever would, but I was comforted knowing He was making an effort to relate to me. Even though Jesus did not go through my exact circumstances, He helped ease moments of nervousness and confirmed He would stay with me even when it was over. He was going to bring me to a place of peace. I know millions of people have had babies with no worries about it, but I had not and I was scared! It may seem silly, but this is how it went:

→ I read about the Last Supper and saw how Jesus was glad to be with His disciples one last time before He had to go away. *Similarly,* I had just finished having my last great day with family and friends before I had to go away.

→ He prayed in the garden asking God, "if possible to let this cup pass," knowing the crucifixion was coming within hours. *Similarly,* I was in my room asking God if it was possible that I could skip all the pain and just have the baby a different way. I did not know what to expect and imagined the worst. I knew my body was going to be physically challenged and I did not want to go through it.

→ I read about how Jesus' friends could not stay awake with Him. Jesus was going through this alone with only His Father to talk to. *Similarly,* Aaron was busy doing something else and I was all alone with only God to talk to, realizing no one was going to get me through this and help my mindset but Him.

→ Jesus was taken away and transported to see different people in charge, beaten along the way. *Similarly,* I was going to be taken to the hospital and see a nurse for this and a doctor for that, getting poked and prodded with needles that were way too big.

→ Jesus was crucified; no one else could do this job—only He alone. *Similarly,* I was going to have this baby, no one else could—only me alone.

→ Jesus' body was laid to rest when it was over. *Similarly,* my body could rest when it was over.

→ Jesus' resurrection brought possibility of new life, through believers being born again, bringing new joy. *Similarly,* the baby was a new life that was being born and would bring new joy.

Well, of course, everything turned out fine. The moment it was over and I held Nicole for the first time, I knew it was all worth it. I do not know how I could have been so worried. I knew life was only going to get better; I had this new, little life full of promise and possibility that Aaron and I got to play with. I was so excited; God had kept His promise and stuck with me. When we have to say goodbye to someone, our heavenly Bridegroom will be with us. Jesus is there during our times of desperation, loneliness, sadness, and anxiousness. The great news is He also will be around during our times of joy, happiness, and accomplishments.

16. Has Good Intentions / Forgives

"You intended to harm me, *but God* intended it for good to accomplish what is now being done, the saving of many lives" (Genesis 50:20 NIV, emphasis added). *Also found in KJV, NLT, AMP, and MSG in Genesis 50:19-21.

This BUT GOD verse is similar to the New Testament verse Romans 8:28 that I quoted in the discussion of BUT GOD #14.

After Jacob's death, Joseph graciously reassured his brothers again that he was not going to have his revenge. Joseph had moved on as he had seen the bigger picture and forgave them. His brothers, though, must have still felt guilty or allowed the enemy to plant lies in their heads. In this verse, they were scared and came to Joseph throwing themselves down before him, saying they would be his slaves. Joseph told them again it was God's plan to use him to save many lives.

Christ Jesus went through horrible suffering to save the lives of many. How many times are we like Joseph's brothers and throw ourselves down before Jesus, telling Him we are sorry for sins we already asked forgiveness for? Why do we continue to believe the lies, feel guilty for situations, and continue to be in bondage when the Lord has already cleansed and forgiven us? Do not let the enemy continue to condemn you (Rom 8:1). Jesus has the power to forgive sins (Matt 9:6). His blood washed and sanctified us so that we would not be stained by those sins any longer. It is up to us to accept this forgiveness once we have asked for it and move on. We can do this because our Bridegroom has authority to make us feel new again. Joseph did not possess this authority, so his brothers had difficulty releasing their guilt.

I like these sayings: "There is no testimony without a test," "There is no message without a mess," and "There is no triumph without a trial." Our Bridegroom has good intentions for us and uses circumstances to refine us (getting rid of ALL impurities) until we are full of amazing stories of grace. He wants His people to come out stronger, bolder, wiser, and full of courage and integrity. We need to be understanding and forgiving.

Our story needs to *look* and *sound* different than those who do not know Jesus. It is a story where we do not have to flavor it with foul language to make people pay attention, or relate in a better way (Ps 19:14). It is a story where we do not end up in the bondage of depression, addictions, or suicidal thoughts. Although Christians do deal with these problems, we can lean on Christ to heal us and help us through them. We can tell a story that portrays us rising above the circumstances so we stand out with integrity and not blend in with society. We need to share our testimony with those who are not part of the bride of Christ so that we, too, can be like Joseph (and Jesus). Then, we will be in a position to show Jesus' forgiveness and how He can save many lives. They will be introduced to God's good intentions. So, once you put on your new self (Eph 4:22-24, Col 3:10, 2 Cor 5:17), stop acting and talking like you are still wearing your old self, clothed in filthy rags. The Lord has removed the guilt and sin from your life and clothed you with splendid robes (Zech 3:3-4). Let these verses help encourage you because, sometimes, being refined is easier said than done.

17. Comes to Us / Helps / Leads

"Soon I will die," Joseph told his brothers, "*but God* will surely come to help you and lead you out of this land of Egypt. He will bring you back to the land he solemnly promised to give to Abraham, to Isaac, and to Jacob" (Genesis 50:24 NLT, emphasis added). *Also found in the AMP and NIV.

Joseph is dying, but reminds his brothers that God lives. I wonder if Joseph remembered and realized how comforting it was to hear these similar words when his father said this to him (#15). When we have lost the one person in our lives that has been the authority and the provider for us, it is hard not to be discouraged. Uncertainty sets in when the one who was your mentor, your go-to person for advice, is gone. Thankfully, our Bridegroom will always be around to lead us where we need to go. He is everlasting and will visit us when we seek His presence. Sometimes He may come when we are not expecting a visit, but live expecting one!

After Joseph's death, the Egyptians were worried about the growing number of the Israelites and forced them into slavery. The Israelites remembered the Lord was their Helper so they prayed. As we will see, the Lord answered their prayers and helped. It is unfortunate, though, that in the midst of being saved from slavery, their faith decreased in the only One who continued to help them. They began doubting Him so much that the generation who received the initial help of escape from slavery was also the generation who missed out on the Promised Land because of their unbelief.

You may be growing weary, always hearing these same lines, "God is our help" or "Jesus is coming back soon to save us." Realize the Bridegroom IS returning for His bride. Remember, it is more than a story passed down; it is truth. Do not lose faith now. Do not let unbelief keep you from the Promised Land.

18. Gives the Facts / Commands

> *"But God* again laid out the facts to Moses and Aaron regarding the Israelites and Pharaoh king of Egypt, and He again commanded them to lead the Israelites out of the land of Egypt" (Exodus 6:13 MSG, emphasis added).

AMAZING! The very next BUT GOD is when God is doing exactly what Joseph (and Jacob) said! Here, God gave the plans to Moses and Aaron to lead the Israelites out of Egypt. God is so consistent; in fact, He used that same word "lead" (#17) in this BUT GOD so you will not miss it—leading them out of Egypt! Our Bridegroom is not only consistent with what He says, but He likes to make you smile along the way when you discover it. He also will go over the plan *again* until we get the facts straight (#4). As we will soon see, there were a lot of facts to go over and Moses was going to need to be bold in Pharaoh's presence.

Another part of the verse that stood out to me was, "He again commanded them." Remember, sometimes Jesus is not only making sure we get the facts straight, but He also wants us to follow through with His commands. If we love Him, we will obey His commands. John 14:23 says, "Jesus replied, 'All who love me will do what I say. My Father will love them, and we will come and make our home with each of them'" (NLT).

Cindy Powell wrote some interesting thoughts I want to share from her book, *The Key to His Heart.*[13] She points out that when change is coming, we might not be prepared and wish we had extra time to adjust. In this BUT GOD verse, He made sure Moses and Aaron were very well prepared by giving them all the facts. If we refuse to move when God moves, we will never take new ground. If that happens, we will be left behind. So when that cloud moves, we need to get up and follow it without looking back. I wonder if that was one of the facts God was going over with them.

In regard to believers today, Jesus reminded us in Luke 17:32 of Lot's wife (Gen 19:17-27). She looked back and missed what God was doing in front of her. Instead of being a part of the future God had set out for her, she became a monument to the past (Gen 19:26). Change is coming and it may be painful, BUT GOD has laid out His facts in the Bible for us to know ahead of time. If we know our Bridegroom well enough, we will know when it is time to go. Like Chris Tomlin's song "I Will Follow" says, "Where You go, I'll go, where you stay, I'll stay, when you move, I'll move, I will follow You!"[14]

19. Uses Our Hearts As They Are

"*But God* made Pharaoh stubborn as ever. He still didn't release the Israelites" (Exodus 10:20 MSG).

Just in case you do not know, this is part of a very famous story in the Bible. Moses goes to Pharaoh and begins to implement the commands, just as the Lord said in the previous BUT GOD. He tells Pharaoh that God said to let His people go so they can serve Him in the wilderness. God sends signs and wonders to show that He is Lord, but Pharaoh hardens his heart and says no. Exodus 7-11 lists the plagues which are as follows: 1-Water into blood 2-Frogs 3-Lice 4- Flies 5-Diseased livestock 6-Boils 7-Hail 8-Locusts 9-Darkness 10-Death of the firstborn.The first two signs Pharaoh's magicians were able to use enhancements to copy, but by the third sign they could not, and told Pharaoh the signs were from the hand of God.

In Exodus 7, God told Moses in advance (verses 3-4) He was going to harden Pharaoh's heart so God could lay His hand on Egypt and multiply His signs and wonders. In Exodus 7:14, we see that even before God had intervened and He had sent in Moses, Pharaoh's heart was hard. This set the stage to let you know what kind of person Pharaoh was before the story even got going. God used this to His advantage.

We read in Exodus 7:22 and Exodus 8:7-15 that Pharaoh hardened his heart. Even when the magicians could not copy God's signs with the lice (they did not even try with the flies), Pharaoh hardened his heart and would not let the people go, as found in Exodus 8:19 and verse 32. In Exodus 9:7, again, we read his heart became hard when all his livestock died.

The first time we read that God *caused* Pharaoh's heart to be hard was when the sixth plague hit—the boils in Exodus 9:12. God allowed Pharaoh to suffer boils, maybe due to all the previous stubbornness he displayed when he had hardened his heart on his own. God may have been giving him a chance to work on his heart to avoid the next plague (the seventh plague), but Pharaoh failed the test. Pharaoh again hardened his own heart when we read in Exodus 9:35 where the seventh plague of hail came down. Seven plagues had passed, and since seven is the number that represents completeness, I think God decided to use Pharaoh's stubborn heart against him.

Exodus 10:1-2 (MSG) says that the Lord told Moses to go to Pharaoh again. He had made Pharaoh's heart hard so that he would be forced to look at the signs. God also wanted Moses to be able to tell his children and grandchildren these stories to show that God was sovereign. Moses knew God was going to cause Pharaoh to go through the next plague. Nonetheless, Moses still told Pharaoh if he did not release God's people, locusts were coming next (Ex 10:3-6). Pharaoh was so frustrated that he told Moses he could go worship, but he could only take the men with him, not all the families or livestock. Well, God was not going to leave anyone behind. So, with that, God had Moses stretch out his hand for the locusts to come (the eighth plague) and devour everything that the hail had not destroyed (v 12). Pharaoh admitted he sinned and asked for forgiveness. He also asked Moses to pray to God that the locusts would be taken away. In Exodus 10:20, we see our BUT GOD verse, and we see God, for the second time, hardened Pharaoh's heart, just like He told Moses He would. Once the request was granted to make the locusts go away, Pharaoh refused to let the people go.

Remember, Pharaoh's heart was already in a position where God did not have to do much. God did not make Pharaoh's heart hard from the beginning; this is how Pharaoh already was! The Lord used that to work for Him to bring about His glory. God made harder what was already hard. God was going to bring more signs and wonders at Pharaoh's expense because He wanted to leave no doubt about who was bringing these plagues upon Egypt. Pharaoh had enjoyed control over the Israelites too long. He had mistreated them so badly that he was going to pay the price as he wallowed in the extra plagues, which were part of God's plan all along anyway. God wanted Pharaoh to sit and think about all these outbreaks the one true God was causing. Interestingly, the false gods that Pharaoh and the Egyptians worshipped coincided with the plagues, so God could prove His sovereignty. Pharaoh would be very aware of who was in charge, and it would not be Heqt (frog goddess), Scarabus (flying bug god), Shu (god of nature), Ra (sun god), etc.[15]

Before our Bridegroom returns to rule, the earth will see similar signs and wonders. These plagues in the book of Exodus are a type or shadow of what is to come. Like Pharaoh's plague with locusts, we read about the fifth trumpet blast in Revelation 9. A star will fall from heaven to the earth causing smoke to rise, darkening the sun and moon. Out of that smoke locusts will come, but will torment like scorpions for five months those who do not have God's seal upon their heads. Many other signs, wonders, and plagues will come, and, unfortunately, the ones in charge are going to be like Pharaoh and have hardened hearts toward the Lord. They will become more defiant against God, not repenting and turning from their ways (Rev 16:9-11). Bride of Christ, let this be a reminder to keep your heart soft! Let us allow our Bridegroom to use our tender and loving hearts and make them even more so.

20. Does Not Want Us in the Dark

"*But God* kept Pharaoh stubborn as ever. He wouldn't agree to release them" (Exodus 10:27 MSG, emphasis added).

Good thing we are doing these BUT GODs in order, because we just finished BUT GOD #19 on the eighth plague and now we come to our next BUT GOD as we discuss the ninth. God kept Pharaoh stubborn. Thick darkness came upon the land for three days. The Bible says in Exodus 10:22-23 only the Israelites could move about because they had light where they were living. Of course they would! God was not punishing the Israelites—He was protecting them—but in the meantime, God was teaching Pharaoh a lesson. During this plague, Pharaoh told Moses he could leave if he took with him only the people—not their herds. Moses told Pharaoh that the animals were needed for sacrifice as part of their worship, BUT GOD hardened Pharaoh's heart, and the Israelites were not allowed to leave.

Did you read in Exodus 10:23 that it was so dark the Egyptians could not even rise from their place for three days? Interesting! Our Bridegroom was in the tomb in the dark for three days and His body did not move either, but the difference is He is the light (John 8:12). I would say people who do not know Jesus are stuck in the plague of darkness. They need to soften their hearts to Jesus and become children of God, so they can be carriers of the light as the Israelites were and as we believers are today (Matt 5:14-16). Until people ask the Holy Spirit to open their eyes to see, ears to hear, and hearts to accept, they will not fully understand God, and may stay blinded and hard-hearted. Sometimes, because He is so gracious and full of mercy, God intervenes and shows people anyway (example Saul/Paul in Acts 9 and Rom 10:20). Second Corinthians 4:6 tells us that it was God who commanded light to shine out from darkness and that light shines in our hearts. We are to share that light of the knowledge of the glory of God.

Since we do not want to be in the dark, we need to keep our hearts tender and our minds alert to our Lord's plans. Do not miss the important signs He is displaying in the land at this time. Our Bridegroom is coming back and He is allowing alignments with nations and leaders to bring about the one world government system that will pave the way for the antichrist and ultimately Christ's return. We have to be still and wait on the Lord while He allows leaders to make decisions according to His purposes and His timeline. Though we do not understand why governments make decisions that seem so ungodly, we need to remember our Bridegroom is divinely intervening to make our release from this world system all the more inviting. We need to remember we are not fighting against flesh and blood but against the powers of this world that use their evil influence on people (Eph 6:12). It is by our prayers that God's warriors can help in the heavenly realms to protect us from the repercussions of bad governmental decisions. We do not look at what is seen, but what is unseen. The things that are seen are temporary, but the things that are unseen are eternal (2 Cor 4:18).

Just like the Israelites in the book of Exodus were not affected during the plagues, I believe the Lord will protect His people as a whole when the judgments begin, if any of us are still here. I certainly do not want to be here. As my pastor said, "I will hope for pre-tribulation rapture, but plan for post-tribulation." Meaning, I will prepare my mind and my heart so my emotions do not overtake me and so I am not mad at God and His plan if we all stay. Jesus is preparing His bride to be ready. He wants us to look at the things of the Old Testament to see the fulfillment in the New Testament. There are shadows of Jesus in stories and pictures of what is to come all throughout the book of Exodus, and we have barely touched on two of them. Another one is going to show up in the next BUT GOD, and it is a good one! Your Bridegroom wants you to take the time to dig deep, will you?

21. Gave a Hidden Rehearsal

"Moses and Aaron had performed all these signs in Pharaoh's presence, *but God* turned Pharaoh more stubborn than ever—yet again he refused to release the Israelites from his land" (Exodus 11:10 MSG, emphasis added).

God made the BUT GODs line up so you would get the whole entire story! God's last sign (the tenth plague) that Moses revealed to Pharaoh was the sign of the death of the firstborn. Moses told Pharaoh every firstborn child in Egypt (including animals) would die. This plague would not be against the Israelites. God told Moses earlier that Pharaoh would not listen so that God's signs would be multiplied. God, for the third and last time, made Pharaoh's heart stubborn during this plague and allowed for the angel of death to enter the land of Egypt.

There are so many hidden signs that, as soon as you open your eyes to one, all of them start popping up. One little sign I noticed concerns the mass death that was about to occur. There are three main times I remember this being mentioned in the Bible: the first one was during Moses' time as a baby (Ex 1:22), the second one was this BUT GOD final plague—death of the firstborn, and the third one was right after Jesus was born (Matt 2:16). Is that pointing to something? Moses was seen as a representation of God in the Old Testament. His life was threatened as a baby, and many Jewish babies were killed, but Moses' life was spared. Pharaoh now threatens Moses' life as an adult (Ex 10:28). Death is something that is important in the story of Moses and the nation of Israel. We know Jesus' life was threatened as a baby, and, as an adult, we know His death was important to the story. When death came, freedom was released!

The biggest sign in this last plague was the picture of what the Israelites were doing (Ex 12). They were given specific instructions from God as to what to do to be saved from death. They had to prepare spotless, male lambs. They were to inspect the lamb for four days and slaughter one per family. The Israelites were instructed to eat the whole lamb. They were to take a bunch of hyssop and dip it in the blood of the lamb and put it on the doorframe of their house (Ex 12:21-23). This is how the angel of death knew to pass over their house so they would be saved. God provided them with full stomachs before their journey. They ate of the lamb and took their dough before it was leavened (it had no yeast) because they were driven from the land of Egypt (Ex 12:33-39). The Israelites were commanded to remember this day annually; it is called The Feast of Passover (Ex 12:24-27). Unfortunately, they had no idea at the time they were participating in a rehearsal of a story that would point them to Jesus.

Abraham believed God, so he was given the gospel message. It was first revealed in the seed (Gen 15), then the fullness of that single seed manifested into the greatness of One Son (through Abraham's son, Isaac, came the Son of God). God revealed the end plan in Genesis 22, where we learn that Abraham was asked by God to offer his son, Isaac, to God on a mountain. Knowing this, Abraham believed that he and Isaac would leave to worship and then they *both* would come back (Gen 22:5). Abraham spoke in faith when he told Isaac, "God Himself will provide the lamb for the burnt offering . . ." (Gen 22:8 NIV). God had promised a future for Isaac and since that had not been fulfilled, Abraham believed God would keep His word (#4). Indeed, God provided a ram for the sacrifice once He saw Abraham's obedience (Gen 22:12-14). Jesus is the Lamb that Abraham prophesied God would provide in the future. God saw in Abraham how it would feel to offer up His only Son, as later, near same mountain, Jesus shed His blood to save us all from everlasting death.[16]

The New Testament teaches us about the time when the real "Lamb of God" arrived. John the Baptist proclaimed it to the people. He said in John 1:29, "Behold the Lamb of God," but still many did not understand. Jesus lived a spotless life and many people "ate" His words. When we partake in communion together, we are to remember His body and His blood (Luke 22:19-20). Just like the spotless lamb was inspected by the Israelites for four days, Jesus spent His last four days in Jerusalem before dying on the cross. The same day the Israelites celebrated Passover was the same day Jesus died on the cross! Jesus defeated Satan and became the bridge that allows us to cross over to the Father and have a relationship with God again (Kent Tucker's book, *In The Red Zone*, helps explain this concept to others). Letting Jesus' blood cover you allows you to be saved from eternal death. Jesus was in the grave on the Feast of Unleavened Bread. To have unleavened bread meant bread with no yeast. Yeast is referred to as sin; Jesus had no sin (1 Corinthians 5:6-8). The Israelites were restricted by God to eat unleavened bread during this week. Jesus rose on the third day, which was also known as Feast of Firstfruits (1 Cor 15:20-23).

Until the Israelites ate of the lamb, they could not come out of Egypt; the blood was a sign that they ate of the lamb. Jesus and His Father both require us to eat of the Lamb and remember what He has done for us. We break the bread and drink the wine (or grape juice) in remembrance of Him, the eternal Lamb. Rarely does one learn about the feasts of the Lord (Lev 23) in churches today, but to study them will increase your understanding of how He came and fulfilled them. Many say that the spring feasts, along with Pentecost, were fulfilled with Jesus' first coming. The fall feasts are said to find their final fulfillment at His second coming (rapture, judgment, and millennium reign). Our Bridegroom reveals Himself in so many ways!

22. Leads

"*But God* led the people about, through the way of the wilderness of the Red Sea: and the children of Israel went up harnessed out of the land of Egypt" (Exodus 13:18 KJV, emphasis added). *Also found in the AMP.

Once Pharaoh's son died in the last plague, we finally come to the conclusion of the story where we see Pharaoh let the Israelites leave Egypt. God Himself led the people with a cloud by the day and a pillar of fire at night. That cloud was probably pretty glorious, I can imagine! God painted an interesting picture that we should notice. Sometimes when He sends us to a place, He will also lead us out of that place. After all, Jacob (#15) and Joseph (#17) both said God would lead them out because God allowed (in His plan) for them to be *sent* to there (#14) in the first place. Eventually, they needed rescuing. In BUT GOD #18 we learned that God laid the plans down for Moses to follow and Pharaoh would not let them go (#19 and #20). But, now here we go . . .

The connection to all the previous BUT GODs are outrageously exciting! The Lord wants to make sure you fully understand the magnitude of His promises and plans for His people. If I skipped any BUT GODs, then you would have missed major revelations of God's great power, heart, and character. Have you noticed that many of the main stories in the Bible (especially about the patriarchs) are included in the BUT GODs? If you never read the Bible, this is giving you a crash course, and we are only on BUT GOD #22!

In this BUT GOD we see God following through with His promise of delivery. One of the reasons God sent Joseph into Egypt was so he could be placed in charge by Pharaoh to prepare for the famine. This way, all of Jacob's family would be provided for. The problem was that after it was over, they stayed there. They were stuck in their routine and became comfortable, so comfortable they did not realize the evil around them and were forced into becoming slaves. God knew this was going to happen as He told Abraham about it earlier in Genesis 15:13. In this BUT GOD verse, we see God was on the move and the Israelites were not going to stand still any longer. That is a good word for the church! Do not let your weekly routine of going to church become stagnant. When you see God moving, do not sit and watch Him go by—jump in the river! Follow His lead! Do not get so comfortable in your seat at church that you just listen about the gifts of the Holy Spirit—exercise them!

We have a great God who gathers His people and leads them to safety. He dealt with the oppressor and now was ready to lead His people to the Promised Land. This is exactly what our Bridegroom has planned to do again. We need to be ready to go once He has put the final plan in motion, so eat up from His Word while you can so you will be full for the journey ahead! Jamie Grace's song, "You Lead," has some great lyrics that remind us that God knows the way and He will guide us tenderly.[17] He has more for us than we can see, and He wants to lead His bride, so let Him lead you on!

23. Knows Accidents Happen / Numbers Our Days

"However, if it is not done intentionally, *but God* lets it happen, they are to flee to a place I will designate" (Exodus 21:13 NIV, emphasis added). *Also found in the KJV and AMP.

God is now training the Israelites in His ways. They had never had any of God's laws written out before, and after being in captivity for so long, they probably needed some guidelines to truly live as people of God. They knew all of the Egyptian's customs, including their beliefs in many gods, and they may have needed some redirection. Yahweh gave laws for His people so they would all live by the same statutes and would know His standards. This way, when judgments were passed, everyone would be on the same page. When certain things happened that were covered in His rules, there would not be any question about the punishment or outcome because God had described it clearly for the Israelites. Most of these laws defined sin, so when they were broken, sacrifices had to be made. Blood was shed to shield them from these sins. This is why Jesus came. He was the only One able to keep all the commands, thus, proving to be the perfect lamb without flaw and the final sacrifice for our transgressions (Hebrews 9:28).

Now that you have the background, this particular BUT GOD comes in the midst of judgments concerning a person's death. Usually, if someone died, it was life for life; the murderer would be done away with. In this case, though, God is acknowledging that sometimes accidents happen. These people did not lie in wait or premeditate how they would murder someone; they could have been in the wrong place at the wrong time or some other circumstance. Regardless, they are given grace and the Lord provides safety for them. (Deut 4:41-42 is where the cities are actually set aside and listed by Moses.)

We can all say we have done something by accident. How great is our Bridegroom that He does not play the blame game, but gives us grace. He lets us find protection under His wings ("He will cover you with his feathers, and under his wings you will find refuge; his faithfulness will be your shield and rampart" Psalm 91:4 NIV). He does not judge us in these circumstances but has made allowances. That is not to say the people around us are going to act so kindly. Think about how quickly we are angered when someone has broken something of ours on accident that was special or expensive. How about when you have to explain to your spouse that you accidently backed the car up into a pole, a garbage can, or another car and smashed the rear fender? I have done all those myself—whoops! How about our dear children—do we overreact about spilled milk? Accidents happen; thank you Lord that you are an understanding Bridegroom and allow for mistakes—even ones as serious as death!

Since God is always in charge, He knows how many days He has appointed for us to live on the earth. Psalm 139:16 says, "Your eyes saw my unformed body; all the days ordained for me were written in your book before one of them came to be" (NIV). Also, Proverbs 10:27 says, "The fear of the LORD adds length to life, but the years of the wicked are cut short" (NIV). Satan does not want people to believe in God and he does not want believers to witness about God. Satan is out to kill and destroy. God ordains our days, but we have free will. So, do not give the enemy the opportunity to end your life or someone else's by being involved in something you should not be. As warriors in God's army, it is imperative we know our adversary and his tactics. Remember to pray and ask God for protection for ourselves and our loved ones every day and night so the enemy's plans against us will be cancelled in Jesus' name.

Satan is a thief. He may succeed in stealing a loved one from us in the form of an accident as this BUT GOD verse references. However, we cannot let him succeed in stealing our joy. We cannot let the enemy use the situation to knock us off track. We need to find a way to forgive and let God heal us, honoring Him in the process (Rom 12:17-21). Just like Matt Redman's song, "Blessed be Your Name" says, "You give and take away, my heart will choose to say, Lord, blessed be Your name."[18] Bless God when accidents happen; don't curse Him.

24. Allows Us in His Presence

"*But God* did not raise his hand against these leaders of the Israelites; they saw God, and they ate and drank. The LORD said to Moses, 'Come up to me on the mountain and stay here, and I will give you the tablets of stone with the law and commandments I have written for their instruction'" (Exodus 24:11-12 NIV, emphasis added).

There are verses that say no one has ever seen God (John 1:18, 1 John 4:12), so why does this BUT GOD verse say that they did? I have two answers. The first reason may be that the Israelite leaders may have seen God, but not in all His fullness. God had spoken face to face with Moses, but not while in *all* His glory (Ex 33:11, 20). Maybe that is why Moses may have asked to see God's glory. When God allowed His glory to pass by Moses, He shielded Moses from seeing His face so Moses would not die (Ex 33:18-23). The second reason may be that the Israelite leaders may have seen Jesus Himself since He permanently houses God's being and glory in the flesh (Heb 1:1-3, John 14:6-9). Can you imagine having Jesus, the Son of God, sit at your dinner table? What in the world would you talk about? It is so exciting to know that we will get to do this with our Bridegroom one day soon!

Since we are talking about characteristics of our Bridegroom, the following seems like an important piece of information to share: since Jesus is Jewish, it appears that God is following some Hebrew customs in regards to betrothal. Revelation 3:20 says, "Behold, I stand at the door, and knock: if any man hears my voice, and opens the door, I will come in to him, and will sup with him, and he with me" (KJV). In ancient Hebrew culture, there were four steps in accepting the groom's proposal once two families agreed to a marriage.

#1 When the groom arrived with his father and knocked on the door, the bride-to-be had to open it if she was going to accept.

#2 If she opened the door, both families would then eat a meal together as they discussed the marriage contract (the Ketubah) and what the bride and bridegroom's responsibilities were going to be.

#3 At the end of the meal, the Ketubah was written up and signed to make it official. They were now legally married. The son would not return to take her to the ceremony until he had prepared a place for his bride.

#4 This was the actual wedding ceremony itself and the point at which consummation was allowable.

At each step, specific people would drink a cup of wine. At the third and fourth steps, only the bride and Bridegroom could drink it. When they drank the fourth cup after their vows, they would stomp on the cup to symbolize exclusivity to each other.[19] Entering into a covenant with the Lord makes you His bride. Knowing this, I cannot help but see a connection.

#1 The first cup of wine that coincided with the first step could be when the Israelites *accepted salvation* by the blood of the lamb when they marked their *doors* with its blood.

#2 The second step and the second cup that was drunk could be seen in this BUT GOD verse. It talks of the Israelites (bride) and God (our Bridegroom) eating and drinking together. Specifically, the ones present here are the leaders, the ones who carry more responsibility.

#3 The third cup was drunk when the Ketubah was written up and signed. This can be seen in this BUT GOD verse where it seems they are done with the meal and the Lord said He would write up His commands.

This is where the cups end for now as reconfirmed during the last supper. On Passover during the Last Supper, Jesus only drank three of the four cups. He would not drink the fourth cup, known as the Cup of Acceptance or Praise. Jesus (our Bridegroom) let us know He is preparing a place for us now and will return (John 14:3). He reaffirmed that He plans on drinking the fourth cup with us when He says, in Matthew 26:29, "I tell you, I will not drink from this fruit of the vine from now on until that day when I drink it new with you in my Father's kingdom" (NIV). Revelation 19:7 reads, "Let us rejoice and be glad and give him glory! For the wedding of the Lamb has come, and His bride has made herself ready" (NIV). Revelation 19:9 says, "And he saith unto me, Write, Blessed are they which are called unto the marriage supper of the Lamb. And he saith unto me, These are the true sayings of God" (KJV).

Well, there it is—the marriage supper of the Lamb where we will drink the fourth cup of wine with our betrothed and beloved Bridegroom and then smash the cup and be eternally His forever! Let this give you new meaning when you participate in communion. Every time I drink of the cup, I say in my head, "I do!" just as I did when I took my marriage vows. I think this is a great BUT GOD verse. I can't wait to drink the fourth cup with my Bridegroom!

25. Instructs

"*But God* told Balaam, 'Do not go with them. You are not to curse these people, for they have been blessed!'" (Numbers 22:12 NLT, emphasis added). *Also found in the NIV.

While the Israelites journeyed in the desert, we are introduced to the story of Balaam. It is an interesting one. King Balak wanted to drive the Israelites out from the plains of Moab, so he sent for Balaam and offered him money to come and curse the Israelites so they would not be a threat and King Balak could defeat them (Num 22:2-6). Balaam allowed the officials to stay overnight as he spoke to the Lord about this. God clearly told him not to go. Instead of telling the officials he could not go and that the Israelites "have been blessed," Balaam said in verse 13, "The Lord *wouldn't* let him go."

Balaam was a false prophet. False prophets accept bribes and their words do not always line up with what the Bible says; they speak destructive heresies. In Numbers 31, we read of what was to become of Balaam in the future. Balaam was killed and he was also blamed for causing people to sin against the Lord (Numbers 31:16, Joshua 13:22).

I was taught the English transliteration of Hebrew words for the story of Balaam from Brian Howard of Nitzahon Ministries.[20] The English transliteration of the Hebrew words used in this BUT GOD verse for "Do not go with them" is *Vielech Emaheim.* Meaning, "You shall not go with them *in common purpose.*" God told Balaam not to go with them (King Balak's men) in order to curse the Israelites.

When we get a clear "no" from our Bridegroom, we must be sure not to hold resentment in our hearts for not getting our way. Let us just be happy the Lord gave us an answer! If we truly love Him, we will honor His way when He instructs us. Let us go only when it is in a common purpose with God, not our own will.

26. Has Righteous Anger

"*But God* was angry that Balaam was going, so he sent the angel of the Lord to stand in the road to block his way. As Balaam and two servants were riding along, Balaam's donkey saw the angel of the LORD standing in the road with a drawn sword in his hand. The donkey bolted off the road into a field, but Balaam beat it and turned it back onto the road" (Numbers 22:22, 23 NLT, emphasis added). *Also found in the NIV.

God is allowing us to see the full story of what happened here by just following the BUT GOD clues. After Balaam did not go the first time, more distinguished officials came back to sweeten the offer for Balaam to entice him to go. God had already told Balaam not to go with King Balak's officials to curse the Israelites (#25). Instead of resisting them, Balaam again let them stay the night to see if God would give him another answer. Balaam already knew what God's answer was, so why did he ask again? Could it be that he really wanted to go see the king and have riches offered? But why would Balaam want to visit a king desiring to curse God's people? Maybe it was because he was a false prophet, and at times did not always do what was right.

In verse 20, we read that God told Balaam he could go this time, BUT GOD made sure Balaam knew he was only to say what God told him to. When God told Balaam he could go, the English transliteration of Hebrew words used was, *Vielech Etam* meaning, "*Go not* in common purpose." Meaning, he could go, but not in the common purpose of coming against the Israelites, as was the purpose of King Balak.

I never understood why it seemed that God changed His mind and let Balaam go and then why God got mad when Balaam went. After all, it seemed that God told Balaam he *could* go. Seeing the Hebrew translation of the words solves my question and makes the answer obviously clear. God really had not changed His mind. God still did not want Balaam to curse the Israelites. He was letting Balaam go based on that understanding. But, we read in Numbers 22:21, Balaam "went with" the princes. The English transliteration of Hebrew words used when describing how Balaam went was, *Vielech Eim*, which means that Balaam "*Went with common purpose.*" He went *in order to* curse the Israelites. This is *opposite* of what the Lord told him to do! That is why this BUT GOD verse says God was angry with Balaam for going. Balaam left early and, despite the donkey's resistance to go, Balaam pushed onward. He then beat the donkey three separate times until the donkey actually spoke to him and Balaam saw the angel blocking the road! We think donkeys are stubborn, but it seems Balaam had an issue with this as well!

When we are stubborn, we cannot see the heart of God. Entertaining "better offers" and thinking we can do things the way we want can lead us into trouble. God does not like when we do not listen to Him the first time. If God allows us to have our way, it might come with contingencies. God did not change His mind about letting Balaam go, He just gave clear instructions on *how to go*. God set obvious boundaries around Balaam's journey. It was up to Balaam to obey them.

We read later in the story that God used Balaam's mouth to bless Israel many times. God expects us to have *common sense* once He provides the opportunities we had wanted. He does not want us to try to be sneaky like Balaam, who left with the princes early in the morning "with common purpose," going against what God had said. BUT GOD #25 and this BUT GOD verse demonstrate that God does not want us aligning ourselves with anyone who would want to curse Israel (Gen 12:3). Those who do will make God angry.

Once Balaam was with King Balak, he began to prophesy. God filled Balaam's mouth with His words. During one of the three times Balaam prophesied to King Balak, our Bridegroom's characteristics were described. King Balak wanted Balaam to curse the Israelites, but instead God controlled the words coming out of Balaam's mouth. Balaam said, "God is not a man, so He does not lie. He is not human, so He does not change his mind. Has he ever spoken and failed to act? Has he ever promised and not carried it through? Listen, I received a command to bless; God has blessed, and I cannot reverse it! No misfortune is in his plan for Jacob; no trouble is in store for Israel. For the LORD their God is with them; he has been proclaimed their king. God brought them out of Egypt; for them he is as strong as a wild ox. No curse can touch Jacob; no magic has any power against Israel. For now it will be said of Jacob, 'What wonders God has done for Israel!'" (Numbers 23:19-23 NLT).

I think it is important to clarify one more thing. Concerning the verse I just quoted from in Numbers, where it states, "He never changes His mind," I believe it is in reference to the fact that God never varies or alters His affections when it concerns His people or

His covenant with them. He would never curse them or apologize for giving them the gracious gifts He had bestowed upon them. He had planned for Israel to inherit the Promised Land, and that was something He would not change His mind about. Just as I stated before, God had not changed His mind about Balaam going *in common purpose* with King Balak's people, and God got angry when His directions were ignored. He was not going to let this king employ a prophet to speak out words that would try to alter His plan for the Israelites.

Yahweh will never change His mind about Israel and the plans He has for them—plans for a future. I say this in reference to Jeremiah 29:11. Once Israel had made it to the Promised Land, they turned to false gods and this angered God. Because of this, God allowed the Israelites to be sent to Babylon, but even in the midst of their captivity, He still had a future for them *because He WILL NEVER change His mind about the plans He has made for His children.* This is why we know we have a blessed hope in Him. We are His children, along with Israel, and will receive happily the plans He has in store for us because they are good (Gal 3:29).

We always hear how we have a loving God, and that is true, but let us not take advantage of His loving kindness. Since God is a holy God, His anger is displayed when righteousness is being denied. God has been angry in the past with people when His holiness, sovereignty, and righteousness are not upheld to His standards. In Exodus 4:14, God was angry when Moses was seemingly unwilling to do what was asked of him. In Deuteronomy 9:8, 19-20, God was angry when Aaron and the Israelites made a calf image. In David Pawson's book about Isaiah, he explains how a whole political situation developed because God was angry.[21] The people of God were living as if He did not exist; they were full of pride. There was injustice and wickedness running wild. God gets angry with the wicked because they deny His righteous authority. He will display His righteous anger again toward the wicked as they will be the ones receiving His wrath and fury as read in Romans 1:18. Actually, all of Romans 1 displays what happens on Earth when God is mad. God gives these people over to their depraved minds. God forgives those who repent, because He is a loving God, but He will stay angry with those who do not repent and are defiant. Do not think that when we purposely ignore our God's instructions He won't care, He will, because He knows it is not in our best interest!

27. Lets Us Know When He Is Not In It
"But God told me, 'Tell them, "Don't do it; don't go up to fight—I'm not with you in this. Your enemies will waste you"'" (Deuteronomy 1:42 MSG, emphasis added).

Who would ever want to go into battle without God on their side? Why would anyone want to do anything without Him? Even Moses asked not to be sent ahead if God did not go with them. Moses knew God's presence distinguished the Israelites from all the other people on the earth (Exodus 33:15-16).

Here is some history to catch you up: the Israelites had made it to the edge of the Promised Land. God had spoken of this promised place to their forefathers for years. We can verify that in Exodus 3:17 which reads, "And I have said, I will bring you up out of the affliction of Egypt unto the land of the Canaanites, and the Hittites, and the Amorites, and the Perizzites, and the Hivites, and the Jebusites, unto a land flowing with milk and honey" (KJV). Now, the Israelites were right in front of it! The Lord was so excited for them to finally be there, He specifically said to them, "And I said unto you, Ye are come unto the mountain of the Amorites, which the LORD our God doth give unto us. Behold, the LORD thy God hath set the land before thee: go up and possess it, as the LORD God of thy fathers hath said unto thee; fear not, neither be discouraged" (Deut 1:20, 21 KJV). Basically, "We are here! Do not be afraid; go get it!"

All the Israelites had to do was trust the Lord's word, but Deuteronomy 1:32 says they *did not* and verse 34 says when the Lord heard this, He was angry (#26). The Israelites' unbelief was unacceptable after all God had provided for them. He had parted the Red Sea as an escape route (Ex 14:21-22), provided bread from heaven (Ex 16) and then quail when they complained for meat

(Num 11), fought battles with them, and made water come from a rock (Ex 17). Even with these miraculous provisions and more, the Israelites were unable to learn how to grow their faith from each blessing and were unsuccessful at believing in God for each upcoming challenge. The Israelites lost faith and were afraid that the Amorites might dominate them in battle. The result was that God had enough and, therefore, did not bless the Israelites because of their unbelief. In this BUT GOD, God told the Israelites not to gear up for this fight anymore because He was not going to let them win. The Israelites' unbelief this time cost them their entrance into the Promised Land. Their generation lost the right to open God's gift to them. Despite what God told them, they did not listen and instead rebelled—they wanted that present! They tried to win the battle without Him, but were unsuccessful (Deut 1:43-46).

When I am participating in an activity that is a big deal, I want to have my husband, Aaron, with me. It is always better when he wants to come. If he is unable to, I cannot wait to tell him about it when it is over so he can enjoy the thrill of it, even though he was not there. Reliving it is half the fun and he is always excited to hear how it went. Of course, there have been times I wanted to do something and he said no. I knew I could still get my way, but if I did it without his support or blessing, it was not as fun. I could not relive any of the moments with him, I could not tell him what I learned, and I could not even enjoy myself fully while I was at the activity. It just seemed to put a downer on the whole thing. Afterward, I would come home and find that he was upset with me because I had done what I wanted and I had not considered what he had said. Having support makes things so much easier and better in every circumstance.

Relating this to our heavenly Bridegroom is easy. With His support, things flow so smoothly! Without His support, I encounter similar problems as I expressed before, but worse. I find myself going into situations with no authority, no power, no safety, and no delight in reliving it. In fact, when He is not in it, there is usually nothing good to speak of that is lasting. It is just not the same. Usually, I spend more time trying to fix the mess that never would have existed if I would have just listened to God in the first place. Thankfully, I have learned if God is not in it, why in the world would I want to be? If He says He is not going with me, then I do not want to go.

In this BUT GOD verse we learn that even though the Israelites disappointed God and did not believe Him, He still protected them by His warning. God could have been angry and just walked away, but He had a covenant with them and still wanted to spare their lives by letting them know He would not fight this battle for them anymore. God had only changed His mind because of their disbelief. Even though He told them not to go, the Israelites went anyway and lost.

If my spouse tells me that I do not have his support, then I need to stop and rethink. Should I still proceed? Is God telling me to still go or is God using my spouse to let me know not to participate in whatever it was I wanted to do. I need to carefully and prayerfully weigh the consequences. We need to be a united front, working as a team, partnering together with our earthly spouse and our heavenly Bridegroom. Nothing will ever succeed the right way if our Bridegroom is not in it. Jeremy Camp has a great song reiterating this point, so, if you can, listen to "Without You" from his album *Reckless*.[22]

28. Expects Our Best

"*But God* was still angry with me because of you. He wouldn't listen. He said, 'Enough of that. Not another word from you on this. Climb to the top of Mount Pisgah and look around: look west, north, south, east. Take in the land with your own eyes. Take a good look because you're not going to cross this Jordan'" (Deuteronomy 3:26-27 MSG, emphasis added).

In the last two BUT GODs, we have discussed God's righteous anger. He has a right to be angry when people deny His authority, His Word, or His power. God was angry because Balaam tried to go against His people, He was angry with Israel because they did not believe Him, and God was angry with Moses, not because of the Israelites, but because Moses was disobedient and did not trust the Lord. Moses had been given a great deal of responsibility by leading the Israelites. God trusted him to be obedient to all of His commands.

In Numbers 20:8-12, God told Moses to *speak* to the rock and it would produce water for the Israelites to drink, but Moses *struck* the rock twice instead. Disobeying God and not making God holy in front of the Israelites caused Him to be angry with Moses. This was the reason Moses would not be allowed to lead the people into the Promised Land. God likes to show His glory in many different ways and He wants all the credit. God had already shown water coming forth from a rock being struck (Ex 17:6). The reason striking the rock only once was important was because the rock represented Christ. Christ only needed to be struck once to pay for our sin. His death was the final sacrifice for sin once and for all (Heb 9:24-28; 10:10). This time, God wanted water to break out differently from a rock. Moses instead did it the way he wanted.

As you have read in this BUT GOD verse, Moses blamed the Israelites as the reason he did not get to go into the Promised Land, but Moses was not reviewing the whole story. Moses gave a commentary on what had transpired and left out a few details, namely what he personally had done. Moses realized that after pleading with God (as the earlier verses state in this chapter), God had not changed His mind to let him go in. Moses blamed the Israelites for complaining, which angered the Lord. Moses then again had to go to the Lord and get a resolution from Him that would satisfy the Israelites. After getting the instructions, Moses did not follow them exactly, which meant that there would be consequences. Remember, Moses was just a man. He was not perfect and he made mistakes, just like the other patriarchs did. The only One who lived a perfect life was our Bridegroom, Jesus.

God did not remain angry forever because He delights in faithful love (Micah 7:18). Moses was definitely faithful, as are many of God's people. Because of His covenant with Abraham, Isaac, and Jacob, God will always have a remnant who have remained faithful and who will receive His inheritance. Because of God's grace, He forgives our sins when we ask and remembers them no more, therefore allowing His faithful love to continue to flow to us. In this BUT GOD verse, Moses played the blame game, saying it was the Israelites fault he was missing out on the Promised Land. The reality was it was his own fault, and God was not *still* angry—God was following through with the chastisement He gave Moses. Moses, along with Aaron, took God's credit for themselves when getting the Israelites water. We see it said in Numbers 20:10, ". . . Hear now, you rebels! Must *we* bring water for you out of this rock?"(NKJV emphasis added). Moses called the Israelites "rebels" when, in fact, he himself was also rebelling by being disobedient to following the Lord's instructions. All he had to do was speak to the rock in front of them and give God the glory for providing them water. Moses and Aaron made a costly mistake, and, as a result, lost their access into the Promised Land. I am sure the Lord was disappointed that Moses now could not go. The rules for obedience had to apply to everyone; there were no exceptions, even for the friend of God (Ex 33:11).

Our Bridegroom has emotions. He can be angry, but that is not what the lesson is here. He wants us to listen and be obedient to Him so we do not miss out on the wonderful promises He has waiting for us. He wants us to trust Him when He says He is going to bring forth a miracle. Deuteronomy 8:5, Proverbs 3:12, and Hebrews 12:6-10 all say God disciplines those He loves. No one likes discipline, BUT GOD uses it to improve our character (Heb 12:11). We need to know our Bridegroom wants the best *from* us and *for* us. As His bride, we need to deliver our best, especially when it involves a task that is important for His will to be accomplished in our lives, as well as our brothers and sisters in Christ.

A side note to show how gracious our God is: He did allow Moses to overlook the Promised Land before he died (Deut 34). Moses died on the mountain after living a full one hundred and twenty years. God Himself buried Moses somewhere in the valley, which means God took care of Moses' body and carried his friend off the mountain. He also let Moses take a special trip to a mountain top in the Promised Land many generations later in the spiritual realm to speak with our Bridegroom (Luke 9:28-36).

29. Holds Us Accountable for Our Actions / Disciplines for Disobedience

"But GOD was angry with me because of you and the things you said. He swore that I'd never cross the Jordan, never get to enter the good land that GOD, your God, is giving you as an inheritance. This means that I am going to die here. I'm not crossing the Jordan. But you will cross; you'll possess the good land" (Deuteronomy 4:21-22 MSG, emphasis added).

Moses again reminded the Israelites he did not get to go into the Promised Land and Joshua would now be the one taking them there. Moses blamed the Israelites because of the unfaithful and ungrateful words they had said which had angered the Lord. The Israelites had complained about everything during their time in the desert and constantly second guessed the Lord's provision. This must have tried Moses' patience and aggravated him to the point where Moses was disobedient to the Lord. Since Moses displeased the Lord, Moses was going to die right outside the Promised Land. The generation of Israelites Moses was talking to in this BUT GOD verse was the next generation which the Lord said *would enter* into the Promised Land. Their fathers had acted in disobedience, voiding that generation's right to enter, so Moses might have been trying to appeal to this next generation by stressing the importance of obedience. Basically, learn from his mistake and the mistake of their fathers.

Moses was educating the Israelites on how important it is to be obedient to God. Moses instructed the Israelites to tell the future generations that obedience is important so they might live long in the land God was giving them. Moses could give a heartfelt lesson on being obedient because He was not obedient and was disciplined for it. He did not want this to happen to any one of the Israelites at that time, since they were so close to crossing the Jordan. Moses himself wanted to cross that Jordan and was more than physically capable of doing it, but the Lord told him no.

Moses could taste the victory of what was to come because he had just witnessed how easily God defeated the previous fortified cities (Deut 3) and he desperately wanted to make it to the end. Think of it like this: it is like watching a really good football game on TV that runs into overtime, and then your TV breaks and you do not get to know the final score. It is like watching a movie and not seeing the happy ending. Moses wanted to know the final score! He wanted to know the ending of the movie! Moses did all he could so the Israelites would get to enter the land this time around. In order to enjoy the fruit, they had to be obedient; they had to trust the Lord! Moses knew everything was contingent on them learning from their forefathers' past mistakes and obeying God. He knew if they did not stay obedient, the Lord would discipline the Israelites, as the Lord had disciplined Moses, and the Promised Land would be taken from them. Moses knew that pain and was trying to give them a pep talk before the "big game" so he could guarantee a win for his team.

How many times have you learned a lesson that you did not want to ever learn again? It had such a deep impact on you that you felt you needed to help others prevent going through anything like it. Maybe it was drunk driving, drugs, stealing, lying to your mom, or cheating on a test. Maybe you got a ticket for not stopping at the stop sign the whole way. Were the disciplinary actions severe enough to make sure you did not repeat it? Was there a consequence to your actions that affected someone else's life in a negative way? Moses was trying to help them by teaching through his experience.

I am sure many of the Israelites thought his punishment was severe because they regarded Moses with such high esteem. Maybe this lesson made such an impression that it facilitated an increased adherence to the laws of God as the next generation entered into the promise. This might have scared them straight—perhaps straight into the act of obedience. Our Bridegroom wants us to be obedient; He does not want to take away the Promised Land from us. We know the commands He has given us. We know how to show our love for Him; we need to trust Him and be obedient (Deut 11:22, John 14:15, 21, 24).

30. Moves Obstacles Out of Our Way

"So don't be intimidated by them. God, your God, is among you—God majestic, God awesome. God, your God, will get rid of these nations, bit by bit. You won't be permitted to wipe them out all at once lest the wild animals take over and overwhelm you. *But God*, your God, will move them out of your way—he'll throw them into a huge panic until there's nothing left of them. He'll turn their kings over to you and you'll remove all trace of them under Heaven. Not one person will be able to stand up to you; you'll put an end to them all" (Deuteronomy 7:21-24 MSG, emphasis added).

Besides the animal problem, God gives us another hint at why the Israelites would not be permitted to wipe the enemies out all at once. In Exodus 23:30, God said He would drive the nations out little by little. He promised certain things *if* they obeyed His voice *and* did all that He spoke (Ex 23:22). He would fulfill the number of their days and they would live to their fullest potential; there would be no miscarriages (Ex 23:26) so that they could increase in number and they would inherit the land (Ex 23:30). God wanted them to grow in number as well as grow in Him. They needed to continue to walk in His ways and listen to Him, not being distracted by the world's ways and their gods (Ex 23:24). The more they followed His lead, the more land He could hand over to them.

Have you ever tried leaving a concert or a ball game? Have you noticed how much easier it is to move through the masses of people when someone bigger is in front of you clearing the way? When I take my kids out of a crowded place, a trail is carved out behind me as we hold onto each other's hands, but as soon as someone lets go or lets someone get in between us, the kids get stuck and stop moving. This is a perfect example of us and God.

Our Bridegroom is making a pathway before us. All we need to do is follow His lead and not let go of His hand or let our eyes stray. We do not want to get lost in the crowd of this world. Let us keep our eyes on Jesus, let us not look at the popcorn or souvenirs on the side the world uses to distract us. Remember Peter in Matthew 14:25-31? He walked on the water with Jesus and as long as he looked upon Him, he was safe. It was when he let his emotions overtake him and his eyes strayed to look at the water that he began to sink. Our Bridegroom wants us to look straight into His eyes and to hold His hands now. Allow Him to direct you and do not let go. He will move all the obstacles out of your way through His glory and power. Do not let the anxieties of this world cause you to lose focus and sink. You will see the impossible possible as long as you keep your eyes on Him and step out in faith!

31. Reveals Understanding

[Moses Blesses Israel on the Plains of Moab] "Moses called all Israel together and said, 'You've seen with your own eyes everything that God did in Egypt to Pharaoh and his servants, and to the land itself—the massive trials to which you were eyewitnesses, the great signs and miracle-wonders. *But God didn't give you an understanding heart or perceptive eyes or attentive ears until right now, this very day*'" (Deuteronomy 29:2-4 MSG, emphasis added).

The Israelites had so much to be thankful for: they were led out of Egypt, given food, promised victories over nations—all the while wearing the same shoes for forty years! The Lord gave Israel understanding that He was their God and He had made a covenant with them. He wanted them, and their future generations, to honor Him by keeping the agreement (Deut 29:14-15).

The Lord made sure the Israelites understood exactly what they were getting into with Him. He did not force them to do what He wanted. He presented His offer through Moses: "Then Moses went up to God, and the LORD called to him from the mountain and said, "This is what you are to say to the descendants of Jacob and what you are to tell the people of Israel: 'You yourselves have seen what I did to Egypt, and how I carried you on eagles' wings and brought you to myself. Now if you obey me fully and keep my covenant, then out of all nations you will be my treasured possession. Although the whole earth is mine, you will be for me a kingdom of priests and a holy nation.' These are the words you are to speak to the Israelites" (Exodus 19:3-6 NIV).

In Exodus 19:8, we find that all the Israelites answered that they would do what the Lord had spoken. The whole congregation of the Israelites heard God speak the Ten Commandments, but chose to have God just speak to Moses after that (Ex 20:18-21). They all knew what they were getting into with the covenant of God and whole heartedly agreed. They said yes to God and yes to making a covenant with Him. They said yes to following Him as their God and yes to obeying His commands as His people. They made this great decision that determined the destiny of their future generations. Unfortunately, no matter how many times God proved Himself faithful to them, they kept failing to put all their hope in Him. They were an unbelieving generation and missed their opportunity of entering into the Promised Land (Num 14:22-23 and BUT GOD #27).

Our Bridegroom wants us to understand we are His. We must honor Him by not forsaking Him and give ourselves away to other things. He has given us so much to be thankful for. Let us keep our commitment to our Bridegroom the way He has committed Himself to us. Let our eyes and ears be open to how great He is. In the New Testament, Jesus continually taught about having our eyes open, ears to hear, and understanding hearts. Our Bridegroom wants us to know His secrets. As we draw closer to Him, He will reveal more of Himself to us. Moses says in Deuteronomy 29:29 that the hidden things belong to the Lord, but the secrets He reveals belong to us and our future generations. Not only will the Holy Spirit give us personal understanding, but He will also use prophets (Amos 3:7). If you are a friend of God, He will trust you with His secrets and reveal to you His mysteries. He may confirm them through His prophets (1 Cor 14:31 tells us that the gift of prophecy is for *all* of us). Some of His secrets reveal the battle plan for the days ahead. It is important that we know our Bridegroom well so that He gives us understanding. We want to be aligned with His will all the time. Surrounding ourselves with Spirit-filled Christians will help us gain more understanding as the Bible says, "we know in part" (1 Cor 13:9 NIV). You may get one piece of the puzzle while the Lord gives another piece to someone else. This is how the body of Christ works together so that we all may understand God's revelations in accordance with His Word.

32. Takes Charge of Us

"When the High God gave the nations their stake, gave them their place on Earth, He put each of the peoples within boundaries under the care of divine guardians. *But God himself took charge of his people, took Jacob on as his personal concern*" (Deuteronomy 32:8-9 MSG, emphasis added).

This BUT GOD is in the song of Moses, all the Israelites learned this song so future generations would know what the Lord had done for them. They also would know what would happen to them should they fail to live their lives the way they agreed with God. God wanted them to know they would be His treasured possession (Ex 19:5). He loves Israel, they are His children and He will continue to care for them always. His promises to the Israelites started with Abraham and have not ended. His Word is just as true now as it was then. Let me say again—He loves Israel. He loved them then and He loves them now.

He also loves His bride; we are very much His personal concern. God founded Israel, encircled them, kept them, protected and carried them, led them, and fed them (Deut. 32:10-14). Oh, how our Bridegroom does the same for us! He cares for us, watches over us, provides for us, and loves us. We are His treasured bride. Together, with Israel, we will be the ones who will reign with Him in His kingdom.

If you have made a commitment to Christ, know that the moment you did so, you became a special person to God. Although these words were spoken about the Israelites, let them wash over you as a reminder of the proclamation the Lord spoke over you also on that special day you accepted Him:

A Special People of God

"This day the LORD your God commands you to observe these statutes and judgments; therefore you shall be careful to observe them with all your heart and with all your soul. Today you have proclaimed the LORD to be your God, and that you will walk in His ways and keep His statutes, His commandments, and His judgments, and that you will obey His voice. Also today the LORD has proclaimed you to be His special people, just as He promised you, that you should keep all His commandments, and that He will set you high above all nations which He has made, in praise, in name, and in honor, and that you may be a holy people to the LORD your God, just as He has spoken" (Deut 26:16-19 NKJV).

Jesus has redeemed us all and made us His own people. We have been grafted into God's promises with Israel and now ". . . are a chosen generation, a royal priesthood, a holy nation, His own special people, that you may proclaim the praises of Him who called you out of darkness into His marvelous light; who once were not a people but are now the people of God, who had not obtained mercy but now have obtained mercy" (1 Peter 2:9-10 NKJV).

33. Gives Us Our Identity in Him

"*But God* faced him directly: 'Go in this strength that is yours. Save Israel from Midian. Haven't I just sent you?'" (Judges 6:14 MSG, emphasis added).

The Midianites were allowed to oppress Israel for seven years because the Israelites did evil in the Lord's sight. The Israelites cried out to God and the Angel of the Lord came to speak to Gideon. We read in Judges 6:13a that Gideon asked Him, ". . . if the Lord is with us, why has all this happened to us? And where are the miracles our ancestors have told us about?" (NLT). Are these not similar to the questions the world asks today?

The Lord had already sent them a prophet to answer these questions as stated in Judges 6:8-10 (they had not obeyed His voice), but the Lord told Gideon that He was going to be with him and he was going to deliver the Israelites (v 16). Gideon referred to himself as the weakest and the least (v 15), BUT GOD saw Gideon as a mighty man of valor (v 12). In the miracles that followed, Gideon's faith increased to help him be the man God purposed him to be—a warrior for His glory!

Just as Abraham accepted the Bridal call from God when asked to leave his country and his father's house in Genesis 12, so must we. God has plans to bless each of us separately, but we must trust Him to redefine who we are. Abraham was 75 years old when he took on this journey, Gideon thought of himself as a weakling, the prophet Amos was just a sheep breeder, one of Jesus' disciples was a mistrusted tax collector, and others were uneducated fishermen. All these people accepted God's call and rose to the occasion. The bridal dynamic includes giving up your name and taking the name of your Bridegroom. Together we are one with His purpose as the bride finds her fullness and her meaning in Him alone. We need to think thoughts of ourselves from that elevated place. If you have a bad thought about yourself, get rid of it and get a new one. Jesus is raising up His bride to see herself as someone who will reign next to Him. The higher up we go, the greater our faith and the stronger the demonstrations of God will be in and through us. We need to take a step above the enemy and know our identity in Christ so we will not be easily defeated by fear and intimidation. Remember the prophetic words spoken over you and live your life with purpose to achieve them![23] God's prophetic words over Gideon pushed Him to have confidence so he could deliver the Israelites. Gideon had God's guarantee that he did not need to fear for his life. The same type of situation happened with David. God told Samuel that David was to be appointed king and since David wasn't king yet, he had no need to be intimidated by Goliath (1 Sam 16-17). Knowing ahead of time that you will go into battle and be victorious should give you great courage!

We have a unique identity in Christ. Sometimes, God changed names of people in the Bible, but only to remind them of who they really were. Abraham, Jacob, and Peter's names were all changed (Matt 16:17-19). If you research the meanings of the new and old names, you will see God made each identity something greater. The enemy will try to rob us of our identities. Do not let him change your name or attach a label to you to make you feel less than you are.[24] Our Bridegroom wants you to walk in the fullness of all that it cost Him to purchase you. Joshua Mills once said, "In the glory realm, God begins to introduce you to yourself. The more you reflect Him, the more He shows you who He has made you to be."[25] Now is a great time to listen to the song by Jason Gray called, "Remind Me Who I Am."[26] The words are perfect! When our identity is secure, so is our destiny![27]

Notice how God addressed Gideon when He first spoke to him. The Angel of the Lord said Gideon was mighty and strong. This is how Gideon was known in heaven. God saw Gideon as part of the answer *before* Gideon voiced doubts about his own ability. Our Father God looks upon us as who He has made us to be—the final outcome—not what we think of ourselves in the process. Sure, He helps us along as we grow in our identity in Him, but when He speaks to us, it is as if He sees us already completed. We can imitate this wonderful example by speaking to our children this way and edifying each other. Jesus looks at His bride as who we are in Him. A good Bridegroom looks past our flaws, both physically and emotionally, and sees us as who and what we are meant to be. Thank you God!

The following are just a few verses to remind you of who you are in Christ. Make a declaration and speak each one out loud to encourage your soul. Notice you take on part of your Bridegroom's name as you say "I am" before each one.

John 1:12	I am God's child
John 8:31	I am a disciple of Christ
John 15:15	I am Jesus' friend
Romans 8:1-2	I am free from condemnation
Romans 10:9-13	I am saved in Christ
Romans 15:14	I am full of goodness in Christ
1 Corinthians 12:27	I am member of Christ's body
Ephesians 1:5-7	I am adopted and accepted, redeemed and forgiven
Philippians 3:20	I am a citizen of heaven
Colossians 1:12	I am qualified to share in the inheritance of the saints
1 Thessalonians 3:13	I am blameless and holy before God's presence
Hebrews 1:3	I am purified from sin by Christ
Hebrews 10:14	I have been made perfect forever in Christ
1 Peter 2:9	I am a member of a royal priesthood—along with all the saints
Revelation 19:7-8, 14	I am the pure bride of Christ—clean, white, and righteous

34. Gives Peace

"But God reassured him, 'Easy now. Don't panic. You won't die'" (Judges 6:23 MSG, emphasis added).

The Angel of the Lord told Gideon he would be the one to deliver Israel from the Midianites. Gideon asked The Angel of the Lord to show him a sign that what He was saying was true. Gideon asked the Angel of the Lord to wait for him to return while he prepared an offering. The Lord waited and accepted Gideon's offering (meat and unleavened bread) by consuming it with fire before departing.[28] Gideon realized it was the Lord with whom he had spoken and must have instantly been overwhelmed. In Isaiah 6 we read that Isaiah saw God seated on His throne and said, "Woe to me for I am undone" and have "unclean lips." Similarly, Gideon must have also realized how unworthy he was next to a holy God. This is why the Lord then imparted peace to Gideon and reassured him that he would be okay. Gideon took this to heart and built an altar calling it The-Lord-Is-Peace (v 24).

When my dad had his quadruple heart bypass surgery, I should have been a nervous wreck, but I did not cry and I actually did not worry. I had a peace that I still cannot explain; I just knew he was going to be okay. The whole situation surrounding my dad was a miracle as far as I am concerned. He went in for a regular physical and the doctor immediately called an ambulance to take him to the hospital. My dad thought the doctor was crazy and said he was fine and would drive himself. The doctor told him he was a walking time bomb and transported him to the hospital where he had emergency surgery the next day. Even though I knew the risk of him dying was high, I also knew God was going to keep him safe. The surgery took forever, but I was not anxious. Any normal person would have been a disaster those two days, BUT GOD gave me peace about the whole situation. Only Jesus can give that kind of peace. He wants us to relax and not stress out. He has all things under control even when we think death is near.

Jesus was not just a man or a good teacher. Isaiah foretold of a child being born who would be named the "Prince of Peace" (Is 9:6). Jesus was the One Isaiah was prophesying about. Jesus is relevant to our time because His life makes a difference in the lives of others. I heard David Brickner, Executive Director of Jews for Jesus, teach that shalom, or peace, is not the absence of strife; it is the presence of God during strife.[29] We need the shalom of God in the midst of troubles that, at times, seem to be spinning out of control. In our own lives, we face storms daily that can be quieted with God's serene and peaceful ways. When Jesus comes back to rule, He is going to make sure the whole world lives in peace. Peace on Earth and good will toward men (Luke 2:14).

35. Lets Israel Win

"*But God*, the God of Israel, gave Sihon and all his troops to Israel. Israel defeated them" (Judges 11:21 MSG, verses 14-27 are grouped together, emphasis added).

Jephthah was elected to lead the Israelites against the people of Ammom. The king of Ammom wanted the land back that had been previously given over to the Israelites at the time of Moses, many, many years before. Here in Judges, the story is recounted, but we also find it originally in Deuteronomy 2:24-31. It tells the story of God hardening the heart of Sihon, Amorite king of Heshbon, so that he would not allow the Israelites to pass through his land. This king brought out his people to fight the Israelites, BUT GOD let the Israelites defeat them. God had allowed this so that He could begin to put dread, fear, and anguish upon all other nations. With this defeat under Israel's belt, the other nations began to worry. This allowed for the Israelites to begin possessing and inheriting the land. In Judges 11:33, we find the Lord delivered Israel again from the people of Ammom through Jephthah.

This situation still happens today. God gives Israel land that other countries want. Israel became a nation again in 1948, but everyone was not happy about it. In 1967, many countries tried to destroy Israel, but Israel won and gained more land. Along with that, they won control of Jerusalem from the Palestinians who would not initially give it up back in 1948 (they are known as the Edomites, or the Philistines, who come from Esau in the Bible).

In 1973, Egypt and Syria went to war with Israel to reclaim the land they lost in 1967, but Israel won the war. In 1979, Egypt signed a peace treaty with Israel, which is currently unsteady due to its civil unrest and new leadership. In 2005, Israel decided to give up the Gaza Strip in hopes of living peacefully with the Palestinians. However, the attempt has been unsuccessful due to Hamas' governing control. Hamas is a group of Palestinian Islamic fundamentalists.[30] Now the Palestinians want to divide Jerusalem (Obadiah 1:11) to possess more of the land. You see—it is ongoing! In fact, on November 29, 2012, the United Nations took a vote to recognize the State of Palestine as a non-member observer state. The motion was passed by an overwhelming vote of 138 to 9. There were many Islamic countries that supported this vote. Islam does not believe that Israel has a right to exist, but Israel does have that right. Though the Palestinian people have suffered just as Israel has with ongoing disputes, dividing the land will not bring about a blessing or peace. Actually, the Lord has made it very clear in Joel 3:1-2 that God will judge all nations who divide the land of Israel.

This BUT GOD story reminds me of how God hardened Pharaoh's heart so that eventually the Israelites would be freed from Egypt (#19). God seems to use unruly leaders' hearts to bring more glory and honor to Him. God has a plan for His bride and He will facilitate situations that will bring us rewards and fulfill His promises. Remember, stories in the Old Testament were to foreshadow events to come. We need to recall these stories in these last days when our leaders make decisions that seem to make things worse for those who believe in Him. We also need to remember this when Israel seems surrounded by enemies all the time. Eventually, Israel will think they have peace, but it will be false and the one who promised peace (the antichrist) will go back on his word. All this is only to bring us to a place where we will be fulfilling the book of Revelation and ultimately be with our Bridegroom forever. Read the end of the Bible—God lets His beloved win! For the Jewish people who have not read the New Testament, the end of the Old Testament is filled with the same information!

36. Provides the Holy Spirit / Is the Water of Life

"*But God* clave a hollow place that was in the jaw, and there came water thereout; and when he had drunk, his spirit came again, and he revived: wherefore he called the name thereof Enhakkore, which is in Lehi unto this day" (Judges 15:19 KJV, emphasis added).

We now turn our attention to Samson. He was a man who was given great strength and was filled with the Spirit of the Lord. From the womb he was purposed to be a Nazirite (Judges 13:5, Num 6) and was predestined to deliver Israel from Philistine rule (Judges 14:4). He had married a Philistine woman who later had her life threatened if she did not get an answer to a riddle Samson had told the Philistines. She got the answer and told them. After paying off the Philistines the wager for solving the riddle, Samson burned with anger and returned to his father's home (Judges 14). Unknowingly to Samson, his wife was given to his best man, as her father explained he thought Samson hated her (Judges 14:20-15:3).

To take revenge, Samson caught three hundred foxes and tied their tails to torches two by two.[31] He sent them into the Philistine's fields which then burned. The Philistines, in turn, burned his wife and her father. Samson attacked them and they were slaughtered. He was later handed over to the Philistines, but the Holy Spirit gave him strength and he used a donkey's jawbone to kill one thousand Philistine men, enabling him to free himself. Samson was very thirsty afterward and called to the Lord.[32] This is where we find our BUT GOD verse. God heard Samson's need and provided the water for him, much like we learned in BUT GOD #8 where God heard Ishmael crying and did the same for him. Therefore, the place was called Enhakkore, meaning "The Spring of the Caller." Whatever our need is, God will provide, just call on Him (Is 58:9-11, Jer 33:3). Whatever the need may be in the future, God will make sure we are taken care of (#14).

The Lord, our Rock, is known as the Water of Life. God demonstrated this fact for the Israelites when they were wandering in the desert. In Exodus 17:1-7, we read that the Lord stood in front of Moses on the rock. When Moses struck it one time with his rod, water came out for the people to drink. Jesus told the woman at the well in John 4:10-14 that the gift of God is living water. Then Jesus said to her, ". . . whoever drinks the water I give them will never thirst" (NIV). In John 7:38, Jesus told everyone at the Feast of Tabernacles that anyone who believes in Him will have streams of living water. Even after dying on the cross, water and blood rushed out of His body after one of the soldiers had pierced Jesus' side (John 19:34—but that is another study in itself).

Water is used to cleanse and purify, quench thirst and satisfy, and to soothe and relax. In this BUT GOD verse, notice that God split the hollow place and water came out. This story of Samson demonstrates physically what was also happening spiritually. When the Holy Spirit has poured into us and we have spent ourselves, He is the only One who can fill us up again. Therefore, we are revived through the living water of Christ. That is why it says Samson's "spirit came again and he was revived." Think of it this way: after a long day of work, most people want to come home, take off their shoes, and sit down with a cold drink. Our Bridegroom wants to bring us that nice, tall glass of water. The water will cleanse and purify us so we are presentable; it will quench our yearning for Him and satisfy our soul. The sound of His soothing voice will calm our anxieties and fears. He gives us water of life full of the Holy Spirit.

37. Is Holy

"*But God* struck down some of the inhabitants of Beth Shemesh, putting seventy of them to death because they looked into the ark of the LORD. The people mourned because of the heavy blow the LORD had dealt them" (1 Samuel 6:19 NIV, emphasis added).

Here the Ark of the Covenant was being returned to the Israelites from the Philistines. The Philistines had been plagued with tumors while it was in their possession, so they called on their priests for instruction. They were told to return it with a trespass offering, so they did. When the ark arrived in the field of Beth Shemesh, the Levites took it down (v 15).

The people had not been living according to the laws of God and had forgotten many of the ordinances He had commanded concerning the handling of His presence. The ark was to be carried on the shoulders by the Levites with the poles. It was to be covered and only looked upon by the High Priest from the line of Aaron once a year during the Day of Atonement after all the appropriate sacrifices and cleansings had been completed. God is holy, and since Jesus had not yet come to be the sacrifice for all, God's presence was not accessible to everyone. For the Philistines, the rituals did not matter as much because they weren't His people; the Israelites were. The Israelites needed to know how to treat God. It was up to them to know and remember, not up to God to remind them to read what was written. Had they not strayed so far from serving Him and knowing His heart, they would have remembered and known who was allowed near the ark and near His presence. Therefore, would not have suffered this tragedy of so many lost lives. The New King James Version of 1 Samuel 6:19 says that God had struck fifty thousand and seventy men of the people. This is actually much more than the New International Version states and is a good reminder that when studying the Bible, it is good to look at many resources, especially ones closer to the original translation.[33]

When you were younger, you may have been taken to Sunday school and learned all about the Bible. As you got older, it was up to you to remember those lessons by staying in His Word. The Scriptures are so important, let's not be like the Israelites in this story and forget parts of God's instructions (found in the front of the Bible). God is holy and His Word is holy; in it, we learn how to be holy people.

Our Bridegroom has written us the most important love letter we will ever read. Remember, it also could be viewed as a marriage contract because it listed the responsibilities between Israel and God (Ex 19:5-6, Jer 31:32, and BUT GOD #24). We need to give our Bridegroom the respect and honor He deserves. It is up to us to read His letter to know what He likes. Hint: He likes for us to *believe* Him and be *obedient* to what He has written. He likes for us to *forgive* others, because He forgave others. He likes for us to *love* God and love one another. So from Genesis to Revelation, we do the best we can in obeying His commands and learning the lessons He shows us, knowing we are also covered by His grace. Since Jesus came there is no need to sacrifice animals anymore, but now by knowing Him, we can enter into His glory any time we come before Him in humility. You can read in Matthew 27:51 that the veil was torn from top to bottom. This symbolized that we all have access into the Holy of Holies to meet with God through Jesus anytime we want. The veil had separated God's presence from man in the temple and access was only allowed once a year to the high priest. Now, there is no separation required between us and our heavenly Father.

The Bible teaches in Ephesians 5:22-23 that a husband is to love his wife and the wife is to respect her husband. We know Jesus loves us, so as His bride, let's not lack in knowing what our Bridegroom likes; let's give Him the glory He is due and the respect He deserves. The bride should reflect her Bridegroom; the Bible tells us how to do that. In 1 Peter 1:15-16, it says to be holy because He is holy. We see in this BUT GOD example how holy God is. The ark encompassed His holiness; our bodies encompass His holiness if we have invited Jesus in! First Corinthians 3:16-17 says God's temple is holy and we are that temple! One way to show God the respect He deserves means honoring Him by loving our bodies enough to control them to do what is right and pure.

I did a study once on "How to be Holy." What I found was that I had to work backwards. The following is how my little study progressed. God's grace (Rom 5:1-2) gives us access to faith in Jesus who justifies us (becoming right with God), so now we can have peace with God through mercy (Titus 3:4-5). Romans 6:19-22 says the benefit of being righteous is being set free from sin; therefore, what *righteousness* reaps leads to holiness. Romans 6:16 says *obedience* leads to righteousness. So, we obey His commands because we love Him (1 John 5:3), which leads us to righteousness, which leads to holiness, which then gives us the ability to inherit eternal life and see God (Heb 12:14). So, our love of God motivates us to obedience, which leads to righteousness, which leads to holiness.[34]

If we choose to be obedient, what does righteous living look like? That question sent me on another journey through the Bible which turned into a devotional poem the Holy Spirit helped me write. I will share it below, but please remember, we cannot earn our way to heaven by good works. We do good works that were created for us to do which God prepared for us (Eph 2:10) because the presence of Jesus is living inside us (Gal 2:20). We need to walk in that identity because we have been transformed. Our spots and wrinkles are being removed as we are washed by His Word (sanctification) and become like a tree overflowing with the fruits of the Spirit (Gal 5:22-23). I believe He shares what righteous living looks like to be a guide on how to show Jesus inside you. Jesus was the only one who lived a righteous life and our Bridegroom is coming back for a holy bride, so let this bless you, not condemn you. And, most of all, remember how HOLY our Bridegroom is!

<u>Walking In the Path of Righteousness</u>   *Tina Miller 2007*
Want to glorify God in all that I do *1 Cor 6:19-20*
To live a righteous life before You *1 Jn 3:7*
Your Word says it's useful for teaching me *2 Tim 3:16*
Want to live a life that is holy, renewing my mind daily, *1 Pet 1:16, Rom 12:2; 13:12-14*
Surrounding myself with good company, *Prov 12:26*
And making sure to guard my integrity *Prov 13:6*
Saying no to evil and yes to self control *Titus 2:11-13*
Godly living helps make me whole *Luke 11:33-36*

The hope is that we will believe *Eph 1:18*
Righteousness credited by faith is what we will receive *Eph 4:5*
Doing "good works" is not what You are counting *Is 64:6*
My opportunities to believe and love is what You are amounting *Jn 20:28, Eph 4:24*
Lord, I believe Your Word is true *Rom 10:17*
Delighting in Your law to see me through *Ps 112*
My faith is complete by what I do *James 2:22-24*
Jesus I put my trust in You *Jn 14:1*

Show me how to sow unfailing love *Hos 10:12*
To seek first the kingdom above *Matt 6:33*
To trust You Lord and have faith as Abraham *Rom 4*
I accept You Jesus as the Lamb *Jn 1:29, Rom 3:21-26, Rev 5*

I will walk in Your ways and obey Your commands *Ps 112*
Accepting eternal life given with pierced hands *Jn 3:16, Rom 6:32*
I choose this because I love You *Jn 15:14-17, 1 Jn 4:8-12*
And Your love has made me new *Ps 146:8*

Hear me Lord when I call out for insight *Prov 2*
Even in the darkness light dawns for the upright *Ps 112*
Turn my ear to wisdom when it talks *Prov 2*
Help me do what's right and have a blameless walk *Ps 15:2, 1 Jn 3:7*
Give me discretion when Your Word enters my heart *Prov 2*
Let me speak what is fitting right from the start *Prov 10:31-32, Ps 37:30*
Let me find knowledge and understanding *Prov 2*
Even after a storm I will be firmly standing *Job 17:9, Prov 10:25*

Help me be generous and lend freely *Ps 112*
Let me care for those who are needy *Ps 107:42, Prov 29:7*
I will speak words that nourish them *Prov 10:21*
Like a fountain of life, leading away from sin *Is 33:5-16, Prov 10:11*
I will weigh my answers before I speak *Prov 15:28*
But be bold as lions for the weak *Prov 28:1; 29:7*
I will mean what I say; my actions will be true *Matt 23:28*
I will not be a fake; I am representing You *Matt 23:28*

I will care for my animals with tenderness *Prov 12:10*
And be an example of Your love and kindness *Titus 3:4*
Sowing in peace and harvesting righteousness *James 3:18, Is 32:13*
Awakened, satisfied with seeing Your likeness *Ps 17:15*
Speaking the truth, I will rejoice *Ps 15:2; 32:11; 33:1*
Helping others to hear Your voice *Dan 12:3*
Let me be remembered for doing what is right *Ps 112*
Focusing and pointing to You with all my might *Mk 12:30, Deut 6:4-5*

38. Has Reasons for Not Replying

"So Saul asked God, 'Should we go after the Philistines? Will you help us defeat them?' *But God* made no reply that day" (1 Samuel 14:37 NLT, emphasis added). *Also found in the NIV.

The Israelites demanded of the prophet, Samuel, to give them a king in 1 Samuel 8. God had Samuel anoint Saul. In this BUT GOD context, King Saul along with his son, Jonathan, went to fight the Philistines. While Jonathan was away from his father,

Saul made the army take an oath not to eat (1 Sam 14:24). How an army is going to fight well while being deprived of food I do not know. Jonathan, not knowing about the odd oath, ate some honey (v 27), which caused a problem in camp and almost cost him his life (vv 38-46).

I think God did not answer Saul for a couple of reasons. The Israelites rejected God from being their only King. Instead, they wanted a human king in front of them like the other nations. King Saul looked the part (1 Sam 9:1-2), but he was not the kind of king God wanted him to be. Because of Saul's rebellion in Gilgal (1 Sam 13:9-14), Samuel said God would not establish Saul's kingdom and would anoint someone else to be leader over His people. Saul continued to make bad decisions (like this oath to not eat) and did not yield his heart to be in tune with the Lord's, so God did not answer him.

Our Bridegroom wants us to have a heart after His own. David, who was the next chosen king, was said to be a man after God's own heart (Acts 13:22). David knew this was important and told his son (who was king after him) in 1 Chronicles 28:9, "And you, my son Solomon, acknowledge the God of your father, and serve him with wholehearted devotion and with a willing mind, for the LORD searches every heart and understands every desire and every thought. If you seek Him, He will be found by you; but if you forsake Him, He will reject you forever" (NIV).

There are times that the Lord is silent for His own reasons, but there are times our attitude blocks our intimacy with our Bridegroom. Always check your heart and ask Him to take away anything that might be blocking your communication with Him. Ask Him to reveal those obstacles to you (Psalm 139:23-24). We have a Bridegroom who wants a relationship with us. He will answer you if you call on Him (Jer. 33:3). It may not be in your timeframe, but it is always in His. Just like the Barlow Girls song, "Never Alone,"[35] we should remember that sometimes when God does not answer—we just have to hold tight to what we know—He is here, and we are never alone (#73). If you have a response to your prayer, it IS an answered prayer, even if it is not the answer you wanted. Know Jesus hears His bride's prayers and will answer them.

39. Feels Disappointment

"Samuel left immediately for Ramah and Saul went home to Gibeah. Samuel had nothing to do with Saul from then on, though he grieved long and deeply over him. *But God* was sorry he had ever made Saul king in the first place" (1 Samuel 15:34-35 MSG, emphasis added).

King Saul was selfish, rebellious, and stubborn—nothing like the righteous King of Kings. In this BUT GOD verse, we see God's disappointment in Saul because He knew Saul's heart was not one that sought to please Him first. Saul made some bad decisions as king and did not follow all the Lord's commands. In 1 Samuel 15:22-23 (NIV), we read Saul rejected the Word of the Lord and that he was rebellious. Jesus does not want us to act this way. He wants His bride to make good decisions when He designates authority and responsibility to us. He wants us to make every effort to make *Him* happy with our decisions and not worry about making men happy (Gal 1:10). Saul struggled with this.

In this chapter, God sent word through the prophet Samuel that Saul was to attack Amalek. He was to kill and destroy all of the people and their belongings. In Deuteronomy 25:19, we see that God had been planning this for a while. First Samuel 15:9 (NIV) shows Saul did not do exactly as the Lord had commanded. By verse 24, Saul admitted to Samuel that he feared the people and complied with their wishes instead of doing what he knew to be right. God decided Saul would no longer be allowed to remain king. Saul did not seem to care about this news at all! All he wanted was to be quickly pardoned so Samuel could honor him in front of the people (v 30). Saul's will was stubborn; he did not consider humbling his heart when the prophet confronted him. He was more concerned about being embarrassed in front of people than being rejected by God.

In the King James Version this BUT GOD verse says, ". . . the LORD repented that he had made Saul king over Israel." The word "repented" is the same word used in Genesis 6:6 that I had mentioned in BUT GOD #2 where it said, "And it repented the LORD that he had made man on the earth . . ."(KJV). The word repented is #5162 in *The Strong's Concordance* and is the Hebrew word *nacham*. The definition of repent is to feel sorrow for sin. So, we can see how these verses would mean that God felt sorrow when man chose to sin, resulting in the need for God to intervene. In this case, that intervention came in the form of replacing Saul as king. God gives people power, and takes it away (Dan 2:20-21, Job 1:21).Saul's disobedience to God cost him his crown and his life (as you will see in #45). God was saddened Saul would not rise to the responsibilities of the call to be king. Saul disappointed God.

Jesus said in Mark 1:15 the kingdom of God is at hand, meaning it is within reach. Some say the kingdom of God is now and not yet. The kingdom of God begins in us, but will not be fulfilled completely until Jesus returns. Since our heavenly Father sent us the Holy Spirit, we should be demonstrating the kingdom instead of only declaring it (Luke 17:20, Matt 4:23). We need to not only tell people about Jesus, but show them Jesus by displaying His power as we touch their lives. When our Bridegroom gives us assignments, we need to be committed. We cannot have the fear of man keep us from doing what the Lord has called us to complete. We cannot be concerned over what others will think when we pray for someone or share a testimony about God. Being a Christian is difficult when our heart is tempted to impress people by choosing their ways over God's ways. We need to have integrity. When God asks you to do something that is not popular or considered normal, it gives people an opportunity to reject you. Whether God picks me to give a word to someone, to be involved in a project, or to be part of His bride, I never want Him to feel He cannot trust me. I would be devastated! If He handpicks me for it, He has a purpose. That purpose may be to test me, train me, and stretch me. It also may be to bless me. I want His kingdom to flow through me as I fulfill the plans He sets before me. In every opportunity Jesus presents, I want to make Him proud, not disappointed.

Father God, thank you for having mercy on our souls. Dear Jesus, thank you for bearing with us humans when we disappoint you. We are destined to live with the King of Kings and exist as co-rulers with Christ. You are training us to live as a royal bride, so let us choose the destiny to which You have called us in this life. Help us be wise in the decisions we make and be obedient when

You ask us to do something, even if it makes us uncomfortable. Remind us not to be fearful of man's thoughts, but let the fear of God be what drives us.[36]

40. Looks at the Heart

"*But God* told Samuel, 'Looks aren't everything. Don't be impressed with his looks and stature. I've already eliminated him. God judges persons differently than humans do. Men and women look at the face; God looks into the heart'" (1 Samuel 16:7 MSG, emphasis added).

As mentioned in BUT GOD #38 and #39, God was not going to let Saul continue to be king. In this BUT GOD verse, Samuel was trying to find whom the Lord had picked to be the next king over Israel. God sent Samuel to Jesse, who was from Bethlehem, to anoint one of his sons. Samuel thought it would be the eldest son, but the Lord did not pick any of the men in front of Samuel. In fact, Samuel asked if all of Jesse's sons were present (v 11). We find out that David, the youngest son, was not even there! He was shepherding his sheep. David was summoned and once he came, the Lord told Samuel *he* was the one.

I love everything about this verse. Our Bridegroom is the one who judges our hearts and who we are as a person, He does not judge our looks. What if we had to compete in a beauty competition with one another or had to compare bank accounts in order to be part of God's bride? That would be awful! He wants to pick us all and anoint us all, just like He did with David. Will we have willing hearts?

There are many facts about David which foreshadow the Messiah. He had a true king's heart, just as Jesus. David came from Bethlehem; Jesus was born from Bethlehem. He was a shepherd; Jesus is the Good Shepherd (John 10:14). David was the least likely to be picked to be king; Jesus' own community of Nazareth did not see him as more than the carpenter's son, not the Messiah, the King (Matt 13:54-58). David's throne was established forever; Jesus' throne is established forever . . . we could go on and on.

As soon as Samuel anointed David, the Bible says in verses 12 and 13 that the Holy Spirit was with him from that day forward. I love that once we accept God's pursuit of us, He gives us a piece of Him to stay with us. Having the Holy Spirit does not change our looks or our status, but can change something more important—our heart. He lives inside of us, the exact place where our Bridegroom looks. He can purify our hearts to make them even more pleasing to our Lord's eyes. Our bodies carry His presence and that makes us living temples. We are carrying truth around inside of us. When we let His light shine through, that makes our hearts beautiful to Him. Do not get sidetracked by being perfectly physically fit or having fortune and fame. These will not get you VIP status in His books. You need to be spiritually fit, and the time to do that is now, during our engagement time to Jesus. This way we will "fit" into our wedding dress during the marriage supper of the Lamb (Rev 19:7-8). Our Bridegroom knows inner beauty is what counts and that just makes me love Him more.

41. Keeps Us Safe / Keeps Our Secrets and Is Our Friend

"David remained in the wilderness strongholds in the hill country of the Wilderness of Ziph. Saul sought him every day, *but God* did not give him into his hands" (1 Samuel 23:14 AMP, emphasis added). *Also found in the NLT, NIV, KJV, and MSG in 1 Samuel 23:14-15.

Do you have problems that seem overwhelming? Sometimes it helps to put them in perspective by comparing them to David's troubles. Do you have a king pursuing you with all his army, seeking to kill you every day? David did for over ten years! If God can keep David safe through all that, then surely He can keep you safe. Are your trials so bad you would consider exchanging them for someone else's problems? Without knowing what you would get, would you do it? It is hard to complain when I know I could be facing much harder dilemmas. If I have a problem and no solution, then it is God's problem, He always has the solution. I need to ask Him for direction fervently in prayer until I understand.

In 1 Samuel 18, we find that King Saul resented David because of his good reputation. Saul was also afraid of David because the Lord's presence was in him (1 Sam 18:12). David had to flee from Saul who was spiteful and sought to kill him often. In this BUT GOD verse, we find David hiding and God not letting Saul find him; God kept David safe. Saul was irrational and untrustworthy. One minute Saul was letting David marry his daughter, the next he sent messengers to seize him. He wanted David dead, but then later said he was sorry, only to behave malevolently again. David could not let his guard down around Saul because he was untrustworthy. He was not David's friend, BUT GOD was. God could be trusted and would keep David's secrets.

How good to know that David, like us, had the Holy Spirit with him so he was not alone. Remember, it was not until Pentecost, in Acts 2, that the Holy Spirit was available to everyone. Here, in the Old Testament, not many people were privileged to have God's presence with them all the time. The Holy Spirit is truly a gift. He is the great Comforter, a welcomed characteristic of our Bridegroom. He will not give us up when we have our destinies to fulfill and are fully committed to obey God. As long as we stay in His will, He will protect us.

Some of His bride are called to be martyrs and are killed for their belief in Jesus. That may be a destiny that is hard to comprehend. I choose to believe that those who go through death for His glory are seeing the supernatural in those moments and the Holy Spirit is giving them the strength and courage they need. This was not in the Lord's plan for David as God allowed him to gain much personal growth and character during these times of displacement while he was pursued by Saul. God kept him safe the whole time and plans on doing the same for His bride.

42. Is at Work in Us

"Forgive my presumption! *But God* is at work in my master, developing a rule solid and dependable. My master fights

God's battles! As long as you live no evil will stick to you. If anyone stands in your way, if anyone tries to get you out of the way, Know this: Your God-honored life is tightly bound in the bundle of God-protected life; But the lives of your enemies will be hurled aside as a stone is thrown from a sling" (1 Samuel 25:28-29 MSG, emphasis added).

Before we discuss the placement of where we find this in the Bible, reread this BUT GOD as if someone were saying this to you (you being the master). Praying Scripture over ourselves, our friends, and our family is something we should do. Sometimes using Scripture is helpful when we do not know what to pray.

What a lift to David's spirit this must have been when Abigail spoke it over him. It calmed him down and restored his temper. She was the wife of a man who did not return kindness to David. From her choice of words to David in verses 24-31, it was obvious she knew exactly who he was, even though her husband did not (vv 10-11). She knew of David's defeat over Goliath as she slyly threw in the remark about the stone in the sling being hurled at his enemies. That had been a defining moment in David's character early on and she was definitely speaking to his character in this speech. Because of Abigail, her household was spared from David's anger. He basically said she and her advice were a blessing (v 33). Ten days later, Abigail's husband died, so David took her as his wife to care of her.

Our Bridegroom is constantly at work in us, refining us and making us dependable all the while protecting us as we honor Him. He does not want us making rash decisions based on anger. We are to fight evil through our character and our prayers. How nice it is when He sends an "Abigail" our way to refocus our attention onto His will for us. Once God's work in us is complete, we will stand together with Him ready for an everlasting life with our Bridegroom.

43. Wants Us to Honor His Timing

"He went on, 'As God lives, either God will strike him, or his time will come and he'll die in bed, or he'll fall in battle, *but God* forbid that I should lay a finger on God's anointed. Now, grab the spear at his head and the water jug and let's get out of here'" (1 Samuel 26:10-11 MSG, emphasis added).

Though Saul was not a kind king, David knew he still *was* king and David honored that. He knew he could end Saul's manhunt against him by killing Saul while he was sleeping, but he did not. David was wise enough to show Saul he could have ended his life with Saul's own spear but chose to spare him instead. He took the spear and the jug of water. If we dig deeper we can see some symbolism it these items. Jesus said He is the Water of Life, so we know water represents life (#36). The spear is used to cause death. David took the spear and the water. David truly was leaving Saul's living or dying in God's timing, just as he stated. Sometimes when we are treated unjustly and unfairly we want the person who is causing it to go away, but it is not up to us to determine that; it is up to God. David knew God had been protecting him and chose to keep on believing in that protection.

Our Bridegroom wants us to be confident in His character and know what He expects of us. We should know whether He wants us to do something for Him or step back and let Him intervene when His timing is right. It would have been so easy for David to facilitate matters for himself, knowing he was already anointed as the next king. He could have decided this was God giving him the opportunity to kill Saul himself, but He knew God's heart—that was David's greatest gift. He knew God well enough to know God would allow David to reign eventually and that rulership would not come by David's own meddling in the affair to help hurry it along.

How often do we get in the mix of what God is doing? We sometimes cause the situation to last longer because He has to straighten out the extra mess we made by "helping" Him. Remember how Sarah's "help" only caused stress later for Abraham in BUT GOD #7? Let us know our Bridegroom well enough to know which situations we need to leave alone by not intervening in them. He will be pleased that we honored Him in His timing of circumstances.

44. Will Not Honor Disobedience

"Saul prayed to God, *but God* didn't answer—neither by dream nor by sign nor by prophet" (1 Samuel 28:6 MSG, emphasis added).

Like BUT GOD #38, this BUT GOD deals with God not answering Saul's prayer. Saul had continued to rebel against God and had intended to kill David many times. Saul was never truly sorry as he continued to let anger and bitterness reign in his life. He wanted to give into his rage, but at the same time expected God to answer him when he needed help. Isaiah 59:2-3 says that our sins hide God's face from us and He cannot hear us. Do not get me wrong, the Lord wants to help us, but we need to help ourselves as well and repent when we have done wrong. We need to stop our pride and not let pride stop us. Be intentional in the way you conduct yourself all the time, not just when you want something, but also when you do not. It is ironic that Saul would ask God to give him favor, asking God how to lead Israel, when he was no longer the one God wanted leading his people. Saul had no self-control, no humility, and he was very self-centered and rebellious. We need to treat God with respect; it is an honor to talk with Him. I am not surprised at God's silence toward Saul.

Even though Saul knew sorcery was wrong (1 Samuel 28:3), he ordered his officials to find someone to help him get answers. Saul was stubborn and that blinded him from obeying God's instructions. God knew Saul's heart had not changed, and so God did not answer. Saul ordered a witch to call upon Samuel (v 11-14). She described what looked like Samuel and then proceeded being the medium for their conversation. (There is doubt that this was really Samuel's spirit, but that is a whole other study.) King Saul was told that the Lord did not answer him anymore because Saul did not obey the voice of the Lord or execute His wrath on Amalek (#39). Saul was also told he would die the next day. Saul immediately was filled with fear, but not repentance.

We cannot live our lives going back and forth between living a worldly life and acting holy and praying for the Lord's direction. It is hypocritical and ridiculous to think living that way would please our Lord and not cause a rift in our relationship with Him (Rev 3:15-16 says, "I know your deeds, that you are neither cold nor hot. I wish you were either one or the other! So, because you are lukewarm—neither hot nor cold—I am about to spit you out of my mouth" NIV). May our Bridegroom always be pleased with the heart He sees in His beloved bride. Do not play Him; He knows our true intentions.

45. Will Decide When to Take Revenge

They presented the head of Ish-Bosheth to David at Hebron, telling the king, "Here's the head of Ish-Bosheth, Saul's son, your enemy. He was out to kill you, *but God* has given vengeance to my master, the king—vengeance this very day on Saul and his children!" (2 Samuel 4:8 MSG, emphasis added).

To catch you up . . . Saul had died in battle as was foretold in BUT GOD #44. Second Samuel 1 explains how this happened. Saul requested a nearby Amalekite to "kill him" because he was already wounded in battle. The Amalekite did it and then brought Saul's crown to David and told him the details. David lamented King Saul's death, as well as Jonathan's death. David had the Amalekite killed because the Amalekite was not afraid to kill God's anointed (King Saul). By the way, the Amalekite would not have existed to kill him had Saul obeyed God's command of cutting them all off as discussed in BUT GOD #39. Further, in chapter 3, we read that David made a covenant with Abner (who was of Saul's command) to join forces with David. Abner had killed Joab's brother (2 Sam 3:30), so Joab (from David's army) told David that Abner was being deceitful and used that excuse to kill Abner. David, not happy about this, said Joab was too harsh, and cursed Joab's future generations. David mourned for Abner (2 Sam 3:31-39) and Saul (2 Sam 1:11-12).

In this BUT GOD, we continue to see men trying to justify slaying others, but really these men were taking matters into their own hands. Ish-Bosheth was Saul's son and had been made king over Israel. David honored him as king, just as he had honored Saul. David at this point was king over Judah. Ish-Bosheth was lying in bed when his two captains, from Saul's previous troops, killed and beheaded him. Again, David, in 2 Samuel 4:10-12, said these people thought they were bringing him good news, when in fact, they were proving they were wicked men killing righteous men. He decided those two captains needed to be executed, so they were.

The people in this story thought they were honoring God and David as the true king by committing murder. Instead, they were digging their own graves. Do not use God as a reason to justify your actions. We already discussed in BUT GOD #43 that David honored God's timing, and here, we have men who assumed they were doing the work of God when they were not. David did not want to see men die undeservingly, especially a king, and neither does God. Our Bridegroom does not want us to do things in His name that do not bring glory and honor to Him. He does not want us to use His name as a reason for us to do something *we* want either. Make sure it is *His* will before giving *Him* credit; He may not want it.

46. Can Get Displeased with Our Decisions
"But God was not at all pleased with what David had done" (2 Samuel 11:27 MSG, emphasis added).

In BUT GOD #28, we learned God expects our best—especially from those who have been given great authority over His people, like Moses had. We find out here that David learned the same lesson. After all, David was not perfect; he was a man with flaws, just like the other people in the Bible (except Jesus). Just as Moses was disciplined for not obeying God's instructions, David was disciplined (2 Sam. 12:7-15). As wonderful as David was, God does not cover up his flaws in the Bible. Here, we see David's sin with Bathsheba. I discovered another piece of interesting information also. The very thing that David condemned the men for in the previous BUT GOD (#45), he now does himself; a righteous man is killed undeservingly.

David lusted after Bathsheba, whom he knew was a married woman, but still took her for himself. When he found out she was pregnant by him, he tried to cover it up by bringing her husband, Uriah, home from war to be with her. When that plan did not work, David had Uriah sent to the front lines where he knew he would be killed in battle. Once David knew Uriah had died, he took Bathsheba as his wife. God knew what David had done, and He would not let him get away with it. God sent Nathan, a prophet, to reprimand David's actions and tell him of the repercussions of his unwise decisions. Nathan began with a story so David would see the depths of his sin. David acknowledged he sinned against the Lord and the Lord forgave his sin, but Nathan told David that his child would die.

Adultery is wrong and trying to cover it up is also wrong. A sexual sin affects the core of our beings and our spirits. The enemy entices people and once they take the bait and act on that impulse, the damage is done. The Lord addresses this subject many times in the Bible as it hinders His relationship with His bride. God often called Israel an adulterous wife, being unfaithful to Him and loving other gods rather than Him alone (#113).[37]

God's view of marriage is more than a commitment; He sees it as a covenant. He is a jealous lover of our souls. He does not want us to share our affections with anything or anyone that we would place as more important than our relationship with Him. Where our attention is, there our heart lies. Where does your heart lie? Are you displeasing your heavenly Bridegroom with the decisions you are making or is your heart truly His and His alone? I am not saying you cannot have an earthly spouse, only to check your priorities. He wants to be the first priority in your heart because that is where He belongs. Your first desire should be to please your Bridegroom. For me, the thought of doing something that would hinder my relationship with Jesus is all the motivation I need to stay in line. My relationship with Jesus is that important, and I hope it is for you as well.

47. Loves Us and Welcomes Us Home / Gives Life

"'Why, then,' the woman said, 'have you done this very thing against God's people? In his verdict, the king convicts himself by not bringing home his exiled son. We all die sometime. Water spilled on the ground can't be gathered up again. *But God* does not take away life. He works out ways to get the exile back'" (2 Samuel 14:13-14 MSG, emphasis added). *Also found in 2 Sam 14:14 NIV, NLT.

One of David's sons, Absalom, had taken revenge on his brother and killed him. Absalom fled afterward and David had not seen him since. Absalom was not permitted to return by the king, but Joab perceived that David was concerned over Absalom and devised a way for his return. The woman in this BUT GOD verse went to David with a story given to her by Joab. This story would stir David's heart to let Absalom return.

As we have learned previously, water represents life (#43). When this BUT GOD verse makes a statement about water being spilled on the ground, it seems that it is referring to death. It says that God is not the one who takes life away, but rather, is actually the Water of Life (#36) because His agenda is to always *give life* (John 10:10). He wants to bring us back to His heart. In this BUT GOD, we read that our Father works out a way to get the exile back. Like I mentioned in BUT GOD #1, though Adam and Eve were told they would die if they ate from that certain tree, they were exiled first from the Garden of Eden. God wanted to bring humanity back to His garden and through Jesus' life and resurrection, now there is a way. Absalom's legacy represents one of a rebellious son, he disrespected his family, and ultimately branded himself with a bad reputation. Yet, his father David still loved him. This is great to remember when praying for loved ones and our backsliding brothers and sisters in Christ.

When I read this BUT GOD, I think of the Parable of the Prodigal Son Jesus told in Luke 15:11-32. God always wants His children to return to Him, no matter what they have done or how far they have run. There is a song written by Martin Smith and Chris Tomlin based on this story called, "Back to the Start (God's

Great Dance Floor)."[38] Listen to it if you get a chance. Also, in the
Parable of the Lost Sheep in Luke 15:1-7 we see that God does not
want even one of His sheep to stray. He will go after the one that is
lost to get him back safely. Jesus says He will not lose anyone God
has given Him (John 6:39), and that includes you. Romans 8:38-39
says, "For I am convinced that neither death nor life, neither angels
nor demons, neither the present nor the future, nor any powers,
neither height nor depth, nor anything else in all creation, will be
able to separate us from the love of God that is in Christ Jesus our
Lord" (NIV).

Our Bridegroom hates sin, but He does not hate us. He always
loves us because our God is love (1 John 4:8). He desires that we
be able to comprehend the width, length, depth, and height of
Jesus' great love (Eph 3:17-19). What a perfect Father God He
is that He would make a way for us to come home again, not
feeling threatened when we returned, but instead loved, adored,
and wanted. He welcomes us home with a joyous smile because
that is the kind of God He is, and His Son, our Bridegroom, is
just like Him!

48. Sticks by Us

"But me he caught—reached all the way from sky to sea; he
pulled me out of that ocean of hate, that enemy chaos, the
void in which I was drowning. They hit me when I was down,
but God stuck by me. He stood me up on a wide-open field; I
stood there saved—surprised to be loved!" (2 Samuel 22:17-
20 MSG, emphasis added).

I often wonder when I hear music on the radio if the lyrics were
written with God in mind. Some of the best love songs not heard
on Christian music stations can be read as a love song from us to
our Bridegroom or from Him to us. When the Holy Spirit opens
my ears to the words actually being sung, I never hear the song
the same again. This happened to me as I was driving home from
the beach one day when a song by Stephanie Mills came on. The
words that struck me were "Never knew love like this before...

what a surprise."[39] I remembered this BUT GOD verse and realized this was the kind of song that would have made David dance around; it is a perfect song for this verse which is repeated again in Psalms (#72).

Sometimes God surprises us with a hug when we least expect it. He overwhelms us with a flood of feelings, and all we can do is stand in awe of the amazing love He shows us. Sometimes His love brings tears and sometimes it brings smiles, just like hugs do. Hugs make people feel supported when they are discouraged. Hugs let you know you will have a friend that will stick by you—just like our Bridegroom! Proverbs 18:24 tells us that Jesus is our friend and He sticks closer than a brother.

This BUT GOD verse contains words from a song that David spoke to the Lord when he was saved from his enemies, including Saul. David's life was constantly threatened because of who he was. The Bible tells us that the Holy Spirit resided with him just as the Holy Spirit resides in us. That marks us as a target to the enemy—but our God will stick by us. He has also provided us with the best armor to defeat evil (Eph 6:10-17). God saved David and continued to be trustworthy time and time again (#41). He delivered David because He delighted in him (2 Sam 22:20), and He delights in us as well (Prov 11:20, Prov 12:22). God's grace allows us to be loved by Him even though we are all so unworthy. It is only through Christ that we are purified, sanctified, and justified to be in His presence (1 Cor 6:11). We are no longer sinners, but saints. It is only because our Bridegroom sticks by us and helps us stand when the enemy causes chaos that we are saved—saved from the enemy and saved from eternal destruction.

49. Commends Us

"My father David had it in his heart to build a Temple honoring the Name of God, the God of Israel. *But God* told him 'It was good that you wanted to build a Temple in my honor—most commendable! But you are not the one to do it—your son will build it to honor my Name'" (1 Kings 8:17-19 MSG, emphasis added).

Solomon was talking here about what became one of his greatest accomplishments. Thanks to his father for listening to the Lord and not taking over, Solomon was able to oversee the building of the beautiful Temple. It took seven years to complete (1 Kings 6:38). Solomon gave a speech to the whole assembly of Israel once the Ark was brought into the Temple for its permanent dwelling place and the Temple was finished. This BUT GOD is part of that speech.

As king, David resided in a house of cedar. David noticed the Lord resided in a tent and wanted the Lord to have better accommodations (2 Sam 7:1-3). David purposed in his heart to build God a permanent dwelling place. David wanted to bless God, BUT GOD blessed David more and told him that He would build *him* a house, meaning He would establish David's kingdom forever. I do not know if David realized this at the time, but David was being commended with the distinct honor and privilege of the Savior actually coming from his family line (2 Sam 7:11-17).[40]

When God is pleased with us, He will bless us. When we come up with an idea and feel led to act on it, it is because it has come from our Father's heart. He places His desires in our heart and lets them become our desires. If we do something He has asked of us or accomplish what we feel we are led to do, it makes our Bridegroom happy. Matthew 25:21-23 tells of a servant who had been so faithful and responsible that his master was full of praise and said, ". . . Well done, my good and faithful servant. You have been faithful in handling this small amount, so now I will give you many more responsibilities. Let's celebrate together!" (NLT). Will Jesus say these words to you? I hope I hear my Bridegroom say this to me.

50. Speaks through Prophets
"*But God* said to Shemaiah, the man of God" (1 Kings 12:22 NLT, emphasis added).

God had decided to let Jeroboam lead ten of the twelve tribes of Israel because, as years went by, Solomon's heart turned away from the Lord and he had not continued to walk in God's ways (1 Kings 11:31-33). Rehoboam, Solomon's son, was telling the House of Judah (consisting of two tribes) to fight against the House of Israel (consisting of 10 tribes). Rehoboam was hoping to restore the kingdom so he could rule over the entire nation. Shemaiah, "the man of God," told Rehoboam and the other men not to fight and to return home (1 Kings 12:23-24). Thank goodness these men listened to God's instructions not to fight (unlike the Israelites in #27) or they probably would have been defeated.

When we are about His business, as Shemaiah was, God will give us His plans. Shemaiah was God's prophet. There are many examples in the Bible where He used prophets to be His mouthpiece on earth. Prophets are used by God even to this day to let His people know what He is up to (Amos 3:7). God uses a prophet's voice to bring about His strategies for the body of Christ so we will be prepared for the days ahead. Once it is spoken into existence, and if it is God's will, then God will fulfill His Word (just like He will be sure to fulfill every word of the Bible—Jer 1:12, Is 55:11).

God's prophets have already let us know what His future plans are through the Bible. There are people who work in the office of a prophet and are used by God to this day who continue to encourage His church. It is up to us as His bride to listen with a discerning ear to make sure that what the prophets say is in agreement with God's Word (Acts 17:11) and glorifies Jesus (Rev 19:10). You also need to discern the lifestyle of the one giving the word, to judge if he is a true representation of the One who sent him ("Beware of false prophets . . . by their fruit you will know them" Matt 7:15-20). Their words should be confirmation of what the Lord has already placed on your heart and revealed to you (1 Thes 5:19-22). Sometimes, if it is a corporate word for the church, there will be many prophets or teachings on the same subject (1 Cor 14:29). In these last days, it is critical we keep our ears tuned to what our Bridegroom is up to and to test the spirits as there are many false prophets who have gone out into the world (1 John 4:1-4).

The Lord awaits His bride to speak His will into existence. You may not be gifted with the office of a prophet, but our Bridegroom hopes you are willing to be used to bring about His glory. Look at the following verse—it is a perfect complement to our BUT GOD study. Second Peter 1:21 says, "For no prophecy ever originated because some man willed it [to do so—it never came by human impulse], but men spoke from God who were borne along (moved and impelled) by the Holy Spirit" (AMP).

Many times we see God use those who already have a relationship with Him to speak a prophetic word, but this is not always the case. God used Rahab in Joshua 2:9 to speak out that God had given the Israelites the land and that fear was on the inhabitants. Even though she was not part of the chosen people and she was a prostitute (Joshua 2:1), this word was a confirmation of what the Lord had told the Israelites already! The Spirit will use whomever He chooses. We read later that Rahab was spared for showing kindness to the Israelite spies (Josh 6:22-25). Her story is so important that her name is mentioned in Jesus' genealogy (Matt 1:4-5).[41]

Interestingly, the next few BUT GODs are now about prophets . . .

51. Will Not be Outsmarted

"Jeroboam's wife did as she was told; she went straight to Shiloh and to Ahijah's house. Ahijah was an old man at this time, and blind, *but God* had warned Ahijah, 'Jeroboam's wife is on her way to consult with you regarding her sick son; tell her this and this and this'" (1 Kings 14:4-5 MSG, emphasis added).

The whole story . . .

The prophet Ahijah was the one who told Jeroboam that ten tribes would be taken away from Solomon's kingdom and given to him. This was because as Solomon got older, he led the people to worship other gods (1 Kings 11:33-35). Rehoboam, Solomon's son, still had rule over the House of Judah. Jeroboam feared the people would be under Rehoboam's rule again if he let them go to Jerusalem to offer sacrifices in the Temple to God, so he had two golden calves made for them to worship in the cities he ruled over;

one in Bethel, the other in Dan. He also created special feasts and high priests for them (1 Kings 12:25-35). These were all against God's laws and ordinances. Jeroboam's sin caused Israel to sin. Unfortunately, many kings after him did not depart from the sins stemmed by him, which brought about many problems for Israel.

Jeroboam's son became sick, so he sent his wife to Ahijah's house to get an answer about his son's future. He told his wife to go disguised so Ahijah would not know it was her. That is where we find our BUT GOD verse. Jeroboam's wife got a mouthful of terrible news to bring back to her husband. Jeroboam had sinned and done much evil against the Lord. Because of these decisions after the Lord had exalted him, Ahijah told Jeroboam's wife disaster would fall upon their house and Israel (1 Kings 14:9-16) and that her son would die. Ahijah prophesied accurately. As she reached the threshold of her house, her son died. In BUT GOD #98 discussion we will see that the house of Israel was destroyed.

Jeroboam sent his wife in a disguise to a blind prophet. What irony. The prophet would not be able to see the disguise, so what did it matter? The cool part is that God told him she would be in a disguise; God will not be outsmarted. He was not going to let blindness prevent His prophet from knowing who he was talking to and how she was going to represent herself when she arrived. Unfortunately, she was representing her husband's foolish decisions (she was called out on it in verse 6) which were the cause of her not getting to see her son alive ever again.

Everything our Bridegroom does is holy and upright, so when *we* represent Him, we can rest knowing *we* will not be representing a foolish bridegroom who makes bad decisions. Sometimes, He may give us all the details of who we are to talk to and what we are to say, just as He did for His prophet Ahijah. Corporately to His bride, our Bridegroom has actually already told us who we are to talk to and what we are to say, as found in Matthew 28:19-20. Jesus said, "Therefore go and make disciples of all nations, baptizing them in the name of the Father and of the Son and of the Holy Spirit, and teaching them to obey everything I have commanded you. And surely I am with you always, to the very end of the age" (NIV). Our Bridegroom wants us to share Him with the world. He wants us to tell the world what He has taught us—how to obey His instructions so new believers can be carriers of the Kingdom of God. Second Timothy 3:16-17 tells us *all* Scripture instructs in righteousness so that the man of God can be complete. With the Holy Spirit, new believers have guidance to understand the basics of all Scripture, but they need someone to be accountable to. We cannot just share Jesus and leave; discipleship must be established for follow through if someone decides to let Jesus be Lord. This provides new believers assistance as they learn to walk in God's foundational truths. Learning how to hear God clearly helps believers outsmart the enemy.

52. Is Gentle and Quiet

"Then he was told, 'Go, stand on the mountain at attention before God. God will pass by.' A hurricane wind ripped through the mountains and shattered the rocks before God, *but God* wasn't to be found in the wind; after the wind an earthquake, *but God* wasn't in the earthquake; and after the earthquake fire, *but God* wasn't in the fire; and after the fire a gentle and quiet whisper" (1 Kings 19:11-12 MSG, emphasis added).

Elijah was a major prophet used by God to do two main things: prepare and restore. He prepared the people to be ready for the restoration of prophets (they were being killed, so many went into hiding) and he prepared Israel to return to God.

This is what happened . . . Elijah had just concluded a showdown on Mt. Carmel in front of Israel for them to determine whether Baal (who they were wrongly serving) or the Lord was truly God. Through Elijah, God showed the people of Israel how powerful He was with a gigantic display of signs and wonders while the priests of Baal could not facilitate anything. This prompted the people of Israel to see the error of their ways and repent before the Lord God. Elijah then slaughtered all the false prophets of Baal. This angered Jezebel, King Ahab's wife, who then threatened Elijah. Neither Jezebel nor King Ahab were at the event, and since these two were still in charge, Elijah was scared for his life and he ran away.

Jezebel was the daughter of Ethbaal, which means "with Baal." Ahab married Jezebel against God's command; she was a foreigner and she brought this false god into the Israelite kingdom. Jezebel was a real person, but the spirit of her still exists today. Many Bible teachers have taught on the spirit of Jezebel.[42] Jezebel's aim was and still is in our day (Rev 2:20) to silence God's prophets to destroy the testimony of Jesus and the spirit of prophecy (Rev.19:10). Something to remember about the spirit of Jezebel is it never repents; it is sarcastic, plays the victim, is seductive, brings confusion, and holds onto a sense of power it does not have. It causes intimidation, fear, and depression, all the while trying to shut your voice. It is the counterfeit of Elijah's spirit and needs to be confronted once its manipulative ways are discovered.

The Lord helped Elijah break off the effects of this spirit. Elijah was hiding in the desert until an angel sent him on a journey to the mountain of God. Elijah slept in a cave there and God told him to come out. Immediately after, the Lord passed by and we find our BUT GOD verse. The Lord spoke with him. Elijah told God his fear and God then released Elijah to move on and gave him his next assignment.

Elijah assisted in the display of God's glory at Mt. Carmel and immediately his life was threatened. The enemy tries to destroy our highs by striking us with fear. Fear causes immobility and inactivity, which is an unhealthy place for the people of God to be. God cannot use us when we are fearful, so like a good Bridegroom, He helps us to get back out again. This is what God did with Elijah. Our Bridegroom knows how to approach us in a way that still shows His glory, but also is sensitive enough to know what we need from Him.

Another concept this BUT GOD shows is that sometimes we need to stand and wait silently to hear Him. There is a lot of chaos in this world and sometimes we can get caught up in all the noise, BUT GOD does not. You may expect God to speak loudly, just like the world, but if you do, you might miss His whispers. The Book of Joel says in the last days that what has been lost spiritually will be *restored* to *prepare* the way of the Lord (2:28-32). Do not be shaken by the acts of nature and all the distractions in these last days (hurricanes, earthquakes, and fires), but wait in anticipation knowing our Bridegroom is going to arrive next (Luke 21:25-28)!

53. Does Not Always Tell Us Why

"But when she reached the Holy Man at the mountain, she threw herself at his feet and held tightly to him. Gehazi came up to pull her away, but the Holy Man said, 'Leave her alone—can't you see that she's in distress? *But God* hasn't let me in on why; I'm completely in the dark'" (2 Kings 4:27 MSG, emphasis added).

Elisha was a major prophet used by God after Elijah was "taken away" (2 Kings 2). This story is about the prophet Elisha and a woman who was hospitable to him. She noticed he was a man of God who often walked by where they lived, so she persuaded him to come eat with them. She also had her husband build him an upper room where he could sleep when he came. Since she was thoughtful toward him, Elisha wanted to do something for her. He asked his servant to find out what she needed. The servant informed him she did not have a son. Elisha prophesied she would have a son by the following year, even though she did not ask him to give her one. She did not want to get her hopes up and asked him not to lie; sure enough, she bore a son at the appointed time. One day, years later, her son complained of his head hurting and died. The woman laid him on Elisha's bed and mounted a donkey to go after him for help. This is where our BUT GOD begins.

Elisha perceived something was wrong with the boy after seeing and speaking to the woman, but unlike the example in BUT GOD #51, this time the Lord did not tell this prophet what to do or say. Elisha followed her home because she would not leave him. Elisha prayed for the boy and laid on him, but he did not wake up. He left the room, walked back and forth, and then returned and laid on him again. This time the boy came back to life. It was by faith that the woman came to Elisha for help, and it was by persistence that God answered Elisha's prayer. Satan tried to cut that boy's life short because he was destined to do great things for the kingdom of God (#23).[43]

Even Elisha, who was a great prophet, was not always in the know about everything. God may have been moving Elisha to a new level in God's power. In this case, it was to bring about His glory in an authoritative and significant way, to raise a boy from death! Without God telling Elisha what was wrong and what would happen, Elisha had to rely on his knowledge of how powerful God is and trust He would answer the prayer. Elisha did not pray harder or with better words, he just continued to believe until the full change came about. He did not settle when the boy's flesh became warm again (v 34); he continued to pray persistently until the full restoration took place and the boy awoke.

Let's discuss signs and wonders for a minute. *Signs* are given to make people *wonder* about God. It gives Christians an opportunity to draw people a picture of God's love for them. When there is an outpouring of the Holy Spirit, signs and wonders will most likely take place. It is not to have the ministry become a show, but to equip people to spread the kingdom further for His glory. The caution is that if the signs become more enticing than the fruit of the Spirit, then the focus has shifted away from God's purposes. When people make the miracle more important than the fruit, it takes glory off of God rather than adding glory to Him. People watch how Christians act, so by demonstrating the fruit of the Spirit in our own lifestyle, new believers can observe what living by faith means (Gal 5:22-23).

Elisha knew something that most Christians do not practice this day but should: how to pray and believe for miracles. In Luke 11:2-4, the Lord's Prayer says, "God's will be done on Earth as it is in heaven." There is no sickness in heaven, so we need not claim it here on Earth. We need to claim that God's will be on Earth as it is in heaven, and cast out disease in Jesus' name. Ask God to supernaturally intervene with the specifics of what needs to be healed spiritually, physically, and emotionally. We need to be persistent with our Bridegroom to provide complete healing. Every circumstance is different, so even when God does not answer us immediately and we feel totally in the dark about our conditions, we still need to do something about it. There could be spiritual blocks that are preventing healing from taking place. We need to ask God to show us what we are missing. We press in and put our words into action about who we know God to be.

Graham Cooke teaches that all of heaven is drawn to the Jesus in us. So, everything that is available in heaven can be available to us on earth as we draw that goodness down and influence the environment around us for God's glory and His kingdom purposes. The Holy Spirit has gifted each of us. As we grow in those abilities, He will give more if we ask. There are definitely people who God has gifted with His healing power on this earth, and I think we are going to see more of that gift. Chris Tomlin's song, "Our God" from the album *And If Our God Is for Us*, states how there is no one like our God; He is Healer and awesome in power.[44] He is greater, stronger, and higher than any other. It is our job as His bride on earth to move in that knowledge of who our Bridegroom is and put it into practice. By doing this, we will truly represent Him and be able to give Him all the glory.

54. Is Gracious, Merciful, and Faithful to Keep His Promises

"Hazael king of Aram badgered and bedeviled Israel all through the reign of Jehoahaz. *But God* was gracious and showed mercy to them. He stuck with them out of respect for his covenant with Abraham, Isaac, and Jacob. He never gave up on them, never even considered discarding them, even to this day. Hazael king of Aram died. His son Ben-Hadad was the next king" (2 Kings 13:22-24 MSG, emphasis added).

Leviticus 26 lists out the rewards for obeying God's instructions and the punishments for disobeying. God warned the Israelites that if they broke their covenant and did not perform all His commandments, then He would set his face against them so that they would be defeated by their enemies, being ruled over by those who hate them (Lev 26:17). God said they would pay for rejecting His laws, but despite this, He would not reject them and remember His covenant promise (Lev 26:43-45). This is exactly what we see happening in this BUT GOD verse. It says that despite Israel continuing to do evil in the Lord's sight, God was still compassionate toward them and followed through with His promise to stay with them.

Before moving on, please note there is a chart you can flip to in BUT GOD #60 for a quick reference to assist with the king's names. Jehoahaz was the King of Israel and he followed in the sins of Jeroboam (#51). Israel's sins caused God to be angry. God delivered them into the hands of Syria/Aram (2 Kings 13:3); Syria harassed Israel and captured their cities. Jehoahaz's son, Jehoash (also known as Joash), visited Elisha, the prophet, who told Joash that he would strike Syria (Aram) three times, but he would not completely destroy it (2 Kings 13:14-19). King Hazael died and his son, Ben-Hadad, was the new King of Syria. In verse 25 we see that Joash recaptured the cities in Israel that were taken in war during his father's reign (Jehoahaz). Joash defeated the King of Syria three times just as Elisha prophesied.

We have heard it said many times that the Lord is gracious and merciful. Now, we have our first BUT GOD story to go along with these words. He was kind to His people when they did not deserve it. It is His nature to be this way. He made a covenant with the nation of Israel; He was faithful to keep His promise (#4). Israel had made a promise to God also (#31). They all agreed to follow His commands, one being, "You shall have no other gods before me" (Ex 20:3 NIV). Unfortunately, the future generations of Israel were not following what their forefathers set up for them. Because of this, they felt the removal of His protective hand and were defeated in many wars as we read through these Bible stories. BUT GOD will never break His Word, and as our BUT GOD verse says, "He never gave up on them, never even considered discarding them, even to this day." That includes THIS day NOW.

Jeremiah 1:12 says, "Then said the Lord to me, You have seen well, for I am alert and active, watching over My word to perform it" (AMP). Isaiah 55:11 says, "So shall My word be that goes forth out of My mouth: it shall not return to Me void [without producing any effect, useless], but it shall accomplish that which I please and purpose, and it shall prosper in the thing for which I sent it" (AMP). He will continue to be their God and our God, even when we sin, because He is faithful to fulfill His promises and His Word, and He is gracious and merciful. Titus 2:11-15 tells us that God's grace will teach us what we need to know. Figuring out what God has said in the time we have is His evidence of mercy.

The forefathers of America set up a similar covenant with God as Israel did. The country of America was to be built on God's principles; we are to live as one nation under God. Now, the future generation of America is doing everything possible to remove God from the system. Our nation may suffer like the Israelites did when they did not honor their commitment to Him. How many times will America say to God, "We do not need You anymore," and then complain when His protection is lifted off of us? If our nation continues to turn from Him and His ways, we cannot be mad at Him when He allows us to be attacked. Not every American wants to remove God, thankfully, but as a nation we may suffer as a whole when our leaders think that way. God has extended His grace and mercy to us in the past and I pray He will continue, because America needs Him in order to survive. America also needs to continue to be friends with Israel because we will be blessed as long as we are (Gen 12:3). God is on Israel's side, and that is where we need to be standing when the line is drawn in the sand.

From a bridal perspective, we know Jesus will continue to stick with us (#48). The day we decided to allow Him into our lives, He promised He would never leave us or forsake us and we can confidently say He is our help (#17, Heb 13:5-6). God originally said He would never leave or forsake Israel to Joshua once he took over leading the Israelites after Moses' death (Deuteronomy 31:6, 23). All the Bible is relevant for us, but this passage is repeated in the New Testament because God wanted us to know that we can apply it to our lives as well. I believe when any part of the Word of God is spoken, you can ask the Lord for those words, promises, and blessings to be for you. His character is unchanging toward you. He is kind to us when we do not deserve it. He is faithful to keep all His promises and will not abandon us, or Israel. By

His grace we are saved (Eph 2:8), and His mercies are new every morning (Lam 3:22-23).

55. Gives Hope

"God was fully aware of the trouble in Israel, its bitterly hard times. No one was exempt, whether slave or citizen, and no hope of help anywhere was in sight. *But God* wasn't yet ready to blot out the name of Israel from history, so he used Jeroboam son of Jehoash to save them" (2 Kings 14:26-27 MSG, emphasis added).

In 2 Kings 14:25, the writer mentions Jonah was a prophet during these times. Since we learned about God's grace in the previous BUT GOD (#54), this is important to note because Jonah says in Jonah 2:8 that those who cling to worthless idols forfeit God's grace that could be theirs. From the previous BUT GODs, we have seen the Israelites with false gods. God wants to give grace all the time. His nature is to forgive and restore. Times of war are hard and the Israelites were warring with themselves (v 12); they were forfeiting much of God's grace because of their false idols. We see that God was "fully aware" of them going through these "bitterly hard times," so, because of His mercy, God gave relief to the Israelites through this king. God had resolved not to blot out Israel.

It has to be a horrible feeling not to have any "hope of help." Fortunately, we know our Bridegroom gives us hope. Colossians 1:27 says, ". . . Christ in you, the hope of glory" (KJV). We have hope for a future (Jeremiah 29:11) and hope for eternal life (Titus 1:2) because He will not lie to us (John 1:14, 17) and He is faithful to keep His promises (Ps 145:13 NIV). In fact, He wants His bride to be ready to give a defense, an answer, to people who ask for a reason for that hope you have (1 Peter 3:15), so you can be a living testimony for Him.

Since our Bridegroom gives hope, let us tell the world why—because God loves you! He created you to be with Him, just love Him back. Love Him enough that you are willing to show Him by obeying what He asks of you. Realize He loved you so much

He sent His only Son, Jesus, to die for your sins so you would not perish, and He rose from the dead so we could live eternally with Him (John 3:16)! So here is the fun part, we can rearrange some of this BUT GOD verse to fit our lives as well.

God is fully aware of (your name)'s trouble, the bitterly hard times. There was no hope of help anywhere in sight. BUT GOD did not want to blot out the name of (your name) from history, so He sent Jesus, son of Jehovah God to save (your name)!

56. Made the Cosmos / Is Majestic

"Sing to God, everyone and everything! Get out his salvation news every day! Publish his glory among the godless nations, his wonders to all races and religions. And why? Because God is great—well worth praising! No god or goddess comes close in honor. All the popular gods are stuff and nonsense, *but God* made the cosmos! Splendor and majesty flow out of him, strength and joy fill his place" (1 Chronicles 16:23-27 MSG, emphasis added).

In Genesis 1:1, God lets you know right from the start that He created the heavens and the earth. John 1:3 says, "Through Him all things were made; without Him nothing was made that has been made" (NIV). Existence of creation reveals the existence of a Creator.

Our Bridegroom is so creative! Have you seen pictures of all the different wonders in outer space? He made various blends of colors with the planets and nebulas. They all align with each other perfectly in galaxies and usually do not run into each other while spinning around in circulating motions. I love looking at the lights in the sky, and He made so many for us to enjoy! Children love to color pictures from their imagination, and so does God. He had an endless canvas, hence the vastness of our universe.

Not too many people realize that He drew a story in the heavens. Have you heard of "The Gospel in the Stars"? I had not until my friend, Arlene, gave me the book compiled and written originally in 1884 by Joseph Seiss.[45] In it, we find God gave His full salvation plan in the pictures seen in the constellations and the stars. The Hebrews called this the Mazzaroth; in fact, some of the constellations are even mentioned in Job 38:31-33. This may be one reason why David begins Psalm 19 by saying, "The heavens declare the glory of God . . ." (KJV). Ultimately, faith comes by hearing the Word of God and the light of the knowledge of His glory is in the face of Jesus Christ (Rom 10:17, 2 Cor:4:6). Remember, though, that before the Bible existed, God gave humanity a picture book that could be passed down to future generations that could not be destroyed. It could be clearly seen because there was no pollution, smog, street lights, or tall buildings to block the view.

Unfortunately, the enemy has, as he does with everything, taken something of God, and twisted it into something that it was not originally meant to be. Astronomy and astrology are two completely different things and unfortunately today, the pictures in the sky are no longer viewed upon as what God created them to be. They are now referred to as the signs of the Zodiac and people use them as a horoscope, placing their trust in the stars and not in God. God's pictures have been perverted into mythology and the religion of astrology. Satan has also perverted God's rainbow into representing gay pride instead of God's covenant promise. Satan has even tried to take away God's credit in purposeful creation and has led people to believe we have evolved by accident because of a big bang. BUT GOD promises in Romans 8:21 that creation itself will be delivered from the bondage of corruption. So, declare and proclaim how majestic our Bridegroom is for all that He has created in the cosmos. David declares that and more in this BUT GOD, which is part of a song he delivered to thank the Lord (1 Chron 16:8-36) after the ark (which held the Ten Commandments) was brought to Jerusalem and placed in the Tabernacle (the tent which housed the ark).

57. Calls Us to Specific Assignments

"David said to Solomon, 'I wanted in the worst way to build a sanctuary to honor my God. *But God* prevented me, saying, "You've killed too many people, fought too many wars. You are not the one to honor me by building a sanctuary—you've been responsible for too much killing, too much bloodshed. But you are going to have a son and he will be a quiet and peaceful man, and I will calm his enemies down on all sides. His very name will speak peace—that is, Solomon, which means Peace—and I'll give peace and rest under his rule. He will be the one to build a sanctuary in my honor. He'll be my royal adopted son and I'll be his father; and I'll make sure that the authority of his kingdom over Israel lasts forever"'" (1 Chronicles 22:7-10 MSG, emphasis added).

We see the Bible recounting this story MANY times, so our Bridegroom must have more to tell us (#49 was the first one of these BUT GODs during Solomon's speech at the temple's completion). David wanted to build a temple for God as a permanent place for Him to dwell. God told David he would not build it, and here, we learn the reason why as he is telling Solomon. David had shed too much blood on the earth. Solomon was going to be the one to honor the Lord by building the temple, not David. The Lord had equipped David with many gifts and personal experiences that honored God, but David realized that building the temple was Solomon's calling, not his.

Do you ever wish you could do someone else's job? I do. I wish I could sing and play an instrument like the worship leaders at church so I could lead people to sing praises all the time, but I cannot. My singing voice is only beautiful to God and I can only play basic songs on the piano. But, the Lord still allows me to participate in worship, singing a joyful noise (literally) to Him. I enjoy writing songs and poems of praise to Him—as many as I want, even though I am not the one leading that task. Here, we have the same thing. David's heart was in the right place to do something for the Lord, but it was not his calling. The Lord allowed David to still participate, though, so that he could rejoice in the work.

David was given many assignments by God, as we all are. Could you be like David in this example and step back by letting someone else take the lead? David had already begun making preparations before he was told he could not do it (1 Chron 28:2).

Would you be able to let go so easily? Maybe you feel you are more qualified than someone who has been given authority above you. David may have felt this way when he said his son was "young and inexperienced" in front of the assembly (1 Chron 29:1). He did though acknowledge that Solomon was "chosen by God" for the task.

Maybe you are given an assignment you don't feel qualified for. Well, the Bible says you ARE qualified in Colossians 1:12. God takes the weak and makes them strong; you are the best God's got, do not let condemnation keep you from helping Him. Do not let negative attitudes from others prevent you from doing an assignment He has called you to do. Do not neglect the gifting the Lord gave you to use for His glory. First Timothy 4:12-16 says not to let people look down on you because of your youth [your inexperience], but continue to do what you are called to; you will encourage yourself and save others. Our Bridegroom hopes we all will participate in His ministry fully equipped in the hope of our calling (Eph 1:18, 4:4). If we can serve Him joyfully in our calling, we can be a delight to the Lord. Psalm 37:23 says, "The steps of a good man are ordered by the Lord, and He delights in his way" (NKJV).

By letting Solomon build the temple, God was helping Solomon establish himself as a leader. By using the spiritual gifts that God had bundled specifically in him, Solomon could fulfill the task that was directed by God for him to do. Did you see the gift God gave Solomon in our BUT GOD verse that would make things easier for him to build the temple? It is every parent's dream: "Peace and rest under his rule." Since my main and special assignment right now is raising three very wonderful and unique children, this gift from God would really be helpful!

Our Bridegroom lets us each have a turn to do something great for Him. It is an honor to be able to fulfill a job He has determined for us to do. What gift could we ever give Him that could adequately say, "Thank you" or, "We love you" except a gift from the heart? Each of us has a special purpose divinely designed by God. We are each called to carry out specific tasks for Him. He has bundled us up with unique characteristics and gifts that will help us accomplish these tasks as we work hand in hand with His Spirit. Since I mentioned that I loved praise and worship, I thought I would share a song I wrote for God based on the Psalms.

PRAISE   Tina Miller 2/7/07

In the presence of Your saints and all the angels above	*Psalm 52:9*
My mouth and my lips will praise Your Holy love	*Psalm 42:8; 149:6*
May Your praise be heard in the heavens and on Earth	*Psalm 69:34*
And in Your sanctuary where faithfulness was birthed	*Psalm 150; 89:2*
You continually refresh me with Your unfailing love	*Psalm 107:8*
You fix Your gaze upon me like eyes of a dove	*Song 5:12*
I love You, God, my whole heart I give	*Psalm 138:1*
I will sing praise to You as long as I live	*Psalm 35:28*
Praise Him, Praise Him	*Psalm 117*
All day long	*Psalm 35:28*
Praise Him, Praise Him	*Psalm 113:1-3*
With this song	*Psalm 40:3*
Praise Him endlessly	*Psalm 71:6*
For His acts are mighty	*Psalm 150:2*
You are good, You are excellent	*Psalm 150*
I will praise You with my instrument	*Psalm 150*
Praise You with dancing to the tambourine	*Psalm 150*
Praise You with the flute and the strings	*Psalm 150*
I will make it glorious to Your ear	*Psalm 66:2*
Sounding the trumpet for all to hear	*Psalm 150*
With clashing cymbals I will proclaim	*Psalm 150*
Praise to Your beautiful and wonderful Name	*Psalm 145:2*
Praise Yahweh, Praise Yahweh	*Psalm 117*
All day long	*Psalm 35:28*
Praise Jesus, Praise Jesus	*Psalm 113:1-3*
With this song	*Psalm 40:3*
Praise Holy Spirit endlessly	*Psalm 71:6*
For His acts are mighty	*Psalm 150:2*
You are greatly to be praised	*Psalm 96:4*
By Your works I am amazed	*Psalm 145:2*
You have done wonderful deeds for man	*Psalm 107:8*
Firm forever Your love will stand	*Psalm 89:2*
I will praise Your surpassing greatness	*Psalm 150:2*
I will praise Your loving kindness	*Psalm 36:7*
Praise Your Word!	*Psalm 56:4*
Praise Your Power!	*Psalm 21:13; 150:2*
I will praise You every hour!	*Psalm 119:164*

58. Shows Us Jesus / Dwells In Us

"*But God* said unto me, Thou shalt not build a house for my name, because thou hast been a man of war, and hast shed blood" (1 Chronicles 28:3 KJV, emphasis added). *Also found in the NIV, AMP, and NLT.

This BUT GOD verse is a quote from David when he is telling the whole assembly of Israel that Solomon is to build the temple. I have noticed that when David told this story (#57, #58), he mentioned how he had shed blood, but Solomon was gracious and did not mention this part (#49, #59). David has been called by some a shadow figure of the Messiah (#40). He was a warrior, worshipper, and a king. Jesus came the first time to shed HIS OWN blood for us on the cross. Jesus is the eternal Lamb who was slain for us. Jesus is the Lamb who conquered the grave. Just as David shed other people's blood, Jesus will strike down many with the sword of His mouth when He comes again to reign as king. David was a mighty warrior; he killed giants and brought victory to Israel. David was a good king, but Jesus IS our mighty warrior and THE conquering King. He defeated death and resurrected and will reign forever (Rev 19:11-16).

Solomon, David's child, was known as the one who built the temple.[46] Believers, God's children (I John 3:10), house God's presence through the Holy Spirit, as our bodies become His temple (1 Cor 3:16). We learn to control our bodies in a holy and honorable way (1 Thes 4:3-8) as we build our own temple by giving God glory and respect (#37). We are all one body, comprised of many pieces being fit together to grow into one united holy temple of the Lord (Rom 12:4-5, 1 Cor 12:12-27, Eph 2:19-22). We learn to dwell in unity with each other because it is good and pleasant (Ps 133). Cedar was the wood chosen by Solomon and David for their home as well as the temple. David Stewart points out in his book, *Healing Oils of the Bible*, that "of all the essential oils in the world, cedarwoood contains the highest level of sesquiterpenes at 98%" (sesquiterpenes deliver oxygen molecules to cells directly and erase miswritten codes in cellular memory). He points out that breathing in "cedarwood increases the ability to think clearly and enhances the awareness needed for effective prayer and meditation." Living in this environment "contributes toward wise judgments and keeps [your] consciousness elevated on a spiritual level."[47] Since we are the Lord's temple, let us also be wise and surround ourselves with an environment full of pleasing aromas. After all, our prayers are as incense to Him and our worship will facilitate an atmosphere shift pointing to His holy presence, which is carried in us (Ps 141:2, Ps 148-150, Rom 12:1, Rev 5:8). Blessed be the Name of the Lord!

Another word for dwelling place is known in Hebrew as tabernacle. The first place the Lord dwelt with man was in the Garden of Eden. The Lord would again meet with man later in the tabernacle built by Moses in the desert. Jesus came in person and called his own body a temple that would be destroyed and raised up again in three day (John 2:19-22). Our Bridegroom's final dwelling place is with men. He will dwell among us and we will be His people (Rev 21:3). He will again "tabernacle" among us when He returns!

To sum it up, David (a shadow of the Messiah) mentioned shedding blood, though it was not his own, the phrase itself reminds me of Christ. Solomon (representing the sons/daughters of God) was the temple builder. Instead of one main temple housing God's glory, now there are temples worldwide found in the body of Christ. We have just completed the third BUT GOD on this same subject and, amazingly, our Bridegroom is about to give one more lesson about who He is using this story.

59. Sets Us Up for Success

"'My father David very much wanted to build a temple honoring the Name of God, the God of Israel, *but God* told him, 'It was good that you wanted to build a temple in my honor—most commendable! But you are not the one to do it. Your son, who will carry on your dynasty, will build it for my Name'" (2 Chronicles 6:7-9 MSG, emphasis added).

This is our fourth time hearing this same verse. It is a repeat of BUT GOD #49 where Solomon was giving a speech because the temple had been completed (#57 was when David told his son, and #58 was when David told the Israelites). Since David could not be the one to build the temple, David found other ways to participate and continue to please God. In order for Solomon to be successful, Solomon would need both God's support and the people's support.

God helped Solomon by providing peace from other nations so he could complete it as read in BUT GOD #57. King David assisted by preparing whatever he could with all his might (1 Chron 29:2). He prepared Solomon by encouraging him and he prepared the plans for the temple. He prepared the supplies, including gold, silver, bronze, iron, timber, stones, and the musical instruments (1 Chron 23:5). He even prepared the divisions of the priests, Levites, and craftsmen for service as well as prepared the leaders and the people (1 Chron 28:21).

David was led by the Spirit (1 Chron 28:11-21) because David was willing to participate *however* the Lord directed him. David said the Lord's hand was on him so that he could understand in writing all the temple plans which he handed off to Solomon. David's gifting of gold and silver helped make the treasured articles. As king, he set a good example. Other people also gave willingly to the project. Proverbs 16:9 says it perfectly, "A man's heart *plans* his way, But the Lord *directs* his steps" (NKJV, emphasis mine). It was in David's heart to build the temple; he got to write up the *plans* and *directions*, and then God *directed* him to hand it over to Solomon! So cool!

How good our Bridegroom is, that He would set up our children's futures. He wants us to participate in the ministry for the next generation. David did this when he told Solomon in 1 Chronicles 28:8 to possess the land and leave the land as an inheritance to his children. God also wants us to hand down our experience, our time, our encouragement, our connections, our talents, and/or our finances (1 Tim 6:17-19). Think of all the worship songs that have been passed down. Even the Bible itself says it was written for us, the future generation, to praise God and believe that we will have life in His Name (Ps 102:18, John 20:30-31).

Whatever He directs us to do to sow into the future for the kingdom of God, we need to heed His voice and do it (2 Cor. 9:6-

10, Gal 6:8, John 4:37-38). He wants us to hand over what we have learned and gained from our lifetimes. I am not saying empty your bank account to a ministry and leave yourself penniless. What I am saying is show God's love extravagantly, however that may be, according to what the Lord tells you. Beg earnestly to our Lord that the anointing He has bestowed on you would be imparted to the next generation (Eccles 12:9, Rom 1:10-12, I like NIV wording best). You can read about a special group called The Golden Candlestick who had done this in Dr. James Maloney's book, *Ladies of Gold*.[48] He discusses how he received a special impartation from these people who had dedicated their whole lives to doing the work of the Lord. We see that Solomon himself remembered his dad's advice from the Scriptures in 1 Chronicles when he wrote in Proverbs 13:22a, "A good man leaves an inheritance to his children's children" (NKJV). Set them up for success; it is what our Bridegroom wants.

60. Has a Plan / Decides Who Will Be King (Jehovah)

"*But God* had decided that this visit would be Ahaziah's downfall. While he was there, Ahaziah went out with Joram to meet Jehu son of Nimshi, whom the Lord had appointed to destroy the dynasty of Ahab" (2 Chronicles 22:7 NLT, emphasis added).

Before we get started on this one, I just want to note, if you look up 2 Chronicles 20:15b, it says, "'Do not be afraid or discouraged because of this vast army. For the battle is not yours, but God's'" (NIV). This study is only inclusive to the phrase "BUT GOD," but I wanted to mention this because it is a good transition to set us up for this BUT GOD verse. As you will learn, this is exactly what Jehu had to do. Jehu had to take an active stance so God could carry out what He had already determined to do. Jehu seemed to already have the courage to do this, but some of us don't. Remember, the Lord will fight the battle, whatever our personal battle may be. God is courageous enough for us all, but we have to do our part so He can participate with us.

This BUT GOD verse is going to be tricky with all the names, so I thought it might be helpful to draw out a graph so you can understand who is related to who (see below). I also included a few more as mentioned in BUT GOD #54. Ahab married Jezebel and did much evil in the Lord's eyes as king of Israel (#52). Joram was Ahab's son (2 Chron 22:5). Ahaziah was King of Judah, the son of Jehoram and Athaliah (King Ahab's daughter). He was trained to follow in their evil ways (2 Chron 21:5-6, 22:1-4). Jehu was anointed by the prophet to be the new king of Israel (1 Kings 19:15-17). The Lord allowed Jehu to destroy Ahab's descendents, as this verse states, and Jezebel (2 Kings 9-10).

Ahaziah was not following the Lord. He was killed while he was visiting Joram. Joram and Ahaziah were supposed to be representatives for God, but instead were representatives for the false counterfeit gods. The Lord was cleaning up the houses of Israel and Judah. God killed two birds with one stone, so to speak. God had appointed Jehu to take down the counterfeit anointing on the throne so Jehu could step into his delegated authority. Jehu became king of Israel.

There is a little more to the story after this BUT GOD verse that is worth telling. Ahaziah's evil mother, Athaliah, made herself queen by killing off all of the royal heirs of Judah except Joash (Ahaziah's son, not King of Israel Joash in #54), who was secretly taken by Jehoshabeath (Ahaziah's sister) into hiding as Joash was only a baby. Joash was kept hidden in the house of God while Jehoiada (Jehoshabeath's husband who was a priest) got the captains, Levites, and chief fathers of Israel together to make a covenant for Joash to be king (2 Chron 23). Athaliah was dethroned when Joash was crowned king of Judah at the age of seven. He restored the temple (2 Chron 24) under the mentorship of Jehoiada, who was a spiritual father to him.

Being the daughter of Jezebel, it was easy for Athaliah to have the Jezebel spirit (#52) and she took by force a position of power. Notice it was a priest (Jehoiada) who was responsible for dethroning her. Jehu, who was God's appointed king, dethroned the unrighteous leaders—the ungodly kings, Joram and Ahaziah. As the bride of Christ, we also are a royal race, made into a kingdom, priests unto God (1 Peter 2:9, Rev 1:6, 5:10 AMP). Therefore, we are to take this anointing and overthrow all spirits of counterfeit that are trying to claim our authority in Christ. Armor yourself up (Eph 6:10-18) as the Lord released a similar anointing on you (His bride) just like Jehu and Jehoiada.[49] We are kingdom of priests, made to war and worship, as we pray to hasten the day of Jesus' return (2 Peter 3:12 NIV).

Though this verse does not talk specifically of God's righteousness, I think it is important to note that the Lord was putting righteous leaders back in position to lead His people; He had a plan. In order to do this, He had to remove the counterfeit. Our God is a righteous King and there is no one who can administer justice like Him. His original plan was to be Israel's King, but Israel rejected that. They chose to be like other nations and have a physical leader over them (#38), instead of having God be their one and only Commander and Chief (1 Sam 8:6-7). Zechariah prophesied that Israel's king would arrive on a donkey (Zech 9:9). Indeed, Jesus did enter Jerusalem on a donkey (John 12:12-16), but later when the chief priests were asked by Pilate about Jesus, they rejected Him as their king (John 19:15). Jesus will come back once again, and this time His title will be clear for the entire world to see—King of Kings and Lord of Lords (Rev 19:16)! Our king will reign in righteousness forever and His royal family will rule with justice (Is 32:1)!

Since we have humans as leaders we are stuck following their laws (to a degree in accordance with God's Word). In this BUT GOD, the kings were allowing evil practices against God's commands and this was God's reasoning for their removal. How often do we watch current world leaders, movie stars, and sports heroes lead people astray because of their positions? Why do we esteem and favor them when many blaspheme the One we love (James 2:5-7)? So many of them are not fellow believers and set bad examples in the values they portray. As His bride, we are also positioned to be in charge of things, but He wants to work in partnership with us. Let us remember to look to our Bridegroom to help us be good role models like He was. Let Him move you to your rightful position of authority, not be removed from one!

As we have already read, Moses was in a position of authority. Before Moses died, God told Moses to commission Joshua, who would lead the Israelites into the Promised Land (Deut 3:28). In the Old Testament, it is imperative we remember to search for clues that point to Jesus. Much insight is gained when investigating the meanings of names. Joshua's name in Hebrew is Yeshua, and Jesus' name in Hebrew is also Yeshua. Moses was pointing to follow Yeshua (Jesus)! Jesus is the One to lead people to the Promised Land. Jehu's name in Hebrew means "Jehovah is he." Jehovah means "I am that I am." When Moses asked God what His name was, God answered, "I AM THAT I AM" (Ex 3:14). So, Jehu's name means "I Am that I Am he." Jesus told us in the Bible that He was the Son of God and I Am (John 8:58; 10:36). Jesus told the group of soldiers, "I AM he" on the night Judas betrayed Him. His words carried so much authority and divine power that the soldiers fell backwards onto the ground (John 18:4-8). Now we can apply a deeper meaning spiritually to this BUT GOD verse. Since Jesus is God, this verse is now also a picture of what Jesus is going to do when He returns. God has said that His Son, Jesus, is going to reign as King. Jesus is going to dethrone the defiant earthly kings in high places along with Satan, the ruler of the air (Eph 2:2, John 12:31, Rev 19-20).

At the beginning of this particular BUT GOD discussion, I pointed to a verse that encouraged God's army to not be discouraged; the battle is God's and all we need to do is show up. Joshua's main commission from God was to take over territory. Joshua was reminded to be strong and courageous numerous times in Scripture. Jehu was courageous in killing Ahab and Jezebel's descendents. Jesus, of course, is very strong and courageous. As God's army consisting of a kingdom of priests, we too must pursue these virtues and overcome any obstacles of fear that would prevent us from fulfilling our destiny in Christ.

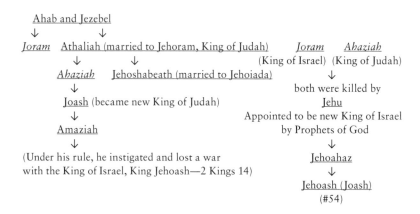

Ahab and Jezebel
↓   ↓
Joram   Athaliah (married to Jehoram, King of Judah)   *Joram*   *Ahaziah*
     ↓   ↓   (King of Israel) (King of Judah)
   Ahaziah   Jehoshabeath (married to Jehoiada)   ↓
     ↓   both were killed by
   Joash (became new King of Judah)   Jehu
     ↓   Appointed to be new King of Israel
   Amaziah   by Prophets of God
     ↓   ↓
(Under his rule, he instigated and lost a war   Jehoahaz
with the King of Israel, King Jehoash—2 Kings 14)   ↓
                                          Jehoash (Joash)
                                              (#54)

61. Is Not Limited by Size / Implements His Judgment

"A year or so later Aramean troops attacked Joash. They invaded Judah and Jerusalem, massacred the leaders, and shipped all their plunder back to the king in Damascus. The Aramean army was quite small, *but God* used them to wipe out Joash's large army—their punishment for deserting God, the God of their ancestors. Arameans implemented God's judgment against Joash" (2 Chronicles 24:23-24 MSG, emphasis added).

As long as Jehoiada (the priest who raised Joash and helped him become king) was with him, Joash did what was right in the eyes of the Lord. Soon after Jehoiada died, however, Joash was easily swayed. He left the ways of God; wooden images and idols were once again worshipped in Judah. God sent prophets and Jehoiada's son, Zechariah, to testify against what they were doing, but King Joash and the people did not listen. In fact, King Joash had Zechariah stoned to death. Because of all of this, the Lord allowed a very small army to come against them and defeat them, leaving Joash severely wounded. Then, Joash's servants conspired against him and killed him because of Zechariah's death (v 25). We read in 2 Kings 14:1-5 that the new king of Judah was Joash's son, Amaziah, and he executed the servants who murdered his father.

Size does not matter to God; He will use whatever means to pack a punch if His people do not heed the constant warnings. To get us back in alignment with Him, He will allow enemies to help "wake us up." We need to do what is right before the Lord, even when we do not have someone as a mentor or father figure around to continue to keep us on the right path. God is very clear that there will be a punishment for deserting Him. He will implement judgment at the end of the age and we will all have to give an account for our decisions. As believers in Christ, we should be able to stand alone in our convictions, knowing already what is right and wrong. Those who rejected Him will be wiped out.

Today, leaders are always surrounded by advisors. God, in His mercy and grace, has always appointed people who were in positions to share His Word and love the leaders, despite their beliefs. Some of these people we see in the Bible were heroes, such as Daniel and Joseph. Daniel was an advisor from the time of King Nebuchadnezzar to the first year of King Cyrus (Dan 1:19-21). Joseph advised an officer of Pharaoh (Gen 39:4), and later, the Pharaoh himself (Gen 41:40). Then we have Jehoiada, who saved, raised, and advised King Joash. God does not want us to open doors to allow enemies into our camp by not obeying His laws, so He will surround us with help (#80). Joash did not continue to lead the people of Judah righteously after Jehoiada died. Joash did not heed any warnings and allowed God's people to disregard the Lord and their covenant with Him.

What kind of position has the Lord allowed you to be in? Are you in charge of a family, employees, or a government? Maybe you hold a key position in your church. Are you disregarding what our Bridegroom asks of you as a leader? Or, are you doing what you know is right in your heart to do? Daily you should seek His face for direction lest an enemy, however small, invade your camp and leave you wounded and unable to lead. Do you have self control and live righteously only when in the company of people from church, or are you the same person alone as you are with others? God requires much of His leaders because we are to be the light that leads others to Him. Let your light shine and do not let the enemy blow it out!

62. Watches over Leaders

"*But God* had his eye on the leaders of the Jews, and the work wasn't stopped until a report could reach Darius and an official reply be returned" (Ezra 5:5 MSG, emphasis added).

We find in 2 Chronicles 36:15-21 that the Word of the Lord continued to be ignored and His prophets were scoffed at until the anger of the Lord arose high against His people. Time after time, as we saw in the previous BUT GODs, the Lord gave new kings chances to follow after His ways, but the people would not listen. The Lord had to deal more severely with the Israelites by not just replacing kings, but having the people taken into captivity. The Lord allowed the king of the Chaldeans to burn down the beautiful temple that Solomon built (#49, #57-#59). The city wall and all of the precious possessions of Jerusalem were eventually all destroyed and survivors were carried away to Babylon. This fulfilled the words of the prophets Jeremiah and Habakkuk. The Israelites were exiled for seventy years. Then, they were slowly allowed to return to Jerusalem to rebuild the temple and the walls.

Ezra was a scribe and priest who led a second group of the exiled Israelites to Jerusalem with valuables the king gave him for God's House (Ezra 7). However, this verse is about the first group that King Cyrus had released (Ezra 1). Interestingly, Isaiah had prophesied about this event before Cyrus was even born (Is 44:28)! The Israelites were allowed to leave and rebuild the temple in Jerusalem, but the surrounding governors felt threatened and opposed their rebuilding until they got King Artaxerxes (believed by many to be the son of Esther) to order the Israelites to cease (Ezra 4:21). Do you remember we discussed how God used His prophets as His mouthpiece in BUT GOD #50? Well, after some time, God sent prophets (Haggai and Zechariah) to encourage the Israelites to begin building again (Ezra 5:1). The surrounding governors again began to harass them after construction had resumed. They questioned who gave the Israelites the authority to build and sent a letter to the current king, King Darius. This is where our BUT GOD emerges. God wanted His people to continue

His work. He had His eye on the ones leading the Jews; He was protecting them and had their backs.

There is a mini lesson if we look at the last three BUT GODs. God determines who will be in authority. He will allow enemies to attack to get our attention if we get off track, but He will always watch over us and will assist us when we are building or restoring righteousness. Psalms 34:15 states that the Lord's eyes are on the righteous. Second Chronicles 16:9 says His eyes are searching throughout the earth to see whose hearts are loyal to Him so He can show Himself strong on their behalf. This is exactly what He is doing here in this BUT GOD. The Israelites were working on His temple to restore what the Babylonians had destroyed. Our Bridegroom wants to support us and strengthen us when we show ourselves loyal to Him and do the work He encourages us to do. He loves to show off and show Himself strong. God was not going to let the tattling governors of the other nations cause chaos. Instead, it backfired in their faces. Once King Darius discovered the Israelites were allowed to rebuild by King Cyrus' decree, King Darius blessed Israel by commanding the other regions to help with providing supplies (Ezra 6). I would love to have seen the faces of the Israelites as they heard the king order their opposition to now contribute to them financially. What a sweet victory with a cherry on top!

63. Saves

"*But [God]* saves [the fatherless] from the sword of their mouth, and the needy from the hand of the mighty" (Job 5:15 AMP, emphasis added).

The book of Job is such a good BUT GOD story. Here is a man who was very blessed and had it all. Satan challenged God by saying Job would curse God if He removed the hedge of protection and the blessings from Job's life (Job 1:10-11). God allowed Satan to test Job's faith and Satan took that opportunity and ran with it. We know that all Satan does is steal, kill, and destroy and that is exactly what he did (John 10:10). He stole all Job's possessions, killed his family, and destroyed his health. Job questioned God, asking why these things were happening to him, and looked to his friends for advice. Unfortunately, his friends judged him and said he must have had a wicked heart; they did not offer Job much mercy in their conversations. God used the situation in Job's favor to help refine Job's character in the midst of his trial. When all was said and done, Job never cursed God; he humbled himself, waited on the Lord, and listened when He spoke back. In the end, the Lord gave to him twice as much as he had before (Job 42:10). Satan tested Job's character and inflicted much misery, BUT GOD sustained Job's life, restored him, and doubled his blessing because Job remained faithful.

In chapter 5 of Job, one of Job's friends, Eliphaz, told Job he needed to bring his cause to God (v 8) and not to despise being chastened by God (v 17). In chapters 15 and 22, he accused Job wrongly of being wicked. Though Eliphaz was not very encouraging or comforting, he did speak *some* truthful words about our God's character. This BUT GOD verse is one of them.

Psalm 35:10 says God delivers the poor from those who are strong against them. That is similar to this BUT GOD verse because it is His character to save. Jesus' name, Yeshua, means "God saves!" God is patient and desires that *all* will be saved, including the needy (2 Peter 3:9, 1 Tim 2:4). God has chosen the poor in this world to be rich in faith and heirs of His kingdom, so do not dishonor the poor man (Matt 5:3, James 2:5-6). We have all seen tyrant leaders who keep their nation hungry and undeveloped while the privileged live in luxury. This breaks God's heart; He wants provision supplied for those who call on His name. God wants to bring the message of salvation to those nations, but some leaders try to keep Yahweh out. God sends missionaries to be His hands and feet. There will always be people less fortunate than us wherever we live (John 12:8). Will you be willing to be His hands and feet? Will you allow your Bridegroom to use you to help save the fatherless and the needy from the hand of the mighty if He asks you? Our God will be their Deliverer and ours too, in our time of need because that is His character and the name of our beloved Bridegroom!

64. Is Just

"The groans of the dying rise from the city, and the souls of the wounded cry out for help. *But God* charges no one with wrongdoing" (Job 24:12 NIV, emphasis added).

In this chapter, Job expressed some opinions that many people have had even to this day. His basic complaint was this: Why is it that people who are so ungodly seem to get away with mistreating people less fortunate than they are? Job spoke of the wicked who are not being charged with wrongdoing by God. He wondered why these violent people were not punished, even as the poor and the fatherless souls cried out as they were dying. Here, Job could not figure out what in the world he had done to have God's protective hand lifted off of him as he continued to be persecuted and inflicted by Satan. It seemed the ones who should be receiving persecution were getting away with murder! All through this testing, Job knew how majestic God was (Job 26) and he did not let go of his own integrity (Job 27:3-6); he knew what the future held in eternity for the wicked people who did not change their ways (Job 27:13-23). The wicked are obviously not interested in following God's laws so they are not being disciplined by God to improve. God chastises only those He loves. Maybe God is not correcting the wicked because they are not listening to Him anyway and do not want God's love, advice, or discipline in their lives.

Our Bridegroom will not force His way on anyone. He presents His ways and each person is given the opportunity to pursue Him or not. Everyone is born with a degree of knowing some right from wrong (Rom 2:14-15). Our Bridegroom will surely execute justice on the wicked. Being a just God means He will be the One who gives a deserved reward or a just penalty. Rest assured that no one will escape the Day of Judgment and the wicked will get what is coming to them.

Also, it is good to remember that even though the wicked seem to get away with crimes and social injustice, we do not know their lives. We do not know how they might be emotionally tormented or what personal problems they may be acquiring along the way. God loves people; He certainly does not want to ever be eternally separated from any one of us. He wants the "wicked" to be healed from their brokenness and surrender themselves totally to Him. I am sure there are many "wicked" people who have turned to our Bridegroom and repented and now follow in His ways. If God charged everyone with death immediately after they sinned, none of us would be alive today. No one would have a chance to ask for forgiveness. This is a time of grace; we are not called to bring judgment on unbelievers (or as Graham Cooke calls them, "pre-Christians").[50] God balances justice and mercy with righteousness. In Leviticus 4, we see that people can sin unintentionally, but when they realize it is a sin, they need to repent. God gives everyone a chance to repent, even the wicked, because God is guided by truth, justice, reason, and fairness. That is the definition of being just. I am so glad our Bridegroom is fair to everyone.

65. Watches the Wicked

"They are scraps of wood floating on the water—useless, cursed junk, good for nothing. As surely as snow melts under the hot, summer sun, sinners disappear in the grave. The womb has forgotten them, worms have relished them—nothing that is evil lasts. Unscrupulous, they prey on those less fortunate. However much they strut and flex their muscles, there's nothing to them. They're hollow. They may have an illusion of security, *but God* has his eye on them. They may get their brief successes, but then it's over, nothing to show for it. Like yesterday's newspaper, they're used to wrap up the garbage. You're free to try to prove me a liar, but you won't be able to do it" (Job 24:18-25 MSG, emphasis added).

Well, there you have it. Job discussed what becomes of the wicked man. Just as discussed in BUT GOD #64, we do not know what the wicked go through emotionally, but we see a glimpse of some of it. They are hollow on the inside, and they think they are secure, but they are deceived. They are forgotten, and no one will proclaim about the legacies they left; God is fully aware of what they are doing and who they are doing it to. He sees when the less fortunate get ran over by their evil schemes. Our Father in heaven will not let their name be remembered with anything successful in His Book. Job was so sure of this; he knew his words would not be disproven.

It is so easy for us to get discouraged when we, as believers, see so much lawlessness going on in society around us. Unfortunately, as time goes on, it seems to only get worse. Jesus said in Matthew 24:12-13 that in the last days, because of the increased wickedness, the love of many will grow cold. My pastor read about a lady in Fresno, California who had been burglarized so many times she put up a sign saying something like, "Please leave me alone, you have stolen from me nine times and I have nothing left!" God knows we are living in the midst of evil and that it is hard for us, but He is powerful enough to take care of it. Do not let it get to you; keep your heart soft like we discussed in BUT GOD #19. God has His eyes on the righteous (#62), but also the unrighteous. He is very aware of what is going on in this world (#11-#12).

Just like Psalm 139 says, He knows everything about humanity and watches everything we humans do. Wicked or righteous, God knows our comings and our goings, when we sit and when we stand. He knows what we are thinking, and whether we are humble or proud. He knows when evil strikes against us. He knows His children need the armor of God for protection: the helmet of salvation, the breastplate of righteousness, the belt of truth, the shield of faith, the sword which is the Word of God, and feet that are ready to spread His Word (Eph 6:10-18). These words are also found in Isaiah 59:17. In looking at the root word for helmet of salvation, we find the name Yeshua. Put on Jesus, you have the mind of Christ, ask for what you need in His name alone.

If there is a God, why do evil things happen? I believe it is because we are in the midst of a spiritual battle. God does not want people to suffer, but He has not fully established His kingdom reign yet on this earth, so in the meantime, He is watchful to which way our hearts will turn. Just like the angels chose sides when Satan tried to gain power, God wants to know which people He can trust to stand by Him. Will you let the enticing worldly power of Satan persuade you or will you have faith in God that He is loving, kind, and compassionate and follow His ways? Being a friend of God allows me to be surrounded with help (#80). He is a fierce warrior beside me (#107); I will not be left to defend myself. I want God to say about me what He said about Job in Job 1:8. I want God to see I fear Him alone and that I turn away from evil. How I want my Bridegroom's eyes to always see the best in me!

66. Is More Powerful than Anyone / Is Sovereign
"But God drags away the mighty by his power; though they become established, they have no assurance of life" (Job 24:22 NIV, emphasis added).

Nothing and no one is more powerful than God. There may be those who have more power or a higher position of authority than we personally are given, but none are more powerful than our Creator. No one can live forever and no one can guarantee they will be alive tomorrow. Only God has that control. He is the only One who can guarantee everlasting life if you accept His Son, Jesus. The wicked seem like they are in control because they rule the way they want and live their lives without following any laws. However, when you look at them with an eternal perspective, it is very different. Satan has control of those who give their lives over to lawlessness, and they will go to hell if they do not repent (1 John 3:4-10). You only have as much authority as the person with the power allows you to have or has themselves. Since God the Father is sovereign, it would be wise to be under His authority rather than siding with Satan. With Holy Spirit and Jesus, God outnumbers Satan three to one, and God has two-third of the angels still on his side (Rev 12:3-4). Many who do not accept Jesus see no need for following His rules. They may not even acknowledge God exists, but even the demons believe in God, so do not be fooled (James 2:19). God still uses people who do not choose Him for His purpose, but they will not get the full benefit of reaping the rewards for doing His work.

Those who do not choose our Father in heaven, whose Son is our Savior, will not be saved; instead, they will choose Satan by choice or by default. Rather than having assurance of life, the wicked and the unsaved will have assurance of death. That is a scary thought. Becoming established in this world does not seem as important when you look at it through eternity's lenses. The "winners" in the world's perspective might actually be the "losers" in eternity. Though we live in this world, remember not to become part of this world (1 John 2:15, James 4:4, Rom 12:2). We believers are only passing through and we do our best to help establish His kingdom on this earth as we await His return and restoration.

Our Bridegroom is showing us all these verses about the wicked in the BUT GODs to try to help us see that if we stay "established" in Him we will have "assurance of life" because we will be saved, despite the wicked's schemes. God will not drag His beloved away, but lead us to lie down in green pastures (Psalm 23). He is all powerful, and He is sovereign. He is God and we are not. After hearing that phrase many times during worship in church, I asked God to help me understand exactly what it meant. Using Scripture, this is the poem the Lord and I came up with.

<u>YOU ARE GOD AND I AM NOT</u>
Tina Miller 12/6/12

You are God and I am not,
Ps 86:10

You are the Potter and I am the pot.
Is 64:8

You have no beginning and no end,
Is 44:6, Rev 22:13

I am a piece of grass fading in the wind.
Is 40:7

You are the One who set the world in motion,
Job 38:4-18

Where was I when You created the ocean?
Gen 1:9-10

You laugh at the wicked's schemes,
Ps 37:12-13

You free us, only Jesus' blood redeems.
John 8:36, Eph 1:7

You alone are righteous and holy,
Lev 11:45, Rom 7:12

Only You give honor to the lowly.
Prov 29:23, Matt 5:3

You are not carved out of metal or wood,
Is 44:15, Jer 10:16, Hab 2:18

Having the mind of Christ, the righteous have understood.
1 Cor 2:14-16

You have all wisdom and all power,
Jer 51:15, Ps 62:11, Rom 16:27

When I am afraid, you are my strong tower.
Ps 91, Prov 18:10

You lead me in Your ways so I will be taught,
Ps 25:9

My smartest idea is your smallest thought.
1 Cor 1:25

You are trustworthy and always good,
Ps 100:5, Ps 118:8

You lived the life no one else could.
1 Peter 2:22

You will provide escape from eternal death,
Ps 68:20

When I have taken my last breath.
Ps 146:3-4

You are the One who reviews our decisions,
Ecc 3:17, Rom 14:10-12

Your Word is sharp enough to make divisions.
Matt 25:33, Heb 4:12

You are the Judge, empowered high upon Your throne,
Ps 11:4

You are the Rock, known as the Cornerstone!
Ps 118:22, Acts 4:11

You are a holy God and will remain,
Ps 77:13, Ps 146:10

Eternally forever, Your kingdom will reign!
Rev 22:5

Only You desire to love us, even after knowing our every thought,
Ps 94:11, Rom 5:7-8

You are God and I am not!
Ps 18:31, Jer 10:6-7,10

67. Is Always Watching

"They may be allowed to live in security, *but God* is always watching them" (Job 24:23 NLT, emphasis added).

The Message Version of the BUT GOD verse as shown in BUT GOD #65 is actually broken down into two separate verses found in BUT GOD #66 and BUT GOD #67. So, again we see God is always watching the wicked, or the "mighty" ones of this world, the ones who seem to get away with everything. Job seems to be saying, "Just because it seems they are living in security now, they might not be for long." These people have come to rely on the fact that their lives will always be this way, that it will always come easy for them, and that they will always be exalted. They are not taking into account that our heavenly Father is watching them. He is not just checking in occasionally either—He is ALWAYS watching them.

This verse seems to make me focus more on the elite of this world, the ones who are always manipulating the system, making secret deals so they stay on top. It makes me glad to know my God and my Bridegroom are keeping an eye on the ones who are scheming against me and against Him. I feel more protected knowing I am connected to someone who knows what is going on. I also find comfort in reading Psalm 91. As long as I stick by Him, He will look out for me.

Lastly, I want to sum up what we have learned in our BUT GODs so far from Job from BUT GOD #63 through BUT GOD #67. I think it is all running together to tell us something. God saves the needy, the poor, the fatherless—but the wicked and the mighty ones still seem to take advantage of them. They actually get away with it too; BUT GOD is just and has His eye continually on the wicked. He will not let them escape death or judgment. It may seem that the "mighty ones" have security in this life, but they really have a false security and will be spending their eternal lives in hell if they continue in their ways. Our Bridegroom knows what's up and will make sure nothing gets by Him.

68. Answers to No One

"Here's what you said. I heard you say it with my own ears. You said, 'I'm pure—I've done nothing wrong. Believe me, I'm clean—my conscience is clear. *But God* keeps picking on me; He treats me like I'm His enemy. He's thrown me in jail; He keeps me under constant surveillance'" (Job 33:8-11 MSG, emphasis added).

Elihu, Job's friend, had listened to what the previous three friends had said to Job and was angry because they did not know for certain why Job was going through hard times, but all condemned and falsely accused him. Now it was Elihu's turn to speak to Job and he responded to what he had heard Job say about this situation. Elihu found no fault in Job's lifestyle, but he found fault in what Job had said of himself and, like his other friends, came up with reasons for Job's problems. He told Job he had added rebellion to his sin (Job 34:37). Elihu argued Job was not right in trying to justify himself by saying he was, "pure and innocent, but was being punished by God." God is allowed to do what He pleased (Job 33: 12; 34:12). Job knew that God was just (#64), but Elihu reminded Job that God does not have to give an account for anything He does *because* He is God (Job 33:13). In Job 35:14-16, he reminded Job that God was not punishing him in anger, and that Job had been talking in vain and speaking without knowledge. He suggested that Job wait for the Lord and that the Lord might be teaching Him something (Job 36:22). Elihu was trying to give good words of advice, but like Job's other friends, no one knew the reason for these times of trouble for Job until Job worked it out with God.

Job was quoted in this BUT GOD verse as saying God was treating him like an enemy. Job did what his three other friends did to him, which was speaking false accusations, but Job spoke them against God. This was why Elihu got on Job's case about the words that came out of his mouth during this time. He wanted Job to remember God was *for* him, not against him. In time, God would give Job help, or answers, because that is how He works; that is His character. God may move slowly at times, but He always moves!

This verse serves as a good reminder to us, the bride. Our Bridegroom wants to teach us something in every situation, every storm, and every hardship. It is an opportunity for us to train ourselves in responding positively to our circumstances rather than reacting to chaos. Jesus lived His life in response to God, not in reaction to the devil. Instead of thinking God is acting like our enemy, we have an opportunity to ask what He is up to instead. It is also a reminder for us not to talk mindlessly about situations we do not understand, lest we might say something inaccurate. Do not accuse God falsely. We need to be established in God, who He is, and what we are doing to further His kingdom, in spite of all the trials we are going through. Granted some trials may throw us for a loop and consume more of our time to get our feet steady again, but do not lose faith in the process! Do not fear either when the troubles come.

Job 38-41 allows us a glimpse into the greatness of God and the mighty works of His hands as stated by Yahweh Himself! His bride will come against trials, but she will be victorious. We will face tribulations otherwise God wouldn't encourage us to be overcomers. This is why it is imperative we know God's character and what He wants. Even when times are tough, Christ's bride will stand firm because she is ready, and she will live for eternity with Him because His character and His Word are true. He is faithful to keep His promises to the end; He will deal with the wicked and His righteousness will reign forever!

69. Steps in Our Situation

"Or, you may fall on your knees and pray—to God's delight! You'll see God's smile and celebrate, finding yourself set right with God. You'll sing God's praises to everyone you meet, testifying, 'I messed up my life—and let me tell you, it wasn't worth it. *But God* stepped in and saved me from certain death. I'm alive again! Once more I see the light!'" (Job 33:26-28 MSG, emphasis added).

Elihu was still speaking to Job here and actually encouraging him on how God works. He reminded Job in verse 14 that God will speak in one way or another, but sometimes man misses it. He goes on to say that sometimes He uses dreams, visions, or inclinations. He can get your attention through pain, or may use messengers or angels. In this BUT GOD verse, Elihu said God may simply answer your prayer so one day you will have a testimony about how He saved you. This is what God did for Job in the end and the book of Job *is* his testimony.

Unfortunately, well-meaning friends do not always have all the right answers. They should talk things out with you so you can accurately assess your situation. Elihu definitely spoke words of wisdom here. He spoke some truths to Job by gently cautioning him in BUT GOD #68, but then here, in BUT GOD #69, he encouraged him with accurate information about our Lord. This is what a good friend should do. True friends do not condemn you for assumptions they have made up, but instead help you in your circumstances. When you start getting sidetracked on an issue, a good friend will pull you back in line, gently correct, and then encourage you. They remind you of God's character and help you look in areas of your life to see if He has given you answers that you might have missed.

Friends are important and if you choose them correctly, you may never need to pay for a counselor! This is why our Bridegroom encourages us to keep good company because iron sharpens iron, and a friend loves at all times (Prov 17:17, Prov 27:17). We need to lean on each other to get through this life. Hopefully, you have friends who will lend a shoulder from time to time and give godly counsel. Sometimes a professional's opinion is a wise option though and can be helpful. No matter who we let in our lives, be it family, coworkers, neighbors, friends, and/or classmates, our outlooks on our circumstances will be influenced to some degree. If we can remember to include our Bridegroom's perspective, we will already be a step in the right direction. We will be able to discern the words to listen to and the ones to throw to the side.

How great is a good testimony? They are encouraging and fun to listen to. People who have been on the brink of death can share how God saved them. Testimonies I have heard include people who have lived a dangerous life partying, a girl who had been mauled by a lion, someone badly hurt in a car crash, war victims, people cured from cancer, survivors from the 9/11 terrorist attack, and even a four-year old girl who received a heart transplant. All of them could easily sing a song of praise to God for stepping into their circumstances and saving them. I'm sure Sarah, Abraham's wife, also could relate to this verse (#3). Now we can add Job to the long list of Bible heroes with great testimonies. Job was on the brink of death BUT GOD delivered him. God blessed him with a double portion as He restored everything back to him. Our Bridegroom is always ready to step in our situations and give a helping hand, making us want to jump up and down and sing something like Jeremy Camp's song, "I'm Alive" from his album *Speaking Louder Than Before.*[51] That could be Job's theme song!

70. Never Denies Justice

"Job says, 'I am innocent, *but God* denies me justice'" (Job 34:5 NIV, emphasis added). *Also found in the AMP, NLT, and MSG in Job 34:5-9.

Elihu seemed to know some aspects of God's character well. In chapter 34 he proclaimed God's justice, and in chapter 36 he proclaimed God's goodness and majesty. Here, he again corrected his friend and told Job that God does not deny justice. In fact, he asks Job in 34:17 an eye opening question: "Are you condemning the One who is Most Just?" He encouraged and reminded Job that God sees all the ways of man (34:21) and that God rewards man according to his work (34:11-12)—BECAUSE He is just! God would never do something wicked and we should never accuse God of doing something that is not true of His character. In chapter 35, Elihu also accuses Job of being self righteous. In Job 29-31, Job had defended himself as he discussed all the things he had not done—thereby claiming his own goodness.

Here, Job was very frustrated with his own situation—he challenged God's character with just one sentence. As children of God, we should know our Father better than that. It is not a sin to be mad. We are made in the image of God; we have emotions. God gets angry, but it is a righteous anger (#26). Jesus displayed righteous anger when he was upset about the temple being turned into a marketplace of thieves (Matt 21:12-13). It is a sin, though, for us to let anger boil inside because we are keeping a record of wrongs (love does not do that—1 Cor 13). Doing this causes sin take root, festering into bitterness which causes one to act out inappropriately. In Job 10:1-2, Job said he would take his complaint to the Lord. This is how we prevent bitterness from taking root. It is important to find the source of your feelings and separate any evil spirit that is feeding you lies. Job said he would tell God not to condemn him and show him why he was being put through this struggle. Job needed to accuse the enemy, not God.

Job, obviously, was a very righteous man to be picked by God to withstand such devastating testing by Satan. God knew Job's dedication to Him would hold true, but Job had a difficult time coming to terms with what was happening to him because he could not find a suitable answer. This frustration led him to make this statement in our BUT GOD verse. He did not curse God, but saying words like this certainly did not please God. Elihu was right in calling Job out on this statement. Job told his friends he desired to reason with God (13:3). However, once God spoke to him in chapter 38-41, Job saw how sinful he was and realized his place very quickly (40:1-5)!

Remember, God allows us to be tested to refine us (Psalm 66:10, 1 Peter 1:6-7). Although Job was a good man, he obviously had some characteristics God needed to tweak. Job was proud and self-righteous and did not see his flaws until it was contrasted against his Creator's holy righteousness. Job was quickly humbled and saw he was "vile" (40:4). He despised himself and repented (42:6). God obviously forgave Job, but now he had to deal with collateral damage. Whereas Job was searching for answers, his friends claimed they *knew* the answers and did not speak what was right of the Lord (42:7). So, Job prayed for them and the Lord accepted their sacrifices, then the Lord restored Job's losses (42:10).

Our Bridegroom is showing us through this verse that He is just (#64). He will refine us through trials when we have sin in our lives or need a character adjustment. He wants us to stay humble because He can mold us and train us easier that way. He does not want us to jump to conclusions and go after His righteous character when it is really ours that needs the fixing. He does not repay righteousness with wickedness. He watches everything—the wicked, the righteous, and all creation. He is all powerful and forgives our proud ways when we humble ourselves and repent. He uses us to pray for others and He restores us. He turns our curses into blessings (Is 61). All these great characteristics of our Bridegroom show through with just this one part of the story. I encourage you to read Job 38-41 if you have not already and be amazed at all He does and is!

71. Is in Charge on His Throne

"*But God* hasn't moved to the mountains; his holy address hasn't changed. He's in charge, as always, his eyes taking everything in, his eyelids Unblinking, examining Adam's unruly brood inside and out, not missing a thing. He tests the good and the bad alike; if anyone cheats, God's outraged. Fail the test and you're out, out in a hail of firestones, Drinking from a canteen filled with hot desert wind" (Psalm 11:4-6 MSG, emphasis added).

This is quite an interesting Psalm with a very timely application given all our earthquakes, tsunamis, and other earth changes in the news each week. The beginning of this Psalm says, basically, if we have put our trust in the Lord, why would we run away to the mountains when even the foundations are destroyed? The mountains are built on dirt and will crumble to the sea (Ps 46). There is no safety in the mountains, but the Lord knows people will run there to hide (Is 2:10-21, Rev 6:15-17). There is only one place with a firm foundation, where we can run and be secure. That is Jesus Christ! If we rely on Him we will not be stricken with panic and will not be shaken (Is 28:16). If we run to Jesus now while there is time, we won't be running away from Him when time has run out (Is 55:6-7). Second Timothy 2:19a says, "BUT GOD's truth stands firm like a foundation stone with this inscription: 'The LORD knows those who are His'" (NLT, emphasis added). Colossians 1:22-23 confirms that if we stay firm in our faith in Jesus and do not wander from the hope found in the gospel then we will be reconciled through Christ's death to be free from accusations and holy in His sight.

What can we do when He puts the righteous and the wicked to the test? Look at the Parable of the Wise and Foolish Builders (Luke 6:46-49). The foolish man built his house upon the sand and when the floods of trouble came down and the waters rose up, his house was washed away. The wise man dug his roots of faith deep into Jesus so when trouble came, his house was not shaken. First Corinthians 15:1-3 says if you hold firmly to the gospel and believe Christ died for your sins, that He was buried and rose on the third day, then you will be saved. Your lifestyle must then change as well, as we are told "Let every one that nameth the name of Christ depart from iniquity" (2 Tim 2:19b KJV).

As we learned in Job, we need to trust God's character. Remember, His eyes are on us and He knows exactly what is going on. We should heed warning and get out of danger, but we cannot stop the earth's shaking or wicked people's scheming. Those are situations where we just need to trust in the Lord that He either will save us or bring us home to glory. The Lord has not moved; He sits on His throne in the heavens. Righteousness and justice are the foundations of His throne (Ps 89:14). The Bible tells us His righteousness is everlasting and His justice endures (Psalm 119:142, 160).

Our Bridegroom loves righteousness because He is righteous. There is still much more Bible prophecy that has to happen before we are in the end of the age, but we are definitely seeing signs confirming we are headed toward that way rapidly. Some say when the Bible refers to the fig tree (as in Joel 1:7), it is talking of Israel. Many interpret the parable of the fig tree (Matthew 24:32-33) referring to Israel becoming a nation in 1948 and/or regaining Jerusalem in 1967 (#35). It says when it is putting forth leaves, know Jesus is at the door and that generation will not pass before they see "these" things. Isaiah 66:8-9 seems to have been a double prophecy fulfilled (being fulfilled partially and then fully) when Jerusalem was restored with Nehemiah and when Israel became a nation in one day.

God is in charge facilitating His plan through His bride as we see His prophecy being fulfilled. Israel is awaiting their Messiah (whom they will soon see was Jesus) and the church is awaiting the rapture and Jesus' return. In the meantime, His church is establishing His kingdom on this earth by introducing people to Jesus. Those who live through the last days need to pray for God's mercy and remember to trust that God will do all that He says He will do. When this happens, do not be one whose heart has grown cold (Matt 24:12) like we discussed in BUT GOD #66. Do not be of the ones who still curse God (Rev 16:9, 11, 21) as He fulfills the written prophecies in the book of Revelation. Hopefully, you know there is no other time than the present to make the choice to be saved, and not just saved, but to be part of His bride. Having a close relationship with Jesus now means you will not be here during the wrath of God later (1 Thessalonians 5:9). Even though there are a lot of people trying to predict when the end of times will occur, as Christ's bride, do not get too caught up in when it will happen—just be ready! There are many different theories, but since God is in charge on the throne, He is the only One who knows for sure. There will be nowhere to hide from the Lord at the end of time, but there is a safe place to run now when we face troubles. Since His address has not changed, we know where to find Him when we need Him. All we have to do is call upon His name and ask for His attention. He has not moved to the mountains, where the foundation is unsure. God's rulership is a sure thing and having faith in His Son Jesus will give you the power to move the mountains (Matt 21:20-22).

72. Is Better than Any Superhero

"But me he caught—reached all the way from sky to sea; he pulled me out of that ocean of hate, that enemy chaos, the void in which I was drowning. They hit me when I was down, *but God* stuck by me. He stood me up on a wide-open field; I stood there saved—surprised to be loved!" (Psalm 18:16-19 MSG, emphasis added).

Does this verse sound familiar to you? You might want to refresh your memory by looking at BUT GOD #48. Again, our Bridegroom had one more characteristic He wanted to reveal through this verse and it is a fun one. Remember, David wrote this Psalm when the

Lord had delivered him from the hand of Saul and his enemies. In
BUT GOD #41, we saw that David was being pursued by King Saul
many times, and many times the Lord protected David.

What I like about this verse is that this time it is found in the
Psalms and, if you read from verse 6, you see a dynamic picture
displayed. David was crying out for help, and God left heaven with
all His glory and entourage en route. He swiftly and powerfully
swooped in and reached from the sky, pulling David out of the
trouble he was stuck in. Our Bridegroom is that same hero who
is ready to come just as swiftly to our rescue with thunder and
lightning, and He has just as much fury for the one causing our
grief. It is like He cannot get here fast enough to save us. Once we
are in His hands, He sets us in the most peaceful place where we
are surrounded by open space and not closed in by any enemies.
This makes me picture Laura Ingles from the show "Little House
on the Prairie," during the closing credits. She is a little girl running
through that wide-open field laughing. She is so full of freedom
without a care in the world. This is how I see David at this point and
how I would see myself. Our Bridegroom is the ultimate superhero.
He also defines what being a true hero means—someone who
gives life and freedom, rescues and guides, and who is humble yet
mighty. A few years ago I wrote the following poem to God. Who
would have known the title would match up perfectly with this
BUT GOD verse other than Him?

HERO   Tina Miller 7/21/07

Father God, you arrive in majesty
And thankful I will be
That you breathed life into me
Because of you, I am here today
And I will gladly say
You are my hero

Jesus you laid down your life for me
So that I could be set free
No one else could've rescued me

From a grim reality
You took my sin away
So in heaven I could say
You are my hero

Holy Spirit you counsel me in wisdom
So I can make the best decision
You guide me in the right direction
You give me gifts and did I mention
You are my hero

Three in one, You are not science fiction
You are the hero definition
Let me give you recognition
You stand for what is right and true
Goodness and justice come from you
You defeat the enemy
We shout for victory
You are humble and mighty
The holy Trinity

73. Does Not Abandon Us / Is a Perfect Father

"You've always been right there for me; don't turn your back on me now. Don't throw me out, don't abandon me; you've always kept the door open. My father and mother walked out and left me, *but God* took me in" (Psalm 27:9-10 MSG, emphasis added).

This is a great Psalm! It declares that the Lord is our Light, our Salvation, and our Strength, so whom should we fear? It speaks to the desire of every believer that one day we will dwell in the Lord's house and we will sing praises to Him. We ask the Lord to teach, lead, and deliver us. This Psalm reminds us to have courage while we wait on the Lord.

This BUT GOD is just a simple prayer asking God not to hide Himself from us as we seek Him. It asks that when we find Him, would He please welcome us and keep us. Hebrews 13:5 tells us He will never leave us, but I am sure God likes to know that we desire His company. I do not know if this happens to you, but sometimes in my quiet times, I am able to feel when He is near. I tell Jesus I can sense Him next to me and let Him know that I desire to always be in His presence. I know that even when I don't feel Him, He is with me, but sometimes there is a shift in the atmosphere that is unconcealed. I love when He speaks directly back to me, even if it is only a couple words. Jesus is such a perfect Bridegroom—I love Him so much!

Something I have not experienced is being parentless, but I have friends and family who are parentless or have been abused or abandoned. I would imagine this verse brings on a whole new meaning if this is your situation, and I am so sorry for whatever you have faced. Rejection by your family is a deep wound that cuts to your identity. That is why it is important to know who you are in Him (#33). He has chosen us, adopted us, and accepted us, and wants to gather us because He has an inheritance for us as His sons and daughters through Christ Jesus (Eph 1:4-14).

A special event on the calendar every year I like to celebrate with God is Father's Day. This BUT GOD verse reminds me there is no other Father like our God. It is easy for me to see God as a loving Father because I have such a great earthly example. When I think of my father, I think of someone who protected me, provided for me, loved me, and did fun activities with me like shopping or bike riding. He taught me new things, and took our family on vacation. He desired to make me happy. When I think of my mother, I think of someone who cared for me, fed me, loved me, listened to me, held me, gave advice, stayed up late to help me with homework, and played games with me. Both of my parents facilitated my growth in the Lord and, of course, they both disciplined me as well. I cannot imagine my life without them or those memories because that was what I grew up with. To know that others do not have that same experience puzzles my mind and just shows what a great space our Bridegroom has to fill in their hearts and lives.

No wonder David is so desperate for God not to abandon Him and so thankful he was taken in! I am thankful my mom and dad were such a good example to me of how to be loving parents. So many aspects of my life never felt empty because of them. I bypassed many of life's bad experiences because I listened to them and obeyed God's Word. I was not perfect by any means, I did things that were wrong too, but my point is I knew not to continue the bad behavior. I knew my parents and God would hold me accountable for my actions. My parents constantly told me how much I was loved and I felt very secure, but they also watched me like a hawk. There does come a point, as you mature, where you grow beyond your parent's restrictions and you need to start taking responsibility for the way you conduct yourself. Based on your upbringing and your beliefs you must decide how you will live. Some parents who are too strict push their children over the edge, and some who are too lenient raise children who have no boundaries. Unfortunately, parents can leave quite a wound on their kids, making it difficult for them to trust the Lord as a loving Father. Many people have never heard their earthly fathers say the words, "I love you." The Lord has to heal that wound in many people. I am sure that when He does, the overwhelming love they feel is indescribable. Our heavenly Father is waiting for the invitation to shower you with His love. Since He is a loving Father, He will hold you accountable for your actions and discipline as needed. Once you have invited Jesus into your life, He will not abandon you. In fact, He promises He will be with you always (Matt 28:20).

74. Fills Us with Him

"Young lions on the prowl get hungry, *but God*-seekers are full of God" (Psalm 34:10 MSG, emphasis added).

This Psalm is full of so many good nuggets that to quote them all would be the same as writing down the whole Psalm itself. Just read it! This verse is so true. Sometimes, my friends and I learn so much and are so full of information about God that we feel like we are going to explode. I am so thankful for the friends God has given me who are just as hungry as I am for His Word. When we get together, we usually do not even have time to talk about our families or other things in our lives. All we want to do is talk about the Lord (boast in Him) and the cool new treasures He led us to discover in His Word or experiences with people He had us minister to.

A group of us meet every so often for breakfast and, on occasion, we sometimes talk until lunchtime! We share books and pass around different CDs, DVDs, and computer links on various topics about God and the Bible. There seriously is not enough time in the day to learn all that we have sitting on our tables from what we have learned at different conferences. Nonetheless, we all feel compelled to go through it because we do not want to miss out on what the other person is so excited about learning. Iron sharpens iron (Prov 27:17) and when we learn something new we can then put it into practice. Once while vacationing with friends, two of my girl friends, Lisa and Tanya, shared poems with me they had written. It inspired me to write a few devotional poems myself. It became a new way for me to express my feelings to Jesus and a way for Him to express His love toward me. As you have seen, I have included some in this study.

Even though this verse says God-seekers are full, it does not mean we do not need any more of God. It means God is making sure we do not lack any good thing and He is constantly feeding our starving appetites until our very beings exude Him. To walk around in the Spirit all day is a goal, but I am far from there; life situations pop up and my mind quickly goes into mommy mode, or referee mode, or whatever else mode. I can definitely say, though, our Bridegroom has really fulfilled this verse in my life, I love that He has given me such a hunger for His Word and He has more than enough food to feed my soul. It overflows onto whoever wants to listen. Thankfully, I have great friends and family who like to participate or else I would be overflowing onto my stuffed animals. Think about some of the revelations He has shown you. How have you shared these with your family or friends? What types of activities do you participate in that help fill you up in God's goodness?

75. Is Not Worried about the "Bad Guys"
"Bad guys have it in for the good guys, obsessed with doing them in. *But God* isn't losing any sleep; to him they're a joke with no punch line" (Psalm 37:12-13 MSG, emphasis added).

The Lord knows what is in store for the wicked, and He lets us know too. They will not inherit the earth and they will not delight in the abundance of peace like the meek (Ps 37:11). The Lord says in a little while the wicked will be no more (Ps 37:10). They will perish and their descendants will be cut off (Ps 37:20-28). There is no one greater than our God, and if all the wicked people joined together against our God, they would still be no match for Him (Rev 19:17-21). The created cannot defeat the Creator. The wicked can make our life more difficult on earth, but we need to find a way to deal with it through God's help until He presses the delete button on them once and for all. The best way to be encouraged is to remind ourselves of our heritage, the rewards for the faithful ones. We will not be forsaken or beg for bread (Ps 37:25), and in the days of famine we will be satisfied (Ps 37:19). He will help us, deliver us, and save us from the wicked because we trusted in our Bridegroom (Ps 37:40). I think God mixed these encouraging words in here because He knows we are the ones who have to live alongside them for now.

Do you remember BUT GOD #63-#67 and all lessons we learned about the wicked already? Sometimes I feel these verses are meant for us to reflect on in the last days when things might be difficult and the wicked are running wild. To read these words is easier said than done for most of us because we are not in situations where this is reality . . . yet. This has been the situation, though, for many in other countries. Christian violence has been majorly underreported, and restrictions to worship God are strictly prohibited with violators being charged with blasphemy. Acknowledging Jesus to some means immediate death. Terrorist attacks on Christians in Africa alone rose 300% from 2005-2012.[52] For those in America, our suffering for the most part has been more about natural disasters like tornadoes, hurricanes, and earthquakes, but we are also very aware of further potential threats from terrorists and wars. God's enemies think they have it all figured out, when actually God is the One laughing at their schemes. The wicked will be the ones regretting their decisions, while the believers in Christ will burn with more passion to spread the Good News.

Still, though, who wants to go through suffering even for a little bit? We want our Bridegroom to come back now, and I say let's skip the part where we have to contend with wicked schemers. BUT GOD is waiting for His timeframe and He wants us to wait patiently for Him (Ps 37:7, 34). God wants everyone to have a chance to turn from their wicked ways and know Him (1 Tim 2:4, 2 Pet 3:9). God wants the enemy to stop reigning in their lives because it causes chaos for them and everyone around them. First Peter 5:9-10 is one of many passages in the Bible letting us know we will suffer because the enemy is always after us, but we need to keep encouraging ourselves with Romans 8:18, which reminds us the sufferings of the present time are not even worthy to be compared with the glory that will be revealed in us. I cannot wait to see that glory!

In verse 25 (NIV) of this Psalm, the writer confirms that during his whole life he has never seen the righteous forsaken. My God who never changes will not change on this fact. If my Bridegroom is not losing sleep about what the wicked are up to, then I should not either. Worrying does not solve anything and, in fact, decreases our health, joy, and faith. Pure joy kills fear, which is why James 1:2 says to consider it joy when going through trials. Do not be fearful about trials or what the enemy is up to, but believe God. God is laughing over the matter and He wants you to see it from His perspective. As Cindy Powell says, "Trials don't rob our joy; unbelief robs our joy."[53] She says that when challenges are seen from heaven's perspective, Satan's schemes are laughable. That is why God laughs at Satan's absurd attempts to thwart His plans. Paul had gone through tremendous trials, but he did not lose his joy. He reminds us in Philippians 3:1 to rejoice in the Lord.

The Lord reminds us to be anxious about nothing and not to worry (Philippians 4:6, Matt 6:25-31). If you can see what is really happening spiritually, you will be able to smile because you have caught on to the game and it will not bother you like it did before. The Lord our God sits in heaven and laughs at those who plot against Him, Psalm 2:4 confirms. It is ridiculous to believe anything the enemy tries to scare us with will be enough to defeat God. The devil's tactics are nothing compared to what he will face in the days ahead. Just saying the name of God's Son, Jesus of Nazareth or *Yeshua Ha-Mashiach*, shakes the enemy and brings him to his knees (Is 45:23-24, Philippians 2:9-11). We have that authority and can say Jesus' name whenever we want. That is what scares the enemy, and he is the only one who should be scared.

76. Makes Us Better

"But all who are hunting for you—oh, let them sing and be happy. Let those who know what you're all about tell the world you're great and not quitting. And me? I'm a mess. I'm nothing and have nothing: make something of me. You can do it; you've got what it takes—*but God*, don't put it off" (Psalm 40:16-17 MSG, emphasis added).

How often do you tell God you are a mess? Every now and then I will say, "I am a wreck!" I am unorganized and feel overwhelmed with all that is supposed to be done when all I really want is to have my Jesus time. When troubles have overtaken our thoughts and we have not had a second to confess our sins to our Savior, we become needy and our hearts are heavy. This is when we need our God to fix us and make us feel better again. Here, David needed God to do that for him, and David asked God to do it quickly. David knew how happy he was when he was not feeling burdened, and he knew he needed God's mercy to save him.

Our Bridegroom has lived on this earth so He knows our struggles. Hebrews 4:14-16 tells us that Jesus, our High Priest, sympathizes with us in our weaknesses. He was tempted in every way, but He did not sin. He took captive His thoughts and focused on all that was true, right, noble, pure, lovely, admirable, excellent, and praiseworthy (Phil 4:8). We are encouraged to think that way to help ourselves. Since He is our partner we need to lean on Him for help, we need to tell Him how desperate we are and He will listen! Jesus knows it is hard for us to do what is right all the time because He walked among us and saw our difficulties. When we feel weak or unworthy, we can approach Him with confidence to receive mercy and grace in our time of need. We can confess our sins to Him. Tell Him your troubles and tell of the ones who are troubling you. He can relate and He can give you the solution. So, God, please make something of us; make us better than we are, and make a masterpiece out of our mess.

When our priorities are in order and we spend time with Him in quiet, He draws us closer to Him which gives us a hunger to want more. That is when we find ourselves "hunting" like this BUT GOD verse says; we go through the Scriptures eating up all we can to learn more about Him. That is when we find ourselves going to church, praying more, and taking on extra things like Bible study or signing up for conferences/retreats or Sunday school classes. Our worship becomes more meaningful and we are happy with His joy. This overflows into telling our friends/family about all He is showing us and we find ourselves boasting about His goodness, just like the beginning of this verse says. To quote Beth Moore, "There ain't no high like the Most High!"[54]

77. Is a Redeemer

"*But God* will redeem my soul from the power of the grave: for He shall receive me. Selah" (Psalm 49:15 KJV, emphasis added). *Also found in the NIV and AMP.

God's not dead—He is alive! Jesus rose from the grave; He has taken the victory and death has been defeated! He is more than capable of redeeming our souls; it will not be stolen away to an unknown place. As His beloved bride, He will receive you with open arms and will not leave you in the grave. To the earth you are dead, but to God, along with our brothers and sisters in Christ, we will be alive forevermore—it will actually be the first day of the rest of our lives!

Dr. Richard Booker wrote in his book, *The Lamb and the Seven-Sealed Scroll*, that "a slave could be redeemed or set free by one who was worthy to purchase his freedom."[55] Jesus was the only One worthy to do this for us. According to Dr. Booker, in biblical times there were five requirements that needed to be fulfilled for one to be a redeemer. They were as follows:

1. Be the nearest kin family member (Jesus became human like us)
2. Be willing to redeem (Jesus willingly gave His life)
3. Be qualified and able to redeem (Jesus was righteous, without sin)
4. Be a free man (Nobody had any claims on Jesus, not Satan or death)
5. Be able to pay the price to redeem (Jesus shed His precious blood as payment)

This Psalm focuses on something else that is important to note and I am sure you have heard it before. Verse 17 says you can take nothing with you when you die. All the riches, splendor, houses, and land will remain. In fact, it will all belong to someone else when you are gone. Verse 20 gives an important lesson; it says just as beasts in the field die, so does a man who has riches without understanding. I believe the understanding is this: do not store up for yourselves treasures on earth, but instead store them in heaven (Matthew 6:19-21). How do you do that? Love God, forgive others, be obedient to the ways of the Lord, love one another even when it is hard, give to the poor, do the works He has set before you, be a good steward of everything God puts on your plate, etc.

My pastor has shared about a certain woman he never met, a woman who had no heirs, a woman who on her own decided to invest in the kingdom of God. She willed her estate to our church (people she never knew), which then allowed us to purchase land that is now the home church to over ten thousand people. This was a woman who had understanding about her riches! Just like BUT GOD #59 where we talked about setting up the future generations, if you have been blessed with riches, then richly bless the future generation to further His kingdom and His glory.

Since our Redeemer lives and our Redeemer is our Bridegroom, do not fear death. When you close your eyes on this earth, you will open them in eternity with your beloved Bridegroom. Remember not to trust the riches of this earth, all the money in the world cannot ransom your soul—no monetary payment is ever enough (Ps 49:8). There is only one acceptable payment—the shedding of Jesus' innocent blood. Though Jesus died a painful death, to Him it was worth it to save us. He wants to present us blameless and guilt free to the Father because we are covered with His precious blood. He wants us to live with Him forever—He desires to be reunited with us (John 17:24). The kingdom was prepared for us (Matt 25:34). Hell was never created for people; it was meant for the fallen angels and Satan (Matt 25:41)! Jesus does not want any of us to end up in hell because He wants us to believe in His Word and believe in Him—it is the only way our soul will be redeemed (John 3:16).

78. Accuses the Wicked and Identifies Falsehood

"But God says to the wicked: 'Why bother reciting my decrees and pretending to obey my covenant?'" (Psalm 50:16 NLT, emphasis added).

This verse reminds me of high school. It was so obvious when someone was being a fake. She pretended to be your friend and acted like she shared your interests just long enough until she got what she truly wanted from you. There were always a lot of different reasons varying from one extreme to the other for her behavior. Maybe she needed to get an answer to a homework problem, or there was an issue in her normal group of friends so she decided to grace you with her attention for a moment, or she wanted to know what that boy said to you. All I know is, when a person made it known that they could care less about you and then randomly acted interested, only to drop you again the next minute, it was obvious she was not sincere. You may think the same thing God says here, "Why bother pretending to be my friend? I know you really don't care." I love that God calls them out on it!

Psalm 50 is cool because the first half is God talking to His people, and the second half is God talking to the wicked. I found it interesting that God did not list the sins of the Israelites, but He spoke of the specific sins of the wicked people. He said that even though He had been silent, He would accuse them in person (v 21). Revelation 22:11-15 talks about those who do wrong and are vile. It says the sexually immoral, the murderers, idolaters, and the ones who practice magic and falsehood will not be able to enter into the kingdom gates—these are the same people God is speaking to in the BUT GOD of Psalm 50. He is again telling them He will rebuke them. They are not honoring Him and, therefore, He will not rescue them by letting them enter into eternity with Him.

God did not rebuke the Israelites (v 8), but reminded them to fulfill their vow. This would honor God and prepare the way for them to see the salvation of God, who is Jesus (v 23). Interesting words, "fulfill vows"—makes me think of saying, "I do" . . .

Do you, beloved bride of Christ, take Jesus to be your wedded husband? To have and to hold from this day forward, whether you are sick or in health, whether you are rich or poor, to love and to cherish, while you are alive on earth and when in death you will never part? Do you promise to obey the laws of God's covenant, to seek His face always, to be faithful and true, to honor your body as His temple, and to find your strength in His arms only? I DO!!!!

Do you Jesus, the Bridegroom, take your bride to have and to hold from this day forward, whether they are sick or in health on earth, whether they are rich or poor? Will you love and cherish them, protect and guide them, strengthen, comfort, and encourage them, receiving them in death with open arms to live in eternity with You and Your Father? Will you wipe every tear from her eye and take away her pain? Will You find her spotless and pure, clothed in white without stain or wrinkle, and provide a home for her to reign next to You in Your kingdom? Jesus says, "I will!" (Rev 19:6-9; 21:4).

Remember, bride, to thank Father God for He is good. He has given us Jesus, our Bridegroom, to be the ultimate sacrifice so we can be with Him. We need to honor Him in all that we do because our thoughts, words, actions, and deeds are preparing our hearts for His return!

79. Strikes Down the Wicked

"But God will strike you down once and for all. He will pull you from your home and uproot you from the land of the living" (Psalm 52:5 NLT, emphasis added).

This is another continuation of how God will deal with the wicked. They boast in evil (v 1), and since their tongues devise destruction (v 2), God will likewise destroy them. This Psalm was actually written about a certain situation found in 1 Samuel 22. David had been hiding from King Saul, who was trying to kill him, and Doeg, someone who worked for Saul, had seen David and reported his whereabouts. The place happened to be in Nob, the city of priests. David had left before Saul got there, nonetheless, Saul ordered the priests to be killed, and many others who resided in the city also lost their lives. So, when reading this Psalm, you can see why David was so descriptive about what kind of characteristics a wicked person displays because he had felt it firsthand. David unknowingly had put the people of Nob in danger, and so he thought he had caused those deaths. A priest had escaped and David had him stay close for safety, since Saul tried to kill him too (1 Sam 22:22-23). David knew he needed to wait on the Lord for the wicked to be dealt with according to God's schedule which is why he says God will strike them down.

If you look at all the BUT GODs we have studied on the wicked (which seem to be a good handful) there is an interesting timeline showing up. We see He watches the wicked (#65) and always sees what the wicked are doing (#67), but it does not worry God and He actually laughs at them (#75). We see He will accuse them (#78), and now we are learning He will strike them down once and for all (#79).

Tattlers like to gain attention; they are arrogant and want to prove they are right or better than someone else. They get a sense of power when they can indulge in giving key information to people in charge. Tattlers are like gossipers, only they are worse because they *like* to see people get in trouble. When Saul ordered the priests to be killed, none of his men would do it, but Doeg did because he was wicked down to the core. David was ready for this wicked man to be struck down and taken away. He did not dwell on when the wicked would get what they deserved; he instead praised the Lord. Interestingly, David compared himself to a green olive tree (v 8). Have you ever noticed green trees do not snap in half? They bend and are strong. We need to be like a green tree. Stay tender to the Lord and do not allow yourself to snap in response to the enemy's provocations—let the Lord do that. He will "uproot" them!

Since we are discussing tattling, I think it is important to note that tattling is not always bad. I have instructed the kids only to tell on someone if they are being dangerous or destructive. You are not always wicked if you tattle. In fact, the Bible encourages it, but for specific reasons only. The Lord did not want His people "turning their eyes away" when someone sinned (Lev 20), or pretend they did not hear an oath that someone should have followed through with but did not (Lev 5:1). He relied on them to "tattle" to keep evil out of their camp.

Our Bridegroom wants us to stay holy and pure, without sin. He wants us to be accountable to Him and each other. We need to confront each other when a brother or sister in the Lord sins. If that does not help, then a third party needs to be involved (Matt 18:15-17). There were times, though, that Jesus did not accept the tattling and responded with correction. Take for instance, Martha and Mary (Luke 10:40). Martha complained about Mary not helping. There were also the Pharisees who told on the adulterous woman to see what Jesus would say (John 8). In these examples, Jesus did not let the ones "telling" walk away without also being corrected themselves.

All this to say, do not talk if you have a wicked intent; it is not pleasing to our Bridegroom. We need to be a bride who is united and pure, working together, not against each other. We are always welcome to tell on whoever we want to God, but then we need to be ready for whatever response He gives. He might give us a gentle but firm reminder that we are not without fault as well. Be satisfied in knowing He will take care of the wicked in His time, and in the meantime, be a green olive tree in His courts of praise.

80. Surrounds Us with Help / Is Our Friend

"*But God* is my helper. The Lord keeps me alive!" (Psalm 54:4 NLT, emphasis added).

David wrote this Psalm when he was again being pursued by King Saul. This story is found in 1 Samuel 23:14-29, when David was hiding in the Wilderness of Ziph (#41). David says in this Psalm his enemies were those who did not seek to have God as their guide; they were strangers, and sought his life (Ps 54:3). David needed to keep the hope of victory when faced with persecution and know it was achievable because God was his helper. God knew that this attitude was important, which is why the Israelites' routine preparations for war included having the priests encourage and declare victory over God's people (Deut 20:1-4).

Fortunately, David was surrounded by those who the Lord had put in his life to help him. We see in 1 Samuel 23:16 that he was visited by his friend Jonathan, who was King Saul's son. This visit helped encourage him in the Lord. David also had a group of men with him who were mighty warriors themselves. They were loyal to David and stuck by him. Second Samuel 23:8-39 discusses the exploits of these warriors. Think about your friends for a moment. Which ones do you trust to keep a secret, which ones do you go to for a hug, which ones make you laugh, which ones make you feel like spending time with you is the best part of their day, which ones cheer you on, which ones hold you accountable, which ones inspire you to be better than you are, which ones entertain you, which ones can you sit next to and not have to say a word, who has seen you at your worst, who will pray with you, who will drop everything if you needed help immediately, and who will listen to your ramblings as you go on and on because you just need to talk? Some of us have friends that are able to satisfy many of these conditions, but we could probably list the best "go to" person who would handle certain situations better than others. One of the most unique qualities about Jesus is that He actually can satisfy this whole list all by Himself—He is the "go to" friend for everything!

Our Bridegroom is a great friend and wants us to be surrounded by great friends as well. It is important to find support from people who have biblical knowledge and who can walk alongside you. Many of these people can be found in small groups from your church. I had never been a small groups kind of person. Doing studies on my own and going to service was fine by me, but the Lord enticed me to finally start attending a women's Bible study at our church. They were going to learn about a book I had always struggled to understand, Song of Solomon, and I had to find out what they were going to say. After sitting for the teaching, I was not interested in sitting again for small group discussion afterwards every single week. That was too much time for me to have to sit still and not eat. Thankfully, my group leader, Sheila, invested her time into our new found friendship. With her encouragement, slowly but surely, I started staying longer and longer until I finally made it through the whole two and a half hours. I went from a nonparticipant to sharing my own personal testimonies. I had never realized that Bible study and small groups could be so much fun. It is like hanging out with all your favorite friends who enjoy God as much as you do. I finally found where all the people who had similar testimonies had been hiding. The thing was though, they were not hiding, they had been out in the open and teaching. I was the one who had been hiding and I did not even know it! By the end of those nine months, I had made lifelong friends. We laughed together, cried together, prayed together, served together, and had become families of the heart. Though staying still is a struggle, I know where to hear all the exciting stories involving my friends and God—in small groups!

The true bride of Christ cheers each other on and attends to each other's needs. Safe places to build close relationships with fellow believers are in small groups. The Bible reminds us we should not give up meeting together so that we can encourage one another—especially as we see the time getting closer to the Lord's return (Heb 10:25). Remember, a bride always has bridesmaids. We are all attendants to the bride of Christ as a whole, to build her up and help her to be ready for the wedding day. "All for one and one for all" should be one of our mottos. Some ways to attend to the bride's needs are serving the body, using your spiritual gifts (1 Cor 12:4-11), praying for her, and adorning her with grace through involvement in forms of worship, instruction, fellowship, and evangelism (interestingly the elaboration acronym of WIFE).[56]

In BUT GOD #48 we discussed that no one sticks by us more than Jesus. Still, we need support while we live here on earth. We need people in our lives who will encourage us and know how to pray for us. It is so important to have someone who is either mature in their faith, or hungry after the Word of God to track with you. You can be accountable to one another as you pursue developing your relationship with the Lord and live according to His instructions. Spiritual growth in the Lord is essential and may be one of the many reasons why God says not to be unequally yoked (2 Cor 6:14). I am not saying to avoid hanging out with nonbelievers, nor am I saying it is detrimental to have friends who do not share your beliefs. After all, Jesus hung out with all kinds of people. We can learn so much from each other, so don't confine yourself to relationships only with believers. What I am saying is watch who you let in your heart, because those are the people who have the power to influence it. Sometimes, healthy boundaries may need to be made. Believers need to compare what their nonbeliever friends say to what God says; our filters need to discern what aligns with the Bible and what does not. You need encouragement from the Lord and a fellow believer can deliver that to you, whereas, an unbeliever may not necessarily convey that you need the Lord's help.

Our Bridegroom wants us to come to Him in our time of need and ask Him for help. He also wants us to ask Him for good friends to help us. People are not perfect, though, and they will disappoint us, BUT GOD never will. He is the only One who is fully trustworthy and will come to our rescue every time. He will give us the strength we need when we feel discouraged and alone, or He may use someone else to deliver the message. Notice that David ends the Psalm with a verse that shows He has seen God deliver Him in the past from His enemies (v 7). I believe David had come to a place of security in his relationship with the Lord where he knew God would keep him safe and continue to help him.

As the bride of Christ without spot or wrinkle, we need to be completely confident in knowing that when we ask for help from our Bridegroom, He will help us. He loves us and has given of Himself to sanctify us, so that we can be holy and blameless (Eph 5:25-27). Our faith in Jesus needs to be strong, and we need each other to build us up and strengthen us in the Lord like Jonathan did for David. So let me help strengthen you right now in case you need reminding and encouragement. Sing part of this song from Casting Crowns' "Praise You in This Storm."[57] Taken from Psalm 121:1-2, it sings "I lift my eyes unto the hills—where does my help come from? My help comes from the Lord, Maker of heaven and earth!" The Creator of everything wants to be your helper—just ask for it!

81. Attacks the Wicked Unexpectedly

"*But God* will shoot an unexpected arrow at them; and suddenly shall they be wounded" (Psalm 64:7 AMP, emphasis added). *Also found in the KJV, NIV, and NLT.

Psalm 11:2-3 portrays the enemy shooting his arrows secretly at the upright and destroying their foundations. The devil is trying to destroy our foundation of faith and trying to make us question the "what" and "why" of our belief. In Psalm 64:3-6, the wicked are described as the ones who are devising plans in secret and shooting arrows against the blameless. The arrows are bitter words. Being the recipient of someone else's bitterness, unkind words, or false accusations can hurt, especially if you are not expecting it. We can be shaken to the core when attacked secretly. People have feelings, and words can pierce us, but we do not have to be wounded. Pastor Henry Wright (www.beinhealth.com) said that wounding is when you take ownership of the piercing. Do not be a victim! Separate yourself from those feelings so they do not become a part of you. That way, you will not become bitter yourself.

When we represent truth and expose sins, whether we know it or not, people will feel convicted and start to attack. Arrows of bitter words or accusations may pursue, BUT GOD is our shield. He will help deflect those assaults against us, but sometimes we make it easy for the enemy and allow his onslaught to penetrate our lives. By allowing him a foothold in an area where we have not trusted who we are in God, and by not asking for forgiveness or healing, we allow the enemy past our defenses.

Remember, God sees the wicked trying to entrap the blameless when they think no one is looking (v 5). It is God, in fact, who is the One that is going to make them stumble over their own words (v 8). The punishment the wicked were planning for someone else will be heaped onto them instead. This verse reminds me of the story of Esther.

The book of Esther does not contain any BUT GODs, but it definitely has a huge BUT GOD lesson in it. It is the story of a Jewish girl, Esther, who becomes queen. There were plans to kill the king, BUT GOD put Mordecai (Esther's uncle) in a position to hear the plan and stop it before it happened. Haman (the king's most honored official) despised Mordecai, BUT GOD humbled Haman. God made Haman the one to lead Mordecai around town proclaiming his greatness for saving the king. Haman wanted the Jews destroyed (he didn't know Esther was Jewish) and persuaded the king to sign a decree agreeing to this, BUT GOD had Esther in position as the queen "for such a time as this" (Esther 4:14). She pleaded with the king that her people would be able to defend themselves since he could not reverse his decree. The king, not knowing that the signed decree had put his queen in danger, promptly agreed and had Haman hanged. Ironically, the means of Haman's death was the very device Haman had planned to hang Mordecai on. What a perfect story for this BUT GOD verse!

Side note: Haman, who was an Agagite, would not have existed had Saul killed King Agag and all the Amalekites as God had ordered (discussed in #39 and #45). We see here in Esther their descendants (like Haman) were still causing the children of Israel problems. An inherited generational hatred for the Jews had been passed down in this particular group of people. The Jews were permitted to defend themselves when the day came for them to be attacked, and God gave them victory over those who tried to annihilate them. The Jews still celebrate this day of victory every year; it is known as the Feast of Purim.

Remember the timeline progression of the wicked we talked about in BUT GOD #79? Now we see *how* the wicked will be struck down—unexpectedly. They will be wounded swiftly and not have time to prevent or stop it. God's surprise attack assures believers that the impact will catch the enemy off guard. Here on earth, the wicked try to do that to us constantly, trying to make us second guess ourselves or feel guilt, BUT GOD will pick us back up (#72) and then will swiftly deal with our enemies.

I heard Damon Thompson speak on January 24, 2012 during TBN's show "Praise the Lord."[58] He said that if the church as a whole would not repeat watered down teachings, then they could recapture the element of surprise ("an unexpected arrow"). When the church exercises their authority in the power of God's Word, fresh messages of what God is saying to the church are delivered. There would be more authenticity in the church's identity, leaving the devil clueless as to what he should do. Damon went on to say that these days, many who attend church seem no different than people who do not. He pointed out that many churches are now "seeker sensitive" instead of being "sensitive to the seekers." He said churches need to start holding members accountable to biblical standards which may not draw crowds, but will ultimately build an army. Since the bride of Christ is also an army of soldiers for God, we need to arm ourselves with the sword of the Spirit, the Word of God. A fresh word and a fresh strategic plan will throw the enemy off his course. Our Bridegroom will strike the nations with a sharp sword—a double edged sword, in fact (Rev 2:12, 19:15). Jesus will come against those who come against Him. Those who persecute the righteous in heart better beware because our Bridegroom loves His Father and wants His Word to be obeyed. Jesus loves His bride and will protect her.

82. Listens to Prayers
"But God did listen! He paid attention to my prayer" (Psalm 66:19 NLT, emphasis added). *Also found in the NIV.

Sometimes when my daughter is talking to me I hear her but do not listen. I acknowledge she is talking, but I have no clue what she is actually saying. She gets frustrated because I do not give the right answer or I give her an incorrect response. This mostly happens when I am very busy or I am upset with her. Praise God that He is never too busy to really listen to our prayers or give us attention. In verse 18 it says, "If I regard iniquity in my heart, the Lord will not hear" (NKJV). Just like when my daughter has done something wrong, but then asks me to do her a favor, I am not about to grant her request (remember #38). I always tell her timing is everything, along with the posture of her heart. The Lord in His grace and mercy often gives us things we do not deserve, but He really does attend to our needs when our hearts are right before Him.

When I was younger, I really wanted to learn how to play the piano like my friends. I asked my parents and they signed me up for lessons; it was an immediate response. Playing the piano required work. If I did not practice then I did not get better. Sometimes, I was not allowed to do other activities until the piano practice timer went off. When it was time for my recital my parents came to listen to me and paid attention to all the hard work I had done.

Just like my parents gave me piano lessons when I asked, our heavenly Father also wants to give us our heartfelt requests. Matthew 7:11 (NIV) says, "If you, then, though you are evil, know how to give good gifts to your children, how much more will your Father in heaven give good gifts to those who ask Him!" I loved when my parents listened to me and paid attention to what I was saying or doing. Just like the piano practicing though (being obedient to the commitment), God may not grant our request for something else (like me wanting to play outside) until the first part is done (practicing and being obedient). There are two important things to remember also about asking God for something. One is that what we ask has to be in accordance with His will and in Jesus' name (John 14:13, John 15:7, 1 John 5:14). The other is that we have to believe He will grant us what we are asking for; unbelief will cancel our request (Mark 11:24, James 1:6-8).

I have one last thought, going back to my kids. I think they have the sweetest prayers—all prayers asked by children are sweet. They are so innocent and so honest in their requests. Mine pray to get good grades on tests, people to be healed from sickness, protection for the soldiers, and future presents they hope to receive. Remember, God listened to Abraham's request (#5), heard Ishmael crying (#8), and will fulfill our needs (#36). Just as you may be passionate about your request, Jesus is more passionate about you and will give you all kinds of attention when you want it, He will be so sweet to you! Ask Jesus anything you want, there is no limit; He will listen to everything you ask of Him. He might not do it all, but He will listen!

83. Smashes the Enemy

"But God will smash the heads of his enemies, crushing the skulls of those who love their guilty ways" (Psalm 68:21 NLT, emphasis added). *Also found in the KJV and AMP.

Striking the wicked with unexpected arrows (#79 and #81) and now smashing their heads. Hmmm . . . I sure do not want to be an enemy of the Lord! He is definitely going to make sure that when He strikes, His enemies will not be getting back up again. He is laying out all His plans here in the BUT GODs! The Lord truly wants us to know He has a strategy against the enemy. Notice I said the enemy, not you. God does not have a plan of destruction against you. Too many people think God is all about discipline, judgment, and doom, but that is not the case. God is loving, He wants people to experience all the blessings He has planned for them. Those who will experience His judgment are the ones who purpose in their hearts to do evil or are the ones who reject Him. God says in His Word that He has no pleasure in the death of the wicked. His desire is for them to turn from their evil ways (Ezekiel 33:10-11).

Psalm 68 is a Messianic Psalm. The very first verse points to Jesus' resurrection (taken from Numbers 10:25-26). Jesus arises and His enemies are scattered! It was through Jesus' death and resurrection that He defeated the enemy (Heb 2:14-15). Ephesians 4:7-10 also quotes Psalm 68:18, showing that Jesus had to descend into the lower parts of the earth before He could ascend. Genesis 3:15 tells us that there would be hatred between the seed of the woman and the serpent. It says, "he will bruise your head." *He* is the Messiah, Jesus Christ. *He* crushed the head of the devil when *He* died and resurrected! The devil will continue to be crushed and defeated by the saints through our prayers and the Lord will throw him into the lake of fire forever.

Many people in this world are being lied to by Satan and allow themselves to be pawns in his attack against God. They are deceived into thinking God does not care about them or that they are too undeserving of His love. Others believe they can continue to live a lifestyle against God's principles without any consequences. God makes it very clear there are going to be repercussions for those who oppose Him. Those who continue living immoral lives are the ones God is hoping He can win over with His love. This is why believers are not to judge people. We are to exhibit God's love even when nonbelievers are involved in their sin. We don't acknowledge it as acceptable, but we love the person. God will bring them to Himself first, then He will deal with their sin after through the conviction of the Holy Spirit.

Jesus does not want to scare people into believing in Him and following His ways. That is not why these verses are in the Bible. They are there because He wants everything out on the table. He wants you to know who He is along with the "how" and "why" you came to be. He wants you to know He prepared a place for you before the foundations of the world (Matt 25:34). Our Bridegroom desires a relationship with you. He will not force His way, because He gave people the right to choose Him. He does, however, want to make it very clear that if you do decide to go your own way, this world's good times will eventually come to an end. Choosing to wait on beginning a relationship with Jesus is a gamble too many take. Eventually you are going to end up on one side or the other (Josh 24:15).

Denying the existence of God is just another lie from Satan. In Acts 19, Paul was teaching about the Lord in the town of Ephesus. Some believed and some did not (Acts 19:9). He was casting out demons in Jesus' name. Only Spirit-filled believers can cast out demons in the power and authority of Jesus' name. The demons have no choice but to submit to who they know are Spirit-filled believers. We have assurance in 1 John 4:4 which says, "You, dear children, are from God and have overcome them, because the One who is in you is greater than the one who is in the world" (NIV).

In Acts 19:15, we see people trying to use the power of Jesus' name without really knowing how it worked. The evil spirit spoke back to them. To the spirit, they were nobodies—their names were not even known to the demon, who admitted to only knowing Jesus and Paul. This particular group of people did not threaten the demon, which is why we read in the very next verse that the evil spirit was able to overpower them. Not positioning yourself alongside God exposes you to chaos. When you do not have the protection of Jesus, Satan can have his way with you—until you choose to stop it.

Recently, my friends and I met a man "Ken" visiting from out of state. He shared about his son "Sam" who had been caught up in an unhealthy lifestyle of alcohol and such for many years and it was heavy on Ken's heart. We prayed that the Lord would begin working to break the stronghold of addiction and draw Sam to Himself. The day Ken returned home from the trip, Sam confessed to his father that he knew he needed to change his lifestyle or he was going to die. Ken was very excited over Sam's admission because he knew it was an immediate answer to prayer. Sam planned to take a walk and then speak with his father later about possibly committing to a program in order to turn his life around. Ken saw much hope and called us for prayer once again for his son. Only a few hours later, we got an email with terrible news.

Shortly after his confession to his father, Sam went outside in an attempt to stop a truck from driving across the lawn and fields. Instead of cooperating, the man got off the truck and proceeded to beat Sam severely. He was critically injured with many wounds to his head and face. We prayed the incident would not be a setback. Satan does not care about people already wasting their lives without his help, but the moment there is a chance they might break free from bondage, he will send out every means necessary to halt the threatening prospect. Thankfully, the Lord healed Sam quickly, and he made the decision to start the program.

The Bible says in Psalm 73:22 that we were foolish and ignorant, like a beast, before we knew God. Satan is happy when people look like his image instead of God's. Eventually, Satan will demand people take the mark of the beast (Rev 13:15-18). Satan wants the ungodly man to look good; consequently, we may see them increasing in riches or being at ease in life (Ps 73:12). Satan does not only lie to nonbelievers, but believers as well. Fortunately, believers have the full countenance of the Holy Spirit and the Lord's protection. Revelation 13:8 tells us that all inhabitants of the earth will worship the beast in the last days, except for those whose name is written in the Lamb's Book of Life. Those who are far from the Lord *will* perish and God *will* destroy those who desert Him (Ps 73:27). You were created to have fellowship with God and Jesus in order that you may be the bride of Christ. As the bride, we will live in eternity with Him and be protected from the evil one and destruction. Psalm 68:20 says the Lord owns the escapes from death. My Bridegroom is the escape route from the plans of the enemy!

84. Is Our Strength

"My flesh and my heart may fail, *but God* is the strength of my heart and my portion forever" (Psalm 73:26 NIV, emphasis added). *Also found in the KJV, AMP, and NLT.

Every time I hear the word "strong," I think of Matthew West's song "Strong Enough."[59] It fits perfectly into what this BUT GOD is telling us! God is our strength! The chorus is fun to sing along to and is perfectly worded. Please listen to it when you have time.

Now, look at the word "portion" in the verse. It also means inheritance; we have inherited a relationship with God forever. That means we have inherited all that is our Savior's. When people die they usually *leave* an inheritance to their relatives. Here, we see that the person who dies, but knows God, is the one who *gets* the inheritance. As active believers in Christ Jesus, we receive eternal life with our heavenly Father and acquire access to everything in Jesus' kingdom because His birthright has become our own!

We can apply this verse spiritually, but we can also look at the physical aspects that it references as well. Once conceived, our bodies begin to develop. Once developed, they start working at full capacity. Just like any machine, maintenance work is required or replacements may need to be issued over time. The medical field has come a long way since the Bible days. These days, if someone lives past one-hundred years old, that is considered a miracle. Before the days of Noah, however, people lived a much longer amount of time; Noah himself lived nine hundred and fifty years (Gen 9:29). The Lord stated in Genesis 6:3, ". . . My Spirit will not contend with humans forever, for they are mortal; their days will be a hundred and twenty years" (NIV). There are some different interpretations of this verse, but we know that Moses lived one hundred and twenty years. He did not become weak and he maintained good eyesight according to Deuteronomy 34:7. I believe it was because Moses followed the Lord's advice and was blessed instead of cursed (Deut 28). Our bodies seem to be breaking down more often, and even at age seventy-five there are not too many who can say they are as healthy as Moses was.

When most people are sick they see a doctor, BUT GOD wants you to remember He is the Great Physician. I am not saying don't see a doctor, I am just reminding you to go to God first. The Bible also instructs us in James 5:14-16 that we are to go to the elders of the church so that they can pray over us and anoint us with oil when we are sick. The Bible says confessing our sins to one another and having faith will also help heal us. A sign of being a believer in Christ is that we are to lay our hands on the sick so they will get well (Mark 16:17-18). Sometimes improvement from the physical ailment is not evident, but we can still find comfort in Him. Some of God's greatest heroes in the Bible had the gift of healing, but yet had health issues of their own. This may all have to do with the concept that the kingdom of God is now and not yet. We may see full health restored now, yet not fully. Whatever the reason, we cannot let a downcast attitude about our health or our circumstances prevent our soul from continuing to give God praise. We need to tell our soul that the joy of the Lord is our strength (Neh 8:10b)!

God wants you to live forever and that was His plan since the very beginning of creation. Sin brought in death. The enemy wants to cut your life short before you have a chance to fulfill all God has purposed for your destiny. Remember, God is the author of life (#47); the enemy is the author of death. Psalm 90:10 tells us our lives last seventy years, or eighty if we are strong, and then some trouble comes and we fly away (Moses wrote that Psalm). God intends for our bodies to be healthy (3 John 1:2). Believing God's Word strengthens our hearts, and even our organs, bones, and body systems as well. Knowing the truth and obeying God's Word strengthens us against the enemy's traps so we can avoid them (2 Tim 2:24-26). God's Word says to love, not hate. God's Word says to forgive, not hold a bitter grudge. God's Word says find satisfaction in Him, not to be envious (envy rots the bones, Prov 14:30). God's Word says to trust in Him, not to worry or fear. When we do not do what His Word says, the enemy is allowed a foothold in and has access to us (James 3:14-16). Our thinking then becomes distorted, which causes our emotions to affect our health. Deep rooted emotional issues can cause blocks from receiving healing. Pastor Henry Wright has put all this information into a very well known book called *A More Excellent Way to Be in Health*. Doctor Caroline Leaf has also done a great amount of research on toxic thoughts' effects on our brains and then ultimately our bodies. This is why we need to be washed (sanctified) in God's Word daily to renew our minds (Rom 12:2). Another great resource is found in Doctor Aiko Hormann's teachings. She teaches how to release negative feelings from the mind through the power of Jesus' name. She also instructs people on how to stop the connection felt in our hearts and guts when negative situations arise.[60]

God is the sole source of healing. Sometimes people have a functional or genetic deficit that could only be healed through a creative miracle. Sometimes God will use His creation to bring you back to health. He created trees for food and their leaves for healing (Ez 47:12, Rev 22:2). God gave us the plants to be used to facilitate healing and healthy living. As we start to rediscover the benefits of this life-source and not try to replace it with man-made drugs we will reap long lasting side-effects rather than ones detrimental to our health. It is sometimes necessary for pharmaceutical drugs to be used for temporary relief or life-threatening situations, but they are not to be used so often that your body becomes either addicted to them or immune. The oils found in plants work together with each other and help to cleanse your receptor sites, erase incorrect information on the cells, and restore the original DNA information that God had intended.[61] Proverbs 21:20 tells us that oil remains in the house of the wise. If we are to be wise for God's kingdom, this is one thing we should look into for our health.[62]

We cannot face trials alone; we need His strength to sustain us through the fight. Hiding His Word in our hearts helps us to not sin (Ps 119:11). It allows our hearts to be strengthened by His truths so we will not be shaken (Ps 15). Leaning and relying on Him to give us the endurance we need is the only way we will finish this race to reach the prize—Jesus and His shared inheritance for us (I Cor 9:24-27, Heb 12:1). We need His strength not only for our physical health, but our mental and spiritual health as well. It is a fact of life that our bodies will fail us, and it is a fact that our God will not (Heb 13:5-6)! God is the strength of my heart! The Bible says many times to love the Lord your God with all your heart, soul, mind, and strength. In fact, Jesus said this was the greatest commandment (Matt 22:36-37). If you purpose your heart to love Him, why wouldn't the Lord strengthen the very thing in your body that beats to His voice alone? If people say, "You have heart," that means you have spirit; you show endurance, persistence, tenderness, and courage. It means you have given your all. Give your Bridegroom your all—He's given His all for you . . . literally!

85. Is the Judge

"*But God* is the Judge! He puts down one and lifts up another" (Psalm 75:7 AMP, emphasis added). *Also found in the KJV.

God decides who will be exalted and who will be cast down. Psalm 147:6 says He lifts up the humble and throws down the wicked. He decides who will be king and who will be overthrown or voted out (#60). If a person has power, it is because the Lord gave him that authority. Jesus told this to Pilate in John 19:11. Abraham called God, "The Judge of all the earth" (Genesis 18:25 NIV). Why wouldn't He be? He created the earth, everything in it, and everything around it (#53). Revelation 20:11-15 declares God is the Judge and that all will stand before Him. He will sit on the great white throne and people will be judged according to their works. The Book of Life will contain the names of those who will not be cast into the lake of fire. Daniel 7:9-11 tells us that the Ancient of Days (God) will hear pompous words from the beast on that day. The beast will then be slain and thrown into the burning flame.

There are some pretty serious times ahead, but for now we have drama on a much smaller scale. Though God is the ultimate judge, we have bosses, teachers, and governing authorities who are over us now making decisions. Theirs do not compare to the justice that God will base (and bases) His decisions on. Everything falls short when compared to the righteousness of God and the standard Jesus set on earth. God works all things according to His plan and purposes, so we need to trust that He has determined who will hold positions of authority as history unfolds. He will move on behalf of believers so unrighteous laws are not passed, but the church must pray.

As a mom I have watched my daughter be a victim of unjust verdicts at school. My daughter Nicole is a straight-A student and is very diligent and meticulous about the work she turns in. She does everything she can to make sure she gets that A. She had a project not long ago that she spent five hours on, knowing that the teacher was going to grade it strictly according to the specifications he gave. He said up front he rarely gave out 100% on this particular assignment. She did extra work to make it more creative and knew it was very different than everyone else's in her class. A few days later, she came home from school extremely frustrated—she got 94%. Of course, that is a great grade, but apparently many others in the class got the same grade and told her that they only spent half an hour on their project or did it quickly the night before. She explained she was mad she had wasted so much of her time, knowing her effort was for nothing. She even went to the teacher just to find out what she did wrong and why she did not get the full 100%. He told her it was based solely on his opinion. There was nothing she could have done; he was the judge. He, of course, did not see her effort, did not know her heart for that 100%, and did not know her inability to understand that following all the requirements was not good enough! God knew, though.

God knows everything, which is why He is the perfect Judge. Whether He puts one down or lifts one up, it is for reasons we may not understand because we do not know everything going on. God executes flawless justice because He follows specific rules that

He put into place. He does not get on a power trip by changing the laws or the requirements. Exodus 12:49 says there will be the same set of instructions for the native born and for the stranger among them. Meaning, Jews and Gentiles must learn and obey His rules as they are for both groups (Num 15:13-16; Lev 24:17-22). When grading us on our works, Jesus will read our hearts accurately. Our Bridegroom is a righteous Judge (#9) and there will be no favoritism (Rom 2:11; Col 3:25). Colossians 3:23-24 says, "Whatever you do, work at it with all your heart, as working for the Lord, not for human masters, since you know that you will receive an inheritance from the Lord as a reward. It is the Lord Christ you are serving" (NIV). What He decides will always be a good decision and He will always be fair.

One last thing, remember that the law does not have the power to save, but was put in place to convict us of our sin when we do not stay within its boundaries. As our Savior, Jesus' blood paid for our transgressions so we will be found innocent when the Judge calls our name. Jesus has the power to save (Acts 4:12). If we have acknowledged Christ before men, He will acknowledge us before His Father in heaven, the Judge of all (Matt 10:32-33).

86. Is Faithful and Gives Help

"When God heard that, he was furious—his anger flared against Jacob, he lost his temper with Israel. It was clear they didn't believe God, had no intention of trusting in his help. *But God* helped them anyway, commanded the clouds and gave orders that opened the gates of heaven. He rained down showers of manna to eat, he gave them the Bread of Heaven. They ate the bread of the mighty angels; he sent them all the food they could eat. He let East Wind break loose from the skies, gave a strong push to South Wind. This time it was birds that rained down—succulent birds, an abundance of birds. He aimed them right for the center of their camp; all round their tents there were birds. They ate and had their fill; he handed them everything they craved on a platter" (Psalm 78:21-29 MSG, emphasis added).

Every time I think about the Israelites in the desert, it makes me wonder how I would react to all the wonders God did if I were there. Would it become so easy for me to constantly complain that it was never enough? Would I be so disrespectful that I would think I could do whatever I pleased despite God's commands? Would I lose trust in Him even when He continued to prove Himself faithful? Would I question the ones He placed in authority over me, knowing they were directly talking to Him face to face? Would I give up my right to talk to my Father face to face because His glory was too great for me and made me tremble? Would I worship in a different way than I was supposed to because it was not outside my comfort zone . . . I would hope not!

I know that God is planning a huge revival where the harvest will be great (especially in the last days—Rev 14:15). There will be miracles after miracles that are going to turn hearts to Jesus. I believe we will be working side by side with God's angels bringing signs and wonders from heaven through our worship and our spiritual gifts. The only way we can do this is if the bride knows her Bridegroom in such a way that it ushers in His presence. We are made to be His hands and feet. We should have so much faith and trust in Father God that questions, like the ones I just mentioned earlier, should not even rise up. We need to reflect Him as much as we possibly can. When we look in the mirror, it should be Jesus we see, not ourselves (1 Cor 13:12). We need to be so humble that He will get all the glory for the miracles without us stealing His spotlight in the slightest. Our heads should stay down, as I decrease, He increases; His fame, not mine. He receives the glory we proclaim.

In BUT GOD #17, we read God would be the one to help Israel. Then, in BUT GOD #18-22, we saw how He came to help His people and led them out just as He said He would. Now, in this BUT GOD, we see yet another promise fulfilled. God knew the Israelites would not trust in His help. Despite everything He did to prove Himself faithful to them, they still lacked faith. They were the generation who saw some of the greatest miracles and who agreed to the initial covenant, so why did they not continue to believe in Him?

The Israelites were used to eating meat in Egypt, and longed for it so much that they started complaining about only having manna to eat (the bread God delivered to them daily from heaven). They complained about leaving Egypt because they thought when they lived in Egypt their bellies were always full (Num 11). This is what made God so upset with them. They were finally out of the place of slavery, and then they wanted to go back. This was a rejection of His deliverance! Of course, I find it ironic God sent them so much meat in response that it became loathsome to the Israelites (Num 11:19-20 NIV).

Nonetheless, the Israelites were the ones God would show His glory through. They were the chosen people who were supposed to demonstrate the ways of God for other nations to notice (Deut 4). Through their lineage, they would bring forth the Messiah (#49). They were the ones commanded to keep God's laws for all the future generations so those laws would not be lost, especially since they were displaced so many times (Rom 3:1-2). Their traditions are one of the many reasons that such a rich heritage has been established within the Jewish community. They have been scattered, regrouped, attacked, and their total annihilation sought time and time again. Their miraculous preservation is a testimony of His faithfulness. Though their eyes were blinded for a time to not see Jesus as their Messiah, that time has passed and now many are seeing and believing.

Likewise, we as His bride are also a testimony of Him. Through the Jews, the Gentile nations are now able to read about the truth of God and know His Word for themselves. Salvation has come to the Gentiles through the Jews denial of Christ. We (the Gentiles) are wild by nature, yet we are embedded in by God's grace. How glorious the day when those natural branches (the Jewish people) are grafted back into their own olive tree (Rom 11)! The Gentiles have an opportunity to help the Jewish people understand who their Messiah is (Rom 11:11-14)! We can also be the ones through who God will show His glory. We are chosen by God to point the way to Jesus for salvation (John 14:6, Acts 4:12, Rom 10:9), and we are to preserve His legacy through the generations. We are the ones who will see some of the greatest miracles in the days to come.

We are the ones, together with the nation of Israel (who will all eventually know Christ as their promised Savior), who will show how magnificent and gracious our God's help really is.

87. Guides Us / Is Our Shepherd

"*But [God]* led His own people forth like sheep and guided them [with a shepherd's care] like a flock in the wilderness" (Psalm 78:52 AMP, emphasis added).

God provided help for the Israelites as they escaped from captivity in Egypt. God caused life for the Egyptians to be miserable through the plagues which finally caused Pharaoh to "let His people go." When time came for the Israelites to leave, God made sure that they had a full meal before they left (the Passover dinner we discussed in #21) and enough riches for their journey (Ex 12:35-36). God led them (#22) and provided a physical leader (Moses) for them to follow while He cleared the way by parting the Red Sea and wiping out the trailing army. I love how God prepared Moses. God had Moses raised in a royal Egyptian household, trained in the Egyptian ways, formally educated, and allowed access to Pharaoh. God also permitted for Moses to learn how to live in the desert and how to be a shepherd before God brought him back to Egypt. God utilized Moses' abilities to stand before Pharaoh and then help the Israelites live in the desert. Despite their forefathers coming from the desert, the Israelites were used to living in Egypt and required an experienced leader. Moses understood what it was like to live in both places due to God's plan of preparation!

The Lord is often referred to as the Shepherd and the Israelites as sheep. This is because the Bible was written for the nation of Israel in a way they could clearly understand. Since many of them raised sheep, they all knew the responsibilities shepherds had and how sheep reacted. It was a metaphor that was simple to relate to at that time. Psalm 23 is another place in the Bible that is well known for this comparison.

The people were led with great care and were given personal protection and personal attention. Even though the wilderness/

desert can be considered a place of great danger or a feeling of God's absence, this BUT GOD verse clearly states that God guided them during this time. The Shepherd is aware of the danger, but also is the ultimate Protector, guiding the sheep to an area of safety. The sheep do not know the destination, but the Shepherd does. The Shepherd took such good care of his sheep that they had confidence in Him and did not fear as they escaped (Ps 78:53).

My father and my friend have been in near-miss car accidents almost identical to each other. They both were headed straight through the intersection when cars to the right and the left of them were suddenly driving toward the sides of their cars. Both of them said they closed their eyes and prayed the Lord would help them through, and, sure enough, when they opened their eyes they were miraculously through the intersection in one piece. Being surrounding on all sides with vehicles that could destroy them, it was as if they were guided through a battle supernaturally. Literally, their existence could have been annihilated. Hmmm . . . where have I heard this before? Oh yes, current-day news concerning Israel. They are surrounded by enemies who actually have said they want to annihilate Israel's existence. Israel needs to remember God will lead their army forth and will guide them when they are in great danger, just like He did for them when they left Egypt.

At the writing of this study, my good friend Christine was letting the Lord navigate her way through her daughter's undiagnosed medical conditions. The doctors finally thought they pinpointed the problem and now Chris' daughter, Alyssa, is currently watching the Lord guide her as she deals with a new onset of a debilitating illness. As He promised to guide the Israelites, He has also promised to guide His bride and care for them leading them to the right place during their times of trouble. Remember, the Shepherd gives personal attention to each of His sheep. After being in a general hospital getting misdiagnosed, she was finally led to a hospital that could give her more accurate care. All along she has trusted the Lord, knowing her faith in Him was building as she focused on Him with all her new-found free time in the bed trying to recuperate. The very first day at the new hospital her mom took a picture of the scheduling board. It read: Grace (nurse) AA (patient) Emmanuel (doctor). The name Grace (meaning: full of grace, good will) and Emmanuel (meaning: God with us) surrounding Alyssa's name was not a coincidence. My friend, Lori, joked with her and said Mercy will come in the morning (like the verse in Lam 3:22-24). The next morning, the head nurse assigned to her was named Mercedes (meaning: lady of mercy)! She and her family see God's hand in her circumstances and we are all excited to see how this testimony is going to continue to play out as we pray for total healing in her body.

To sum it all up, we see our Bridegroom as the one who guides us. We can ask Him to lead us as we willingly follow, realizing He knows the best way to get where we need to go. He will make sure we have been filled up on the Word to sustain us through the journey and that we have the jewels we need to keep us going. We may have to make some turns in dangerous, troubling areas, and we may be in the dark, not able to see if He is still there, but we need to trust that He always is and will be. Revelation 7:17 says that the Lamb sits at the center of the throne and He will be our Shepherd and lead us to springs of living water. That is our Bridegroom!

If we have learned anything by this point through the BUT GOD verses, I hope it is this: God is faithful to the ones He calls His own (#86), He is their help (#86), and their guide (#87). He listens to us (#5 and #82), He does not abandon us (#73), He gives us hope (#55) and peace (#34). He sets us up for success (#59) once He gets us where He wants us because He loves us (#47) and has good intentions for us (#16). So, bride of Christ, do not fear as you escape your wilderness, because we can be confident in our Bridegroom. He can and will lead you because He is strong and mighty to save.

88. Hates When Sin Allows the Enemy Access

"But God, you did walk off and leave us, you lost your temper with the one you anointed." (Psalm 89:38 MSG, emphasis added).

Psalm 89:30-34 emphasizes that if the Israelites forsook God's laws and did not walk in His ways they would be punished, BUT GOD would still remain faithful and keep His covenant to them. This BUT GOD explains that the Israelites saw the repercussions of their unwise decisions come to pass, but even so, they still blessed the Lord, as we read toward the end of the Psalm. We need to follow this example and praise the Lord no matter what we go through.

This BUT GOD reminds me of God as our Father. When we do not listen or follow the rules, we may get a warning, but if we continue to disobey, we will get in trouble. Hopefully, we will learn from our mistakes and make better decisions in the future. Parents discipline because they love their kids enough to make sure they know right from wrong so they can grow up being responsible and trustworthy members of society. God cares enough about us to do the same (Prov 3:11-12, Heb 12:6-10). It is important to remember God does not discipline us by sending someone to hurt us; the enemy does that. (John 10:10 says the enemy comes to steal, kill, and destroy). Usually, it is because we, or a person of authority over us, gave Satan access by opening a door that uncovered us spiritually. We suffer the consequences of someone else's bad decisions, or our own, as Satan unleashes his fury on us.

We are so blessed to have a Father in heaven who lets us complain to Him, even when we bring the problems on ourselves (#28 and #29). We wallow in our sorrow at how bad things are, when, if we would just be obedient to the Word of God, the playbook for life that tells us how to keep out of trouble, we would not have to go through it at all. When we complain to Him, we should not say something about His character that is not true (#68). In this BUT GOD verse, it says God lost His temper, but we know God is in control and would never lose His temper even when He is mad (#119). The word in the King James Version of this verse is "wroth" and is the Hebrew word *abar* (#5674 in *Strong's Concordance*) meaning "turned away from" or "provoked to anger." I think these definitions would be more accurate. God's righteous anger shows up when His people do not obey His Word. When there is no repentance, even after warnings,

God will eventually turn His face away and His protective hand will be lifted.

The Bible gives instructions and promises for the bride of Christ. The enemy wants us to break God's laws and forget our vows to Jesus. Each of us struggle with something different (lying, lust, idolatry, rebellion). What may be difficult for you to overcome may not be a problem for someone else. The enemy knows where we personally are vulnerable and implants thoughts to weaken us, trying to make us fall into his trap. If we are tempted by his ways and react the way the enemy wants, the Holy Spirit will convict us to repent. We do not want to allow the enemy access, and the quicker we shut the door, the less time Satan can establish a foothold.

In BUT GOD #24, the Bible was compared to the Ketubah, our marriage contract, with Jesus. There is a part that describes His responsibilities, and there is a part that describes our responsibilities. His is to go and prepare a place for us in His Father's house, and ours is to make ourselves ready to present ourselves as the pure bride of Christ. How are we to be pure if we have to be disciplined for disobedience? We need to live according to the covenant we agreed to with Him when we said yes to His proposal. Thank goodness for grace because no one can live a sin-free life (except Jesus). Remember though, grace does not give us a license to sin (Rom 6:1-2); it frees us from the consequence of sin, which is death. We still need to keep working on purifying those areas in our lives where we consistently fail the tests. Jesus will finalize making us pure when we see Him in His fullness. Right now we can only reflect Him, like in a mirror—dimly, but when we will see Him face to face we will be able to reflect Him fully in all His glory (1 Cor 13:12)![63]

89. Is Our Hideout

"Can Misrule have anything in common with you? Can Troublemaker pretend to be on your side? They ganged up on good people, plotted behind the backs of the innocent. *But God* became my hideout, God was my high mountain retreat, Then boomeranged their evil back on them: for their evil ways he wiped them out, our God cleaned them out for good" (Psalm 94:20-23 MSG, emphasis added).

One of the many characteristics of God is that He has a soft spot for us when we need to use Him as our hideout. In Him we can find a safe refuge to obtain rest while we wait out the troubles we face. While we are there, we can confide in Him and reset our thinking. We can come out of that hiding place confident that when we face the situation we will do so with clear minds. We will not fear because we will have just returned from a refreshing time with the Lord and sought His counsel on how to overcome the trial. We will respond in a way that He has shown us during our time with Him and we will find peace about the situation. Remember, He is our strength (#84) and He is always with us, even after we leave our hideout. His Spirit is present, guiding us through our circumstances when we let Him.

My hideout times with the Lord includes worship music being played as I sing along. It is amazing what a friend we have in Jesus. He sweetly draws me to Himself and I begin to see what is truly important and what is not. My troubles usually consist of situations with the kids, paying the bills, or the housework piling up. Those troubles are nothing when compared to troubles outside my little life. Wickedness clearly stands out when I think of the injustices going on around me. Things such as child abductions, anti-Christian teachings, addictions, abortions, and child prostitution undoubtedly have evil at their root. These things influence people's overall well being. Knowing the Lord the way we do, it is clear He will execute vengeance on anyone who brings wicked acts against the innocent. However, the Lord will not bring vengeance on anyone who has repented from their poor decisions; Jesus' blood washes every sin away of all who ask for forgiveness and turns to Him for change. There is, therefore, no condemnation for those who are in Christ Jesus (Rom 8:1).

Just as He has a plan for the righteous, He has a plan for the wicked and part of His plan is using their wicked acts against them. Jeremiah 49 and Ezekiel 38-39 discuss a time when countries will come against Israel; both books discuss how God will destroy those nations. It is unclear if these are two separate occasions or if it is discussing the same situation, but during these times when we currently see evil rising, we need not be discouraged because the King of Kings has already shown us what to expect.

We know we are getting close to the coming about of these prophecies as we look at all the wicked leaders who have been removed from their positions in the Middle East. Most of them were tyrants who allowed many injustices in their countries at the expense of the people who lived there. Unfortunately, those leaders are replaced with another person who is just as corrupt. They were torn out of their positions after being found in their hiding places. Our hiding place is much more comfortable under the shelter of God's wings; there is healing (Mal 4:2) and refuge (Ps 91:4) as we are surrounded by songs of victory and shouts of deliverance (Ps 32:7).

Since we are studying the characteristics of our Bridegroom, remember that He wants us to run under His protection and not look elsewhere because He alone is our covering. He is the One who will provide our hideout during any trial we are going through or during the last days. Look at Revelation 12:6, certainly God has a hideout prepared for the "woman" in the wilderness for 1,260 days during the tribulation. Just like we have read about David, Elijah, and soon Jeremiah, the safest hideout we will ever find is under God's protection and care.

90. Takes Good Care of Us

"*But God*, dear Lord, I only have eyes for you. Since I've run for dear life to you, take good care of me. Protect me from their evil scheming, from all their demonic subterfuge. Let the wicked fall flat on their faces, while I walk off without a scratch" (Psalm 141:8-10 MSG, emphasis added).

How perfect! BUT GOD #89 is all about God wanting us to run under His protection, and now this verse says just that! We are in the midst of a battle and there is only one God who can protect us from it (#1). Ephesians 6:12 says, "For our struggle is not against flesh and blood, but against the rulers, against the authorities, against the powers of this dark world and against the spiritual forces of evil in the heavenly realms" (NIV). We know who our real enemy is, and only the Lord can protect us against the evil spiritual realm.

When I was little and had a bad dream at night or I was scared, I ran to my parents' room. That was the safest place to go to for protection; it was just instinctive. My father would get up and go check out any noise I heard and look under the bed and in the closet for me. Once he was involved I felt safe and secure knowing he was handling the situation. My mom would pray with me and things were better after I stayed in their bed for a bit. No one messed with my dad—he is a big and tall man. When I was six, I was allowed to ride my bike five houses down and then back again. One day, as I was turning my bike around in a neighbor's driveway, the owner yelled at me, thinking I was going to hit his car. I rode my bike as fast as I could back home and told my dad. He immediately walked over to that house. As I hid behind my dad's leg and held his hand, he told the man to never yell at me again. My dad towered over the man and the neighbor quickly apologized. My dad was my hero. He protected me and took care of my situation.

Make the decision to run to God so He can be your hideout like we talked about in BUT GOD #89. He will take good care of you. In Revelation 12:6, we see God takes care of the "woman" by providing her food to eat while she hides in the wilderness. We know God has plans to protect us when we choose to let Him. Battlefields require fortresses for safety and that is what He is (Ps 18:2 and 91:2, Prov 14:26 and 18:10 NIV). The band Kutless sings it perfectly, "You are my strong tower, shelter over me, beautiful and mighty, everlasting King . . . a fortress when I'm weak."[64]

We need to stay purely devoted to Him. When we keep our eyes on Him, it lets God know how committed we are to Him. For me, Jesus is it; I am sold out completely to Him and everything He has said. I have already "run for dear life" to my Bridegroom. There is no Plan B—it is Jesus or nothing. My hope is completely put on Him. I expect Jesus to protect me as I am under His shelter. I cannot compete against Satan and his schemes, but I know the battle plan has already been drawn. Just like when I was a little girl, I will run into my Father God's arms and Jesus will fight the battle for me, leaving me without a scratch.

91. Gives Us a Good Life

"Disaster entraps sinners, *but God*-loyal people get a good life" (Proverbs 13:21 MSG, emphasis added).

AMEN!!! Let me ask you, what is a good life anyway? Wealth? Fame? Awards? Though they are really nice, they all can have problems or obligations associated with them. Most people that have lived through a tragedy like homes burning down or a natural disaster, would say they were just glad they and their loved ones were safe. If they were able to save some photos, then that was considered a bonus. So, according to these situations, the basics of a good life would be to have your general needs met, be surrounded by those you love, and be able to share memories. From Jesus' perspective, He may hope His bride might say a good life is one who enjoys His company often and gives God glory. I am writing this at 9:45 PM on October 30, 2011 while watching Pastor Bill Johnson from Bethel Church in Redding, CA on their live web stream.[65] They, as a church, are literally encamping around God's presence right now and Bill just said, "God will entrust us with as much as we will jealously guard." Meaning, He will give us good gifts but wants us to give Him the glory for them all. God does not want us to distort those gifts into something that would be used to manipulate people or steal His fame. He is entrusting us with His reputation. We *get* to have the presence of God in our lives, we *get* to experience His joy, and we *get* to experience a good life *because* He is a good God!

"Disaster entraps the sinners" because one sin leads to another. You know how it goes, you try to cover up one thing and then deceit enters as you continue to lie more and more to cover up the initial lie. Another "disaster" that entraps people is falling into a pit in life. It could mean being stuck in an addiction or a decision that alters the course of your destiny and you become trapped in the sin. Unbelievers do not know how much better life can be because their sin follows them. They do not know that the truth can set them free (John 8:32) because they feel free already—in their sin. They are at the bottom of the lake without the realization that they are drowning. Until their eyes are opened to the only One who can heal them and help them, they will stay unaware and in bondage.

Praise the Lord that He has chosen us to be His bride! We are His sons and daughters; He delights in us as we delight in Him. We are all on different walks with the Lord, but we are all *with* the Lord and that in itself is a good thing. Our Bridegroom is planning a great life for us once He returns. No matter what economical status you fit into, if you are a believer, then you are surrounded by a great group of people who can enjoy the same good life in Him as you do. As His bride, we must walk through the narrow gate; it leads to the good life, and few find it (Matt 7:13-14).

92. Likes to be Included in Our Plans

"[Everything with a Place and a Purpose] Mortals make elaborate plans, *but God* has the last word" (Proverbs 16:1 MSG, emphasis added).

Wow! I can say a lot on this one. Do you make plans? Sometimes our family has so many plans in one day I honestly do not know how it all fits in. There have been times when our weekends were booked up for two months straight with festivals, visitors, vacations, sports games, appointments, outings, or experiences that we just did not want the kids to miss out on. Being busy with activities seems normal to me but sometimes drives my husband crazy. I love to Go! Go! Go! He's okay with the "G" and "O" part, especially if we add the letters "L" and "F" after it. Hahahaha! When I look at my calendar sometimes I wonder what else I can squeeze in. My husband teases me and says that what I do in one day with the kids is what he would do in one summer growing up.

I try to always accommodate what my husband wants to do, but I have been known to be spontaneous and add more to the day if we have free time. That is fun for me, but for people who like to schedule activities ahead of time, it can be frustrating.

There have been many times the Lord has halted me in the middle of my day. He does not want me to be busy; He wants me to have a purpose. He definitely lets me know when I need to slow down or stop for the good of my family and myself. When I do not partner with Him on my schedule planning, I make my family miserable. God wants us to balance our plans. I am still in the process of working on this, but I have learned if there is something I really want to do, I need my earthly spouse *and* my heavenly Bridegroom to agree with the schedule. If I do not book every day, it leaves open available times for His appointments and opportunities that He has waiting for me.

Not long ago, I had a busy month and was finally going to have a day all to myself. I had a full day planned at the beach while the kids were at school. I paid for six hours of parking and planned to walk on the beach, play in the water, do some shopping, eat some ice cream, read my Bible, etc. I spent the first two hours talking with Jesus, walking up and down the ocean and sitting watching the surfers. It was perfect weather and I was so happy. Then, Jesus told me that I had stuff to do and I needed to drive toward home. Wait . . . what? That was not my plan, but I said okay and left. He had me schedule two separate but equally important lunch dates with people that were surprisingly available last minute. Those meetings were life-giving and during one of them I randomly got a call from the school. They told me flag football practice was cancelled, so I needed to pick up my son early. I would have been an hour away had I been at the beach, but now I was only ten minutes away and my last meeting would be over at the exact time that I would need to leave. God had my day planned in such an organized, time-specific schedule, that He was the only One who could have orchestrated every event to fall into place as perfectly as it did.

In James 4:13-15 it says, "Now listen, you who say, 'Today or tomorrow we will go to this or that city, spend a year there, carry on business and make money.' Why, you do not even know what will happen tomorrow. What is your life? You are a mist that appears for a little while and then vanishes. Instead, you ought to say, 'If it is the Lord's will, we will live and do this or that'" (NIV). Tomorrow is not guaranteed, we only have today. I have discovered that I will make my heavenly Bridegroom happy when I add the letter "D" to my GO! GO! GO! days. I must check with God before I go because no matter what elaborate plans I may make, God has the final say.

Include Jesus in your plans and do not be surprised if one day your Bridegroom comes for you in the middle of them. The Bible says in Matthew 24:36-44 that in Noah's days, people were eating, marrying, and going on with their normal lives until Noah entered the ark. That will be the same way our Bridegroom will come. People will be working and not know at which hour He will come. As the bride of Christ, though, we are expected to know when the time is at hand. The Lord said when we see certain signs to be ready so the last days would not take us by surprise. We are to look up because our redemption is near (Luke 21:25-28, 1 Thes 5:1-11). God will have the final say in the end of days when the wicked will be no more and His justice will rule. Jesus wants to include you in *His* plans. He hopes you will choose to include Him in *your* life plans!

93. Has the Last Word and Final Say

"Make your motions and cast your votes, *but God* has the final say" (Proverbs 16:33 MSG, emphasis added).

I thought it was interesting that the beginning of Proverb 16 (#92) tells you that God will have the last word, and then it also ends the Proverb by saying, "God will have the final say." Just a small bit of God's light humor you might have missed.

What you choose to make important in life will matter. You can live the way you want, vote the way you want, and make decisions the way you want. Remember BUT GODs #25 and #26? Even though Balaam consulted God, he thought he could do whatever he wished; He actually intended to curse the Israelites, BUT GOD only let blessings come out of his mouth. Whether you choose to be a part of His plan or not—His will *will* be done, He's purposed it! In the end, God has the final say on everything, including who will be blessed and who will spend eternity with Him. The book of Revelation definitely brings home this truth of the character of God. I have two more thoughts about what it means to have the "final say" and the "last word."

Final Say: Verse 4 of this Proverb says that God made everything with a plan and a purpose. Have you ever heard of Dr. George Washington Carver? I never did until my friend, Becky, loaned me a small book by Glenn Clark called, *The Man Who Talks with the Flowers.*[66] It was a book about Dr. Carver. He would get up early every day to find specimens in the woods and fields to use for his work in a lab. He would also spend that time communing with the Lord. One time, when he was in his workplace, he asked the Lord why the peanut was made. The Lord showed him how to take the peanut apart and put it back together again. From that process many products were invented. Some of them are butter, shampoo, face powder, dyes, rubber compounds, instant coffee, and an ointment used as a treatment for infantile paralysis. The Lord showed him many things about the plans and purposes of this small part of His creation. Dr. Carver let God use him to develop many items that benefit us today. If you are part of the bride of Christ, you need to remember you have something important to contribute that can bring Him glory. Who we give credit to matters to God. Dr. Carver made sure he gave the credit to God. Do not forget that your decisions reflect a representation of Him. Let our Bridegroom show you what His plan and purpose is for you so He can have the final say on your legacy.

Last Words: Last words are always important, and our Bridegroom's were some of the most famous in history. In all four of the gospels you can read His last words from the cross. There are seven different sentences cited for us to see. Matthew 27:46b, "My God, my God, why have you forsaken me?" (NIV) shows us how alone He felt, calling out to God in His time of need. It actually also is the first line to the Messianic Psalm 22, which is important to remember. He was reminding the Jews who were listening to recall that Psalm, pointing to Himself as the Messiah as He fulfilled it in their sight. Luke has three quotes which are found in chapter 23, verses 34, 42-45, and 46. These refer to when Jesus asks God to forgive the people crucifying Him, when He spoke about paradise to the thief on the cross next to Him, and when He spoke to God, giving up His spirit. In John 19:26-27, He entrusted John with taking care of His mother. When He said, ". . . I thirst!" (John 19:28 NKJV), He received the sour wine that was offered from the sponge on hyssop (the Passover lamb's blood was also put on hyssop to mark the Israelite's doorways—Ex 12:22). In Matthew 27:34 we see Jesus tasted it, but did not drink it.

The seventh and final statement found in John 19:30 (NKJV) fulfilled Jesus' mission as He said, ". . . It is finished!" The Greek word for "finished" is found in *Strong's Concordance* #5055. It is the word *teleo* meaning "to complete." The Hebrew word for "done" in Psalm 22:31 is *asah* (*Strong's* #6213) meaning "to do" or "to accomplish." This is important because it now demonstrates how Jesus' first and last words bookended one of the main Psalms that prophesied about Him (Psalm 22). The Jewish people listening would have known this very well as many had the Scriptures memorized. Interestingly, in Revelation 16:17, at the end of time God will say something similar when the last bowl of His wrath is poured out. It is the Greek word *ginomai* (*Strong's* #1096), meaning, "be brought to pass," "be ended," "fall," or "finished."

There could be a complete in depth Bible study on Jesus' last words alone, but I will leave you with this: last words are important. People usually emphasize what is most important for you to know before they leave, die, finish a speech, etc. Take time for yourself to see what instructions He gave the disciples on their last night together, or what famous last words Jesus said just before ascending into heaven. I urge you to study these events; I promise you will learn something new. Famous *last words* are important and with Jesus dying on the cross and saying, "It is finished," He had the *final say* on how to perfectly bridge the gap that separated us from our heavenly Father.

94. Overthrows the Wicked

"The righteous man wisely considereth the house of the wicked: *but God* overthroweth the wicked for their wickedness" (Proverbs 21:12 KJV, emphasis added).

Alright! After having their heads smashed (#83), the wicked are now overthrown! As the anointed bride of Christ we have authority to come against the enemy—remember we can have that Jehu anointing (#60). We can pray against our enemy; he is the one who is trying to persuade us to do his will instead of our Lord Jesus' will. It is clear to us how he twists and perverts things; we can see right through his plans and laugh at him (#75). Our Bridegroom will act out against him and redeem any place Satan has tried to overtake as we bind the wicked and loose the righteousness of God to reign on earth. Our Bridegroom has given us that authority, but we must be willing to use it (Matt 16:19; 18:18). When we sin, we need to repent. When the wicked sin, they continue in their transgressions until God gives them a wakeup call and they repent.

There have been a few times I have had to overthrow a spiritual wicked attack and regain authority in my own house. When I was a new mom, sleep was a luxury not to be wasted, especially at night. One night an evil spirit woke me up and tried to bother me. I was so annoyed at it (and sleep deprived), not one ounce of fear overtook me, and I cast it out of my room in Jesus' name. Not even a second after I thought I had thrown it out and could go back to sleep, it spoke to me and said, "I will go bother your daughter then." Sure enough, a half second later, Nicole was awake and crying in her crib. Now I was mad! I got out of bed and marched straight towards Nicole's room. I stepped into her room and the whole atmosphere changed. A huge chill ran through me and I realized I had to get Nicole out of there. The Holy Spirit instructed me that I needed to bind the evil spirit and to tell it where to go, so it would not come back. I said, "I command you in Jesus' name to go straight back to the pit where you came from, to be bound and never return." With that it was gone; I brought Nicole in my room and we slept through the rest of the night, no problem.

Another time I was asleep in my room and was awakened by a dark evil presence. I knew what to do to get rid of it, but it was not obeying any of my commands. After a while, I was so tired of warfare with the thing and did not know what else to do but ask God to help me because it was not listening to me. I wish I would have thought of that sooner as the help that came was AWESOME! Within moments I heard singing that grew louder and louder until it filled my room. A choir of angels with instruments flooded my room with praise and worship to Jesus. You can imagine how the enemy fled so quickly I do not even remember it going! The angels sang songs I had never heard before, yet somehow I knew! I saw only glimpses of them as they hung out in the air above my head and I wished I was not so tired. They sang until I was just about to fall asleep. I then watched them float out and heard their voices become dimmer and dimmer until they disappeared. It was a magnificent experience!

From these two stories I learned a few important lessons about overthrowing the enemy. We need to cast out and bind the enemy in Jesus' name, but we also need to tell it where to go so it does not pick on someone else (reminds me of when Jesus sent the demons into the pigs in Matt 8:31). I learned that God might be waiting for us to ask Him for help before He intervenes. I was also reminded that worship drives out the enemy more quickly than sitting in silence. We also see a perfect example of this in the Bible. In 2 Chronicles 20:21-24, the Lord ambushed the enemy with confusion as praises were sung. God will fight our battles and give us victory as the enemy is utterly defeated!

Our Bridegroom holds the keys to this kingdom and when He returns He will overthrow all the wicked (Rev 19:19-21) and put them out of business. Satan will one day be overthrown into the lake of fire (Rev 20:2-3, 9, 14-15). Our Bridegroom, Jesus, will take His rightful place as King of Kings on this earth and govern us in righteousness.

95. Is "I Am" and All Powerful

"Who *but God* goes up to heaven and comes back down? Who holds the wind in his fists? Who wraps up the oceans in his cloak? Who has created the whole wide world? What is his name—and his son's name? Tell me if you know!" (Proverbs 30:4 NLT, emphasis added).

This reminds me of that spot in Job where the Lord is asking him, in a roundabout way, similar questions. In BUT GOD #70, I encouraged you to read Job 38-41. If you skipped it or need a quick reminder, you might want to do so now. Let us go through each one of these above questions and see where they take us.

Our God is awesome! The Bible recounts several times in the Old Testament where it seems the Lord came down from heaven to visit man. In the New Testament, the Lord was revealed as Jesus when God sent His only Son down to earth and physically died to save us. After His resurrection, Jesus went back up to heaven again (John 16:28—"I came forth from the Father and have come into the world. Again, I leave the world and go to the Father" NKJV). Ephesians 4:8-10 also discusses how our Savior descended and ascended. Do you know what happens in the ancient Jewish wedding custom after signing the Ketubah (# 24)? The Bridegroom would leave gifts for the bride to remember him by. He would not return to take His bride to the actual wedding feast until he had finished *preparing a place* for her (which was a room addition in his father's house*)*. Only when his father said it was done (much like having the "last word and final say" #92 and #93), then the Bridegroom was allowed to go get his bride. Is this not reminiscent of what our Bridegroom said to us in John 14:2-3? And, is not the Holy Spirit, with all His gifts, our engagement ring of promise from our beloved Bridegroom while we await His return (1 Cor 12:7-11)? John 16:7 says, "Nevertheless I tell you the truth. It is to your advantage that I go away; for if I do not go away, the Helper will not come to you; but if I depart, I will send Him to you" (NKJV).

What a perfect segue we have now as we move on to speak about the wind. The Holy Spirit was sent by the Lord just as He promised and the sound of Him rushing in was like the sound of the wind, Acts 2:2 states. In the Bible it talks about the wind obeying Jesus when He was on the boat (Matt 8:27). Jesus took control of the weather and God will control all the elements of the future. In Mark 13:27, it says that God will send His angels to gather His elect from the four winds from earth to the heavens. Surely we do not know from where the wind is coming or going, as John 3:8 says, and we can be blown to and fro, BUT GOD has a hold on that wind as this BUT GOD verse states, and He has a hold on His bride as well.

The ocean! Did you realize that God told the ocean it could only come so far (Prov 8:29)? That is amazing to me! Every time I am at the beach and watch each wave crash I see how even the ocean is following the orders that God gave it from the creation of the world. Every time the water sinks into the sand and rolls back into the sea it is an act of obedience. God has wrapped the ocean with all kinds of mystery. The only way to find them is to dive in and seek those buried treasures. Just like the sea, we have to dive into His Word to discover hidden truths and treasures that reveal the mysteries of God. I hope you are already discovering some fun treasures as we have been diving into the BUT GODs of the Bible revealing our Bridegroom's characteristics.

We already discussed this next and easy question in BUT GOD #56. "Who has created the whole wide world?" God, of course! Not only did Moses write in Genesis that God created the world, but in Isaiah 45:18, God speaks directly through His prophet and declares that He Himself is the one who created the earth to be inhabited. I love how Psalm 148 reiterates all that we have talked about so far—the wind, the sea, and all creatures on heaven and on earth and everything that exists; all creation should praise His name for His splendor. All things can praise Him because God created them (Gen 1:1) through His spoken Word (who is Jesus, John 1:1-5) and through His Holy Spirit (Gen 1:2).

When Jesus rode on the donkey into Jerusalem on Palm Sunday (as we like to call it) multitudes rejoiced and praised Him as king. The Pharisees told Jesus and His disciples they should stop the people, but Jesus said if they stopped praising Him, then the rocks would cry out in their place (Luke 19:40). Even the rocks would praise Jesus as He passed by His creation into Jerusalem. This was the week Daniel had prophesied about in Daniel 9:25-26, ". . . from the going forth of the command to restore and build

Jerusalem until Messiah the Prince, there shall be seven weeks and sixty-two weeks . . . and after the sixty-two weeks the Messiah shall be cut off . . ." (NKJV). The command Daniel refers to is found in Nehemiah 2:5-8. It shows that the decree went out by the king for the Jews to restore and rebuild Jerusalem. So, if they had been counting, all they had to do was add seven weeks (meaning 49 years) plus sixty-two weeks (434 years). This told them that it would be sixty-nine weeks (or sixty-nine multiplied by "sevens") until the Messiah was "cut off." That time pointed to the exact year at Passover when Jesus was in Jerusalem! They were told in advance when He would be before them. The Author of Life (Acts 3:15) was to be killed and all creation shook when it happened (Matt 27:51).

God's name is Yahweh, I AM THAT I AM (Ex 3:14), and His Son's name is Jesus, Yeshua, our Beloved Bridegroom (#60). Wow! Jesus name means "The Savior of Yahweh." After writing all this and reading a little expansion on just a few of the great things God does to exhibit His power, it is amazing that we get to belong to someone like Him! Jesus has a great Dad, and so do we! We have authority in His name because His power backs us up.

Have you ever word searched in the Bible the Lord's name? I thought I would see where "I Am" led me. Here are some of the results: I Am the Lord who heals you, who sanctifies you (Ex 15:26; 31:13), who separated you (Lev 20:24), the God of Israel who calls you by your name (Is 45:3-4), who teaches you to profit, and who leads you (Is 48:17). A couple more read: I Am the Lord who divided the seas and who speaks (Is 51:15; 52:6). These seem to go in line with our above discussion about the oceans and speaking creation into existence. An important one to see is in Ezekiel 39:28 where God says He is the One who sent Israel into captivity, but also brought them back to their land and left none a captive. In the New Testament in John 8:16, Jesus says, ". . . I am with the Father who sent me" (NKJV). In John 12:45, Jesus said, "And he who sees Me [Jesus] sees Him [GOD] who sent Me [Jesus]" (NKJV, inserts added). Meaning: Jesus is God! Which, of course, we already know, but it is nice to know where it is proven in the Bible.

Looking up the words "I AM" brings you to a whole new set of interesting descriptions of our God. The Hebrew word *Ani* means

"I AM" and is seen several hundreds of time in Scripture. *Anokhi* means "Because I AM" and is used over one hundred times in the Hebrew Scripture. This word emphasizes the importance of God's characteristics when He points out to you all that He is.[67] Once you start looking at them, it is hard to stop, let me just tell you two more. Isaiah 43:25 tells you God is the I AM who erases all your transgressions and will not remember your sins anymore. Isaiah 44:24 says the Lord is the I AM who formed you in the womb, the One who makes all things. Again, this verse tie you back to the BUT GOD verse! I love how God's word is so consistent! No matter what words you decide to study, God's character will always shine through.

In verse 8 of this Proverb, the writer asked the Lord to keep falsehood and lies away from him. What a wise thing to ask, especially when looking for answers to the questions asked in this BUT GOD verse. Let not the bride be deceived about answers to questions concerning her beloved Bridegroom. We want to know everything about Him and since He is the truth, let the truth be told! He is not the same god as the Muslim god, Allah, and our God is not a higher source or energy in the universe or whatever other new age name spiritualist people give Him. He is the God of heaven and earth. He is Yahweh and He is all powerful. Through the Holy Spirit we can feel His presence with us always. His Son's name is Jesus, the King of Kings and Lord of Lords and there is no one like Him. He died, was buried, and rose again on the third day. He is faithful and good all the time, and He promises a guarantee of eternal life for those who believe in Him. Phil Wickham's song, "At Your Name (Yahweh, Yahweh)" is a beautiful way to end this devotion.[68] I suggest you listen to it and shout the Lord's Name. As Psalm 66:4 says, "Everything on earth will worship you; they will sing your praises, shouting your name in glorious songs" (NLT).

96. Is the Only One Who Can Satisfy

"He has made everything beautiful in its time. He also has planted eternity in men's hearts and minds [a divinely implanted sense of a purpose working through the ages which nothing under the sun *but God* alone can satisfy], yet so that men cannot find out what God has done from the beginning to the end" (Ecclesiastes 3:11 AMP, emphasis added).

This is why we struggle to survive; we have eternity "planted" within us. We were not meant for death, we have eternity set "in our hearts and minds." Our whole bodies know they are not meant to die, so they strive to survive. God designed us to live forever and when sin entered, death was allowed to take life away from us. Thankfully, He designed a way for us to live eternally again through His Son, but until death is destroyed, we will all die here on earth.

This verse comes after the famous passages in the Bible where it talks about there being a time for everything, a time to live/die, plant/pluck, kill/heal, break/build, weep/laugh, and on and on. God saw that everything He created was good and He set in motion all things according to their purpose. Remember how we learned some of the purposes of a peanut in BUT GOD #93? He made everything beautiful and in its time, its purposes will be exposed.

God made us with a purpose and only He can satisfy the yearning to know what our function in life should be. Many people do not feel satisfied in their lives, jobs, marriages, etc., but our unique purpose can be fulfilled when we let God use us for the purpose He created for each individual. Only He can satisfy what He put inside of you. If you are not feeling satisfied in life, it may be because you are not fulfilling God's design for your life. Granted, many of us would like to do God's business all the time, but we still have to live in this world and be responsible for all of life's challenges. We have to navigate each day with the many jobs we are in charge of: education, family responsibilities, paying bills, employment, etc. If you examine your schedule, you may find you have more time for God stuff if you include Him in your planning (#92).

My husband, Aaron, has an incredible ability to rehabilitate people who have all sorts of hand and arm injuries and his schedule is often overloaded with patients who request to see him specifically. He has found his niche in helping people and I think he is a great example of Jesus' tenderness in caring for those with injuries. It is Aaron's specialty that he has trained for and he is very good at his job. I told him I envision him one day using his position to pray for healing in Jesus' name right in the clinic and actually see it happen—just like in 1906 during the Azusa Street Revival.[69] Of course he prays for people now, but the opportunities are limited. What he wants to spend most of his free time doing, though, is any sort of sport. He has a ridiculous amount of sports information and ability. He feels that is also supposed to be part of God's purpose for him, but he has yet to figure out what exactly to do with it.

Many people can use their jobs as stepping stones to be able to fulfill their God-given gifts. My friend Lisa works diligently at her church. She networks with many people there and knows who needs what. She is also an incredible writer, a horse trainer, a mother, a wife, a friend, an event planner, and a pastor. God gave her many gifts and she has been able to find satisfaction in all of them by letting God lead her to where she needed to be. She grew up around horses and loves all things girly. She has a unique heart for young girls. If she can bring someone out to the stable, give her a riding lesson, or teach her about makeup, then she gets to have fun while being able to witness, fellowship, and/or mentor all in one shot. She has also helped to develop a nonprofit riding stable designed to minister to kids, which at one point had a waiting list! She has often had to sacrifice her time, but she would tell you it was well worth it for the reward she received of seeing the transformation in someone's life. She has realized that God's divine purpose in how He created her can help facilitate a positive change in someone else. She would tell you it is very satisfying to know you can make a difference in helping others. In our church, we would call this "standing on your number." Meaning, be satisfied in the place God has put you and do not long to be standing on someone else's number trying to fulfill their purpose. You have a unique calling; be happy with what He has purposed in your own heart.

Your Bridegroom has intended for you to live eternally with Him. During your time on earth He will have many assignments for you that will bring satisfaction as you glorify His name (#57). Only He can fully satisfy your desires and fill in the empty spaces in your life. All you have to do is ask. Learn what it is about yourself that fills you up with His joy. With that knowledge, see if there is anything He has put on your plate that would bring Him glory while feeding your appetite for fulfillment in that specific activity. Let your life be an offering to Him as He satisfies your soul. He will make all things beautiful for you in His time.

97. Gives Enjoyment as a Blessing

"God gives some people wealth, possessions and honor, so that they lack nothing their hearts desire, *but God* does not grant them the ability to enjoy them, and strangers enjoy them instead. This is meaningless, a grievous evil" (Ecclesiastes 6:2 NIV, emphasis added).

It is God's gift to us when we enjoy the fruits of our labor and have fun with what we have worked for. Ecclesiastes 3:13 says, "And also that every man should eat and drink, and enjoy the good of all his labour, it is the gift of God" (KJV). Not everyone has that gift from God, and not everyone is able to enjoy their personal possessions—it is a blessing. Since you cannot take what you have earned materially from this life when you die, you will leave this earth with the same amount of stuff as you came with—nothing. You do not know what will happen tomorrow. All your work could be in vain, and if something happens to you, someone else will get your possessions.

I have had patients who have worked their whole lives to enjoy their retirement together with their spouse. Tragically, once they started to enjoy their golden years, a spouse dies and/or suffers a stroke, hip fracture, a heart attack, or some other medical diagnosis and all their plans become meaningless. Their possessions sat idle as they waited to see whether or not the person recuperates. It is a tragedy to watch, but as long as we (the bride of Christ) put our hearts into what really matters, we do not have to let our plans be meaningless. Not all of us need wealth or possessions to be satisfied; having possession of the blessings of the Lord can be fulfillment enough.

If we look at our lives from a heavenly perspective, we will not have tight grips on our earthly possessions and will be able to bounce with the changes. My friends, Jeff and Tara, purchased land and built a beautiful home in Maui overlooking the beach. They have a rule in their family they try to live by called "loose grip living." This means they do not hold on too tightly to anything, because the harder you hold onto something the more difficult it is to let it go. They do not make their life revolve around what they have and where they live, but about whom they can bless while they maintain good stewardship over it for as long as God allows.

Jeff and Tara are an exact opposite example of this BUT GOD verse because they *have been enabled to enjoy* this now. In the future, a stranger may own that house and will enjoy what has been built. He may live there without knowing the depths of how blessed he is, though, because there is something very special about that house. Messages have been written within the framework, because when they built it, Jeff and Tara took seriously the Bible verse that says, "Fix these words of mine in your hearts . . . Write them on the doorframes of your houses . . ." (Deut 11:18-21 NIV). Consequently, there are many Bible verses written all over the inside of those walls.

Knowing my friends are enjoying what they have in itself is a blessing from God. It is to God's glory that they are able to have fellowship there with other believers and allow friends and family a free place to stay while on vacation. In contrast, I have read about many Hollywood stars and CEOs who have multitudes of wealth but lack internal fulfillment. They, instead, turn to drugs and alcohol to feel a high that really only God can satisfy (#96). Unfortunately, those would be the ones this BUT GOD verse would perfectly fit, and those are the ones who need to see through spiritual eyes that their lives do not have to be about their status from the world's viewpoint, but rather from God's. There is no reason why Hollywood cannot turn itself around and be a city full of God's glory. Believers are not immune and can also get caught up in the hype of maintaining their excess. Remember, our Bridegroom will allow you to enjoy your blessings when your heart is pointed in the right direction.

98. Is Trustworthy

"*But God*, the Master, says, 'It won't happen. Nothing will come of it because the capital of Aram is Damascus and the king of Damascus is a mere man, Rezin. As for Ephraim, in sixty-five years it will be rubble, nothing left of it. The capital of Ephraim is Samaria, and the king of Samaria is the mere son of Remaliah. If you don't take your stand in faith, you won't have a leg to stand on'" (Isaiah 7:7-9 MSG, emphasis added).

In BUT GOD #50 we discussed that after the days of King Solomon, Israel was divided. They fought amongst themselves and split into two. Ten tribes stayed in the North and kept the name Israel, also sometimes were known as Ephraim, and had their capital in Samaria. The other two tribes (Benjamin and Judah) were in the South and were known as Judah. They kept the royal line of David and their capital was Jerusalem. David Pawson's book, *Come With Me Through Isaiah,* helped me decipher this section. He explained that Israel made a pact with Syria to destroy the remnant of Judah. Judah was fearful and decided to make a pact with Assyria, thinking their help could save the nation (see 2 Kings 16:7). Judah needed to fear God and know He would protect them. David Pawson writes, "If you have the one right fear in your heart you will have none of the wrong ones."

In this BUT GOD verse, God sent His prophet Isaiah to the king of Judah to confirm the plot against them. Isaiah reassured him of God's protection. The king of Judah, Ahaz, may have struggled putting his trust in God (Is 7:10-12, KJV). The Lord encouraged him to believe they would not have to worry about Israel and Syria and that those two countries would be wiped out. History proved God's promise, and in sixty-five years, Israel and Syria were attacked by Assyria (2 Kings 17).[70]

In BUT GOD #51 we discussed how Israel became separate from Judah. Jeroboam's decision to bring in counterfeit gods, priests, and feasts began Israel's downfall. It was prophesied at that time that disaster would fall on the house of Israel. Their bad decisions gave Satan access to bring destruction upon them, because God said He would allow this if they did not obey His commands.

My friend, Pastor John Hill, explained prophecy this way; Being in front of the situation makes it difficult to know which prophecies may have a double fulfillment, but there are many that we can see that Jesus said He came to fulfill and did (Matt 1:23).[71] Prophecy does not always make sense until it happens. All prophecy is discursive, meaning there are multiple views. It can be talking about past, present, and future.

What I think is most important for us as the bride of Christ to focus on is the last part of this BUT GOD verse. We need to take a stand in our faith even in the midst of conflict. We need to believe and act on God's Word. Every generation goes through tribulations and may think the Lord is coming back during their lifetime. Our generation is no different and, as His bride, we need to stand strong. Evilness will progress before Jesus can come back and reign here in righteousness. When we see trouble on the horizon, as King Ahaz saw in this BUT GOD verse, we need not be frightened into making alliances with the wrong people. Those people come against us in the long run, just like Assyria did later to Judah (2 Kings 17-20). The Bible says in Matthew 24:37-41 that the coming of the Son of Man will be like the days of Noah where people were eating and marrying. This seems to indicate that the economy will be going well in the world, but we will know by the increased "birth pains" on the earth that the time is near (Matt 24:7-8 NIV).

We need to place our trust in our Bridegroom. We need to know His character and the stories that prove them so we will have confidence in His faithfulness and protection. We cannot waiver and look elsewhere for security; we need to look to Jesus, especially since He is the One telling us to believe Him! Have faith! When evil begins to rear its ugly head, we need to rejoice because we know God's glory is going to come next (#52). God has given us two legs for a reason, if we stand on only one, we will have a weak stance, an unsure foundation. Let's not wobble in our faith; let's stand on His sure foundation, the one with which He equipped us with! God can be trusted. Everything Jesus said is true. Let us believe our

Bridegroom as we stand with Him. As Michael W. Smith's song states, "I'll stand, with arms high and heart abandoned, in awe of the One who gave it all."[72]

99. Is the Lion

"Oh, how I grieve for Moab! Refugees stream to Zoar and then on to Eglath-shelishiyah. Up the slopes of Luhith they weep; on the road to Horonaim they cry their loss. The springs of Nimrim are dried up—grass brown, buds stunted, nothing grows. They leave, carrying all their possessions on their backs, everything they own, making their way as best they can across Willow Creek to safety. Poignant cries reverberate all through Moab, Gut-wrenching sobs as far as Eglaim, heart-racking sobs all the way to Beer-elim. The banks of the Dibon crest with blood, *but God* has worse in store for Dibon: A lion—a lion to finish off the fugitives, to clean up whoever's left in the land." (Isaiah 15:5-9 MSG, emphasis added).

God judged the nations surrounding Israel based on their treatment of His people. In this chapter, Isaiah is prophesying against Moab. He grieved for them because of the horrible destruction that was coming to them. No one likes to give someone bad news and here Isaiah had to give it to a whole nation. On top of that, not only was the destruction going to be bad, but just when the remaining people thought they had survived the worst, God would send a lion in to invade their neighborhood to get rid of them—Yikes!

The Moabites were actually descendants of Lot, through his daughters, who clearly had distorted moral views (Gen 19:30-38). This may have been due to their time in Sodom and Gomorrah (#5) or it could have been due to the loss of their mother (Gen 19:17-26). God saw the nation of Moab as His washpot (Ps 108:9). They were haughty and proud (Isaiah 16:6) and they prayed to false gods (Isaiah 16:12, Ruth 1:6-8, 15).

One famous Moabite was Ruth. In the book of Ruth, we read about Naomi's family who decided to move from Bethlehem to

Moab. The men in Naomi's family died in Moab. Naomi decided to move back home and told her daughters-in-law (who were Moabite women) to return to their gods. One of the girls, Ruth, refused to leave; she was determined to stay with Naomi. God may have allowed the move to Moab, and Ruth's marriage into the family, for the divine purpose of pulling Ruth out of that land (it reminds me of the Parable of the Lost Sheep in Matthew 18:12-14). Deuteronomy 29:1-8 tells us the land of Moab had been conquered and inhabited by the Israelite tribes of Reuben, Gad, and Manasseh. Unfortunately, like many of the Israelites, they turned from obeying God's instructions, intermarried, and worshipped false gods. Although Ruth was not identified as an Israelite, she attached herself to the God of Israel and was grafted into His ways. She told Naomi, "Your God *is* my God, your people *are* my people" (Ruth 1:16-18 paraphrased). Ruth moved back to Bethlehem with Naomi and met Rahab's son, Boaz, whom she later married. Both Ruth and Rahab were strangers that sojourned and lived among the Israelites and learned to keep the law of God as some of the exiles from Egypt had done (Ex 12:48-49). The story of Ruth is amazing. In it, the bride of Christ is symbolized in Ruth, our Bridegroom Jesus is symbolized in the kinsman-redeemer Boaz, and Naomi represents Israel.[73] Ruth and Boaz were the great grandparents of King David (#49), from whose line Jesus came (Matt 1:1-17).

In Matthew 25:32, Jesus said He would judge the nations. He said the people of the nations would be separated just as the shepherd divides the sheep from the goats. I think that there is a time in the near future when the Lord is clearly going to see which nations are the sheep and which are the goats. Those who vote in favor of going against or dividing Israel will clearly be goat nations. I hope the United States stays a sheep nation as we stand with Israel, but if the United States eventually turns away, we as individuals need to stand up for God's people as individuals. People of a nation can still be in line with God even if their country is not.

I wish people would not make the fatal mistake of going against God again, but in Revelation 16:14 we read that people will actually make war with God. Like Isaiah grieved for Moab, it is a sad reality when we read about those who remain proud and haughty and worship a false god. Just like this verse, God will send in the animals to clean up the people after striking them down with the sword coming from His mouth (Rev 19:21).

What is it about our Bridegroom He wants us to see clearly here? I think it is the fact that our Bridegroom has the worse in store for those who continue to reject Him. In this BUT GOD verse, the fugitives were the ones who were "finished off" by "a lion." Fugitives are defined as running away or fleeing from the law; "the law" could refer to "God's law," which is His set of instructions on how to live. Some fugitives go on the "most wanted" list. Usually, the most wanted are those who have avoided punishment and are the most dangerous; they have slipped away, like a snake. The most wanted in the end times will be the beast, the false prophet, and Satan/antichrist. They will have deceived the kings and their armies. Jesus will kill with the sword (the Word of the Lord) in His mouth (Isaiah 1:20, Rev 1:16; 2:16; 19:15, 21). We also see that Jesus is ". . . the Lion from the tribe of Judah, the Root of David . . ." (Rev 5:5 KJV).[74] So we know that "a Lion" is a reference to Jesus and Jesus is "the Lion" in the end days who will "finish off the fugitives," cleaning up the unrighteous ones left in the land!!!!

100. Rebukes the Nations

"The nations shall rush like the rushing of many waters: *but God* shall rebuke them, and they shall flee far off, and shall be chased as the chaff of the mountains before the wind, and like a rolling thing before the whirlwind" (Isaiah 17:13 KJV, emphasis added). *Also found in the AMP and MSG in Isaiah 17:12-13.

In BUT GOD #98, we learned Israel made a pact with Syria, BUT GOD promised King Ahaz that Syria would be destroyed. This chapter shows a more descriptive picture of that and also may hold a prophecy for the future of Damascus. Some believe Damascus is going to be a ruinous heap in the near future (Isaiah 17:1). As we watch the news unfold, we see how current events relate to the prophecies connecting to the book of Revelation which truly shows Christ's return is imminent. During a conversation with my friend, Pastor John Hill from Sunrise Church, he said, "When the Lord allows prophecy to be fulfilled in our time we need to ask ourselves, 'What is the reason He is showing us this?' The answer is so that we can see the urgency in which to show others the way to God as the time is drawing closer to the end." God shows prophecy fulfilled so people will believe in God.

Let us think about the nations "rushing" for a second. Most of us have been in a loud and crowded place like a concert. To converse with another person requires raising your voice to hear each other, and you can forget about talking on the cell phone. Thank goodness for texting, right? Now, think of this level of noise, but multiplies a hundred times over. The Message Bible describes the sounds as thunder, crashing waves, massive waterfalls, and roaring nations. With one word, God silences them all. NOISE, NOISE, NOISE, then quiet! So quiet you could hear a pin drop because God had rebuked them and they were no more—Syria is destroyed. God removed them, with only a remnant left being chased far off.

God will judge the nations. He will rebuke those that go against His ways. In BUT GOD #94, we read He overthrows the wicked, and here we read He rebukes the nations. The end is coming and it is literally going to be life or death! Our Bridegroom is righteous and is coming back to reign in that righteousness. He will gather His elect out and rebuke the "goat nations" (#99). In Revelation 20:7-10 we read after one thousand years of Christ reigning and Satan being bound, Satan will be released again to deceive the nations. Revelation 20:14-15 reads that death and Hades are thrown into the lake of fire along with those who were not found in the Book of Life. It sounds like a comic book movie, but it actually will happen. Thankfully, our Bridegroom will be protecting us the whole time.

This is a reason to tell everyone you know about Jesus. Not to scare them into knowing Him, but to tell them that not knowing Him is forsaking their eternal inheritance and protection. God spoke into existence all creation, and with one word can rebuke it all and make it disappear. Thank goodness God loves us, not because of who we are, but because of who He is, and through our Bridegroom we are safe.

101. Will Not be Held Back by "Even Ifs"

"Can plunder be retrieved from a giant, prisoners of war gotten back from a tyrant? *But God* says, 'Even if a giant grips the plunder and a tyrant holds my people prisoner, I'm the one who's on your side, defending your cause, rescuing your children. And your enemies, crazed and desperate, will turn on themselves, killing each other in a frenzy of self-destruction. Then everyone will know that I, God, have saved you—I, the Mighty One of Jacob'" (Isaiah 49:24-26 MSG, emphasis added).

There are a million even ifs . . . even if things do not look perfect, even if you are divorced, even if you are broke, even if you made a bad decision. None of these excuses matter to God; as long as you are His child, He will make beauty out of ashes (Is 61:1-3). In the midst of our conflict, He has a plan. How we trust and rely on Him will determine our future.

My friend, Chantel, was told when she was thirteen years old that she had an unpleasant singing voice and that she should not pursue singing. Chantel loved to sing though and has an amazing talent to play the piano. She determined that *even if* the teacher thought she could not sing, she knew Jesus could help. So, she and her amazing mother started praying the Lord would give her that ability. Sure enough, He did, and she is now one of our church's favorite worship leaders! Her voice is so beautiful that she has accompanied Christian recording artist, Moriah Peters, in a few concerts.

My mother's best friend, Diane Hardesty, who is like my second mom and the one who led me to the Lord when I was eight, wanted to be a nurse. She knew that would be a challenge, but she was determined. *Even if* she was thirty-nine and had a family to take care of, unlike the 20-somethings in her class, she trusted God to hear her prayers and heart. By 45, she was finishing at the top of her class. She worked daily and prayed with her patients and their families who were on hospice care. Before retiring many years later, she had brought hope into the lives of many patients and led them to Jesus before they died.

My mother-in-law, Sherry, has been through a truck load of even ifs. She works at the church my husband and I grew up in and has always been a dedicated employee there. Within a ten year time span, she suffered a stroke, faced the brink of death from breast cancer, was cheated on by her husband of thirty-plus years, unwillingly divorced, watched her father die, and through it all only became more endearing to everyone. *Even though* she suffered through all the humiliation and medical problems and *even though* she walked through the valley of the shadow of death (Ps 23:4), God did not leave her. He defended her and gave her additional favor as she grew more intimate with the Lord after each battle. She has since been asked to speak at conferences and retreats to give her testimony on forgiveness, faith, and hope. *Even if* it is hard for her to understand why, she still gives glory to God and is an encouragement to everyone around her.

God does not give up. He does not think all is hopeless, letting the giant problems or the tyrants with harmful words and deeds win. He sticks by us (#48 and #54) to help (#17 and #86) and to defend. With His presence, the enemy cannot advance because they never beat God (#66). This makes the enemy frustrated and, in their desperation, they get crazy, turning on each other in self destruction. We all realize we would lose the battle without God's help. God is in the battle for the long haul; the enemy may seem to make some advances, but we should not let that be a reason for us to throw in the towel. God stays steady, winning one victory at a time until the final triumph. We need to stay in it with God, praying against evil and praising Him when we have a victory. God is on our side no matter how bad things look. He is the friend who sticks by us, the defense attorney, the warrior, the hero, and the military all wrapped in one on a rescue mission. *Even if* a giant comes at us, *even if* a tyrant imprisons us, *even if* the mountains fall into the sea, *even if* . . . whatever, we need to not let our faith be shaken.[75] God will save us from every circumstance so everyone will know He is God and He will get the glory!

102. Has His Glory Arise on Jerusalem

"[People Returning for the Reunion] Get out of bed, Jerusalem! Wake up. Put your face in the sunlight. God's bright glory has risen for you. The whole earth is wrapped in darkness, all people sunk in deep darkness, *But God* rises on you, His sunrise glory breaks over you. Nations will come to your light, kings to your sunburst brightness. Look up! Look around! Watch as they gather, watch as they approach you: Your sons coming from great distances, your daughters carried by their nannies. When you see them coming you'll smile—big smiles! Your heart will swell and, yes, burst! All those people returning by sea for the reunion, a rich harvest of exiles gathered in from the nations! And then streams of camel caravans as far as the eye can see, young camels of nomads in Midian and Ephah, Pouring in from the south from Sheba, loaded with gold and frankincense, preaching the praises of God. And yes, a great roundup of flocks from the nomads in Kedar and Nebaioth, Welcome gifts for worship at my altar as I bathe my glorious Temple in splendor" (Isaiah 60:1-7 MSG, emphasis added).

There is a song called, "Arise, Shine" and it happens to be taken from this verse in the Bible. Part of it goes like this: Arise shine, for the Light has come . . . and the glory of the Lord has risen over you. Have you ever had a certain song bring back a fond memory? How about a smell that reminds you of someone you once knew? Have you ever looked at pictures from a vacation when you had such a great time you could not wait to go back? I sometimes wonder if this is how God feels about Jerusalem. Psalm 132:7 reads that God's tabernacle is His footstool and in Isaiah 60:13 (NIV), God says He will make the place of His feet glorious. At one time

Jerusalem housed His permanent residence, thanks to David and Solomon (#57 and #59), and during David's reign it had nonstop worship day and night (1 Chron 15-16). It is the city where God's chosen people celebrated His feasts. In Ezekiel 5:5, God says He set Jerusalem in the center of the nations. It is believed by some scholars that God placed the foundational stone, the corner stone, for earth there. God has a lot of memories attached to that city. He has had His eye on it for such a long time, and Jesus said He longed to gather Jerusalem's children together as a hen gathers her chicks under her wings (Matt 23:37). Jesus will return to that city again someday soon (Zech 14).

In this BUT GOD, we see that all these people came to Jerusalem with camel caravans, bringing gold and other gifts. Many believe it is making two references. One reference may refer to the building of the second temple we discussed found in the book of Ezra (#62). Another reference may be speaking of a future prophecy where God is going to restore Jerusalem. He is raising up "one new man" (Eph 2:15-16 KJV) as "a rich harvest of exiles are gathered in from the nations" (excerpt from this BUT GOD verse). Israel will be restored completely, BUT GOD has allowed access for the Gentiles to be grafted in as well (Rom 11). In Luke 21:24 we read, ". . . Jerusalem will be trampled on by the Gentiles until the times of the Gentiles are fulfilled" (NIV). Then there will be signs in the sky and the Son of Man will return (Luke 21:25-28). Isaiah 60:3 refers to the Gentiles coming to its [Jerusalem's] light. Jerusalem's light is the Lord and God will be the glory of Jerusalem (Isaiah 60:19 NIV).

Since 1948, Israel has been reestablished; God promised they will not be uprooted again (Amos 9:14-15), and now, the restoration of the tabernacle of David has begun as the Jewish people return (making *aliyah*).[76] Amos 9:11 says God will restore David's tent as it used to be. Since 1967, Israel has had control over Jerusalem and they are not ever going to willingly give it up. There is no other city in the world that is more discussed and debated about than Jerusalem. Zechariah 12:3 says Jerusalem will become an issue for the world and that is definitely the case today. As the day of the Lord approaches it will be even more so.

There is something else significant about Jerusalem that is very important for the believer to understand. Jesus will not forcibly take the kingship over Israel. He will not come back to Jerusalem until the leaders of Israel ask Him to. Jesus said this in Matthew 23:39 when He quoted Psalm 118:26 (NKJV), ". . . you shall see Me no more till you say, 'Blessed is He who comes in the name of the Lord!'" Peter reaffirmed this by telling his brethren in Acts 3:19-21 to repent and be converted so that times of refreshing can come that God might send Jesus Christ. Jesus had already come once, and Israel is now reminded that He will come again. Israel's representatives have to repent and invite Jesus to be king. Satan's strategy is to keep the leaders of Israel from receiving Jesus as king. Satan will try to eliminate the Jewish race (throughout all history they have been persecuted—our previous generation saw it through Hitler and now we watch through radical Islam). If he can accomplish this or create offense toward Jesus, they will never receive Jesus as king. This is why Satan wants to control Jerusalem. Satan wants to stay out of eternal prison. The enemy desires extermination of the Jewish people so a remnant from Israel cannot invite Jesus to rule as their Messiah (Heb 2:1, Rev 12:13-17, Rev 20). This will not happen, though, as Zechariah 13:8-9 and Zechariah 14:2 say a remnant will be saved and they WILL call on His name.[77]

Acts 15:16-17 says Jesus will return to restore. The remnant and the Gentiles who bear His name will be able to seek His face. There are many places that are shadowing the tabernacle of David's 24/7 worship and prayer. One prominent establishment is in Kansas City, called the International House of Prayer. My friend, Dava, took me there and it was amazing! They are forerunners to the Lord's return and are providing people the opportunity to join in preparing the way of the Lord. Jesus will completely restore David's tabernacle when He returns as He establishes His righteous governmental rule over the world. We, the bride, need to pray for Israel (Ps 122:6, Is 40:1-2, Is 62:11-12). We need to be the watchmen on Jerusalem's wall, praying consistently until ". . . He establishes Jerusalem and makes her the praise of the earth" (Is 62:6-7). We want to usher in our Bridegroom's return.

103. Is Real and Living

"*But God* is the real thing—the living God, the eternal
King. When he's angry, Earth shakes. Yes, and the godless
nations quake" (Jeremiah 10:10 MSG, emphasis added).

I know God is real because I have conversations with Him daily;
I hear Him through my spirit and I hear Him through the Word.
God's not dead—He is alive! We serve a living God, not a wood
or a metal statue. Statue idols of anything are worthless, have no
breath, and cannot talk to you, bring you good luck, or save you
(Jer 10). God does not want us to make a statue of Him and bow
at its feet; He wants us to bow our hearts, wherever we may be,
when we feel His presence with us. The reason God did not let
the Israelites see an image of Him in the pillar of fire at night or
the cloud by day is because He knew they would probably make
some image to worship in its likeness (Deut 4:15-16). I think that
could also be the reason God buried Moses' bones (Deut 34:4-6).
This way, the Israelites would not know where Moses' body was
and could not be deceived by Satan into worshiping his grave as a
shrine (Jude 1:9).

Idols are not only man-made objects. An idol can be anything
that becomes more important to you than it should be. We need
to keep in perspective that we have a very jealous God (Deut.
4:24). He wants to be number one in our lives, and when things
start competing with His time with you, or push you out of His
alignment, He will make you well aware of the issue and may have
a very real conversation with you. I can say this from experience,
because it happened to me.

Many years ago I had a bad habit, and one day decided to let
it slide into my Jesus time. It was on that particular day, in that
moment, when God decided to address it. I was doing my Bible
study, listening to worship music, *and* watching a soap opera
on TV all simultaneously. I am sure you can see the problem;
my choice in the TV program was conflicting with my biblical
principles. I had been feeling a tugging about it for a while, but
kept dismissing the feeling. The problem was that it had become
too important to me. Every day, this show had been dictating my

life in an unhealthy way, just like an idol. I scheduled things around it so I would not miss an episode, and it caused me to have false expectations of how romantic my life should be. God interrupted my distracted studies and spoke directly to my heart. He said very clearly, "We have a good relationship Tina, but if we are to go any further, you have to give this up." Turning off the TV was no problem because it was with the notion that I would do my Bible study and then just watch the show later on a recording. Well, as you can imagine, that did not fly. The Lord then said, "That is not what I meant, I want you to give it up the whole way."

It was hard at first to let go, but then I realized I needed to decide what was more important—a real, living, personal relationship with my heavenly Bridegroom, or a fake reality in a box? There really was no comparison. Then He said, "You need to repeat after me, out loud, that you are going to give it all up." If I said it out loud, I knew I was going to have to keep my word, which is exactly why those instructions were given. After trying to negotiate and receiving no lenience, my heart began to understand the importance of this moment, so I let the show go and let the Lord rule. Next, He led me in what I was to say. He would speak and then He waited for me to repeat what He said. I affirmed how and why I was going to give up the show. He even went so far as to make me verbally agree to not pick up a soap opera magazine during checkout in the grocery store just to see the story line!

Immediately after our "talk," I moved on and decided to turn up the music and worship the Lord. One of the first few songs I sang was from David Crowder Band called "No One Like You."[78] I had heard it on the radio many times so I knew the words, but it was the first time I had listened to it on my iPod. I sang the verses out loud as the song started, but to my surprise, when I began to sing the chorus, Jesus joined in with me! As I sang to Him that there was no one like Him, He sang back to me that there was no one like me! I was laughing and smiling every time the chorus came up because never before had He actually sung *with* me. The song ended and all of a sudden a voice said, "That was terrific! We should sing together more often!" That was the first time I heard those words on this song before. My mouth dropped to the floor! I made the song play again so I could see if that was just my imagination. Those words came on again! I was beside myself! How cool was that? That was not a random coincidence; it was a specific message for me. God just proved, within moments of my decision, how much more fun we were going to have together because I chose Him over the soap opera. Just so you know, I kept my word and have not ever watched or read about the soaps again. I am so glad the Lord set me free.

Only Yahweh will take that kind of personal interest in your well being; no other god is going to have a conversation with you about what you should watch or sing with you about how special He made you. Remember your Bridegroom knows that "There has never ever been anyone like you!" and He wants you to know that about Him as well. He is the only Living God. Have you ever noticed that His chosen nation, Israel, is so similar to the words IS-REAL. God Is Real!

104. Is the Creator / Is the Only God with Power, Wisdom, and Understanding

"*But God* made the earth by his power; He founded the world by his wisdom and stretched out the heavens by his understanding" (Jeremiah 10:12 NIV, emphasis added). *Also found in the NLT.

Colossians 1:16 reminds us all things are created through God and for God. God is full of power that creates something from nothing. Do you have that kind of power? Is anyone able to make a living human being from dirt? God created the world with wisdom (#95) and the universe with understanding (#56). Knowing facts give you wisdom, but applying that information requires understanding. God has both! He knows all the scientific facts about space velocity, gravity, and measurements because He is wise. He knows how to prevent all the planets traveling through space from running into each other because He has understanding. He can apply wisdom and understanding in our everyday lives because He used them to create us. Though Jesus already had understanding before He enveloped His likeness in human flesh, we are comforted knowing He experienced firsthand all of our weaknesses and can sympathize with us (Heb 4:15).

God told Solomon to ask for whatever he wanted God to give to him. Solomon knew how important a discerning heart would be to govern God's people, especially because he was still young, so that was what he asked for. God was so pleased with his request, He gave him both wisdom and understanding, as well as fame, riches, etc. (1 Kings 3). Solomon's wisdom was known throughout the land and rulers from other nations came to visit him. Many of Solomon's bits of wisdom are found in the book of Proverbs.

In this BUT GOD verse, Jeremiah compared who our God is in contrast with any other thing called a god. Atheists would have you believe there is no God. Kris Vallotton from Bethel Church had a clever quote: "Atheists have to believe in God in order to make Him disappear." It takes more faith to *not* believe in God than *to* believe.

Allah, Buddah, Baal the sun god, Moloch, Remphan, Asherah, Krishna or other Hindu gods, the Dalai Lama, Greek gods, emperors, pharaohs, cosmic powers, and any other false authorities that have been erected by man did NOT create anything and will NOT save anybody. These are evil spirits who manipulate humanity through their unmitigated lies. Throughout the years of our civilization, they have weaseled their way into the system. When people talk about reincarnation and give details of their past lives, all I see is an evil spirit manifesting in the person and feeding him lies.[79] Statues are made of material (wood, metal, plastic, etc.) and are worshipped as if they embody the real thing. Remember the Mount Carmel showdown with Elijah and the priests of Baal (#52)? Our God showed up mightily to prove His existence with all odds against Him. The priests of Baal had nothing to show for it. All gods besides Yahweh are frauds and will burn up becoming extinct; they do not have anything worthy of praise. They are only around to be distractions from honoring the one true living God.

People have an innate ability to worship because we were made to worship the One who created us. Yahweh has made it clear in His Word that He loves His children and He loves the fragrance of worship and prayers. Unfortunately, some people insist on worshipping and sacrificing to a false god, but there is no satisfaction found because they are lacking the mutual connection you can only find with the one, true God. We were not made to worship the one who fell from heaven and who wanted to be like God. Somehow Satan has finagled his way into getting that worship from people who think they know the truth, but they are only being greatly deceived by the great deceiver himself. Satan wants to be worshipped, but as long as God does not receive glory either, there is no need for him to intervene in our already sinful lives.

If you think you have gained any wisdom from a god other than the God of Israel, Adonai, than it is from an imposter inhabited by an evil spirit. They are leading you astray from the truths God wants to impart to you. If an unbeliever was truly searching and asking Jesus sincerely if He is real, God would absolutely show up to let them feel His love. Jesus is waiting for the opportunity to tell us all how much He loves us. He will say it or show us in a personal way because He is a personal Savior, not a public figure on display. Do not trade the real God for a fake god. Do not worship a god that was manmade instead of the God that made man (Rom 1:22-25).

Currently, if you are not accepting of the terms the enemy has made popular like "coexist" or "tolerance," then you are categorized as being intolerant or against peace. Paul tells us in 1 Thessalonians 5:12-22 to live in peace, warn those who are unruly, and see to it that no one delivers evil for evil, but pursue what is good, and abstain from all evil. To be tolerant means you believe all truth is personal and people can believe whatever feels right and is best for them; there are no absolutes. I cringe every time I see a bumper sticker with the word "coexist" on it with the letters transformed into religious symbols spelling out the word. We are not called to "coexist," we are called to "come out from among them and be separate . . ." (2 Cor 6:17 NKJV). At the end of time we do not want to hear God say to us, "Well, you blended in really well." No! The ploys creating these words to be popular are by the enemy himself trying to make the believer compromise or look bad by not agreeing.

People are expected to tolerate and coexist with anything except God or Jesus, and His commands found in the Bible. This is the one thing Christians should not be tolerant of! We know that there is an absolute authority (God) and there is only one way to Him (through His Son, Jesus). He has clearly defined right and wrong. Christians cannot compromise the Word of God or silently stand by as they hear lies being fed to nonbelievers seeking truth. God has given us the "mind of Christ," and God's Spirit helps us understand spiritual things, so let us share His wisdom with those who are lost (Philippians 2:1-11, 1 Cor 2:12-16)! At the same time, we need to keep in mind that the Scripture say not to quarrel, but be gentle to all (1 Pet 3:15-17). In humility we are to correct those in opposition. God may grant them repentance and then they will come to their senses (2 Tim 2:24-26).

On September 11, 2012, the Libya US Embassy was raided and attacked, killing the US ambassador and others. The US Secretary of State, Hillary Clinton, reported in her speech given after the attacks urging the audience "not to be discouraged by the hatred and violence that exists, but instead resolve to do something tangible to promote religious tolerance in their own communities."[80] This situation turned out to be a terrorist attack which the government tried to cover up by blaming it on what they called an "intolerant" video. If we keep promoting religious tolerance, radical Muslims will continue to strike until they have made everyone submit to what they want. Radical or not, Islam's objective is to dominate, not coexist. We will not let a false religion claim their god is creator as well. Yahweh is the one true Creator. It is by His power, wisdom, and understanding that all things came into existence. John 1:1-14 tells us that Jesus was the Word that became flesh and dwelt among us and that all things were made through Him. The Bible is not corrupted, it speaks the truth of the Word of the only God, who was and is and is to come.

It is true that America is known for its freedom. That freedom allows people to have a choice about their beliefs. The Bible itself also shows us that we have freedoms. It is up to each individual to choose which options they will believe. Joshua 24:15 says, "But if serving the LORD seems undesirable to you, then choose for yourselves this day whom you will serve, whether the gods your ancestors served beyond the Euphrates, or the gods of the Amorites, in whose land you are living. But as for me and my household, we will serve the LORD" (NIV).

105. Is Here / Is Faithful / Does not Wander

"We know we're guilty. We've lived bad lives—but do something, God. Do it for your sake! Time and time again we've betrayed you. No doubt about it—we've sinned against you. Hope of Israel! Our only hope! Israel's last chance in this trouble! Why are you acting like a tourist, taking in the sights, here today and gone tomorrow? Why do you just stand there and stare, like someone who doesn't know what to do in a crisis? *But God*, you are, in fact, here, here with us! You know who we are—you named us! Don't leave us in the lurch." (Jeremiah 14:7-9 MSG, emphasis added).

God let Jeremiah know the future events that would be coming against Judah, and in this BUT GOD verse, Jeremiah prayed to God to not let it be. Jeremiah stood in the gap trying to intercede on his nation's behalf. That is what we all should do as believers: pray, especially when He has given you a specific word for an upcoming circumstance. The problem was that in Jeremiah 11:14 and Jeremiah 14:11, God told Jeremiah not to pray for the good of the people because they had broken the covenant with Him by worshipping false gods. God was not going to accept their offering or hear their cry because their hearts were full of iniquity (Ps 66:18) and He had already established judgment already.

We read in 2 Kings 21:10-15 and Jeremiah 15:4 it was because of the sins King Mannasseh had committed that God had to wipe Jerusalem and Judah clean. Mannasseh had done every abominable thing and made all Judah sin with him. In 2 Kings 20:16-18, God had determined this judgment was going to happen already and had his prophet, Isaiah, tell King Hezekiah (Mannasseh's father) during his reign. God's righteous anger (#26) was justified and He told his prophets what He was going to do. We read proof these events came to pass in 2 Kings 24:2-4 when the Chaldeans, Syrians, Moabites, and people of Ammom came and destroyed Judah. Then King Nebuchadnezzar of Babylon besieged Jerusalem and carried everything away (2 Kings 24-25). To read a firsthand account of some of the things God's people went through while living in captivity, read the book of Daniel. There were no BUT GODs in that book, but there were some very good BUT GOD moments!

Jeremiah's heart was in the right place in that he tried to talk God out of this tragic judgment, but remember God will have the final say (#93), and if His ways are not kept, He will remove leaders (#60). God was extremely upset with the children of Israel; they kept being influenced by the society around them. God told Jeremiah that Israel loved to wander away from His ordinances. Their kings continued to go astray and the Israelites would follow, even when it was in direct conflict with what God said to do. The king was supposed to lead his people righteously; he was supposed to be doing what God directed. Instead, kings continued to let the power go to their heads and as a result brought everyone down with them in their bad decisions.

Jeremiah knew God was mighty and did not want Him to reject His people and refuse to help. God would not help, though, because He turned Israel over to the things they loved more than Him. Those things gave the enemy access into their hearts (#88). God had promised punishment if they did not repent. Deuteronomy 28 lists out the blessings for obedience and curses for disobedience. Remember the verse I quoted in the beginning of the study? Exodus 34:7b says God "punishes the children and their children for the sin of the parents to the third and fourth generation" (NIV). God followed through with His words, and reminded them it was because of King Mannasseh, as I discussed.

God allowed the consequences to happen, but had every intention of setting things right again. If a wife kept cheating on her husband over and over, there would be consequences. It would be ludicrous to expect her husband to not be upset. That is what happened with God's people. God was Israel's husband and He was going to speak up in a way that made a difference in his wife's decisions. God will never cheat on His people; our Bridegroom will never cheat on His bride. He will always be faithful and true; He will not wander (2 Tim 2:13).

106. Knows When We Help and Share His Word
"[Giving Everything Away for Nothing] Unlucky mother— that you had me as a son, given the unhappy job of indicting the whole country! I've never hurt or harmed a soul, and yet everyone is out to get me. *But, God* knows, I've done everything I could to help them, prayed for them and against their enemies. I've always been on their side, trying to stave off disaster. God knows how I've tried!" (Jeremiah 15:10-11 MSG, emphasis added).

Poor Jeremiah! He was despised by his people. He never prophesied good news to them. He only told them of God's impending judgment, and the people had enough of it. Jeremiah would have rather said nothing than continued bad news, but when he was quiet, he felt as if he was burning on the inside and had to let it out (Jer 20:9). He never physically harmed anyone, but his condemning words caused the hatred of the Israelites toward him. They were not interested in hearing about all their sins and would rather Jeremiah stay quiet. All Jeremiah wanted to do was try to help his people; he tried to stop the impending destruction. He interceded for them, as we saw in BUT GOD #105, and he tried to talk God out of His decision.

Jeremiah felt bad for his country, but also for his mother. As a parent, it is true you do not want anyone disliking your child. You do not want people coming up to you and asking what is wrong with your son and why he says the things he does. I wonder how Jeremiah's mother felt, whether she was supportive or embarrassed. Since the people of God were enjoying a lifestyle full of sin, it was difficult to hear that they needed to change their ways. As a child of God, though, their spirit should have already been conflicting within them. I wonder if the Israelites could feel any struggle within at this point since they had closed their ears to hearing from the Lord for so long. They had grown so distant that they only knew *of* God rather than knowing God. They must have liked the way their lives were going and did not want to change. I do not think the Israelites believed the impending disaster was coming as soon as it was, if they even believed it at all. They were acting so much like the pagan nations around them that it was hard to distinguish that they were the nation supposed to show others God's holy ways.

As believers, our core values come into direct conflict with what is accepted as tolerable in our society (#104). We see backlash immediately if one person gives an opinion that is not the standard anymore, even though that opinion was the majority when this country was founded. It is as if society has flipped their morals and what was good is now bad and what was bad is now good (Is 5:20). Take, for example, Kirk Cameron's appearance on CNN's Piers Morgan show, on March 2, 2012. He was asked what his opinion was on gay marriage. Kirk stated he did not agree with it and that he believed what the Bible said—one man for one woman (Matt 19:3-6). The media attacked him immediately for weeks after. There was also a backlash against the fast-food chain Chick-Fil-A in July 2012 when the president of this Christian company (which is closed on Sundays) said they supported "the biblical definitions of the family unit." Thankfully, many Christian families waited hours in line at their restaurants in an effort to show their support, and the business was blessed as a result. Yet, another example is the comparison of two sports stars. As one internet picture I saw posted, the football star is bashed for being a Christian and promoting a Bible verse while the basketball star is praised for announcing his homosexuality. The Bible tells us that the world will hate us, so we should not be shocked when it happens.

As the bride of Christ, we need to be doing everything we can to help the lost. We need to intercede for the ones who are potentially going to be part of our spiritual family. Our Bridegroom has enabled us to hear His voice, so when we hear Him, we need to be willing to share what He wants us to say. Jesus is also very aware of what we are doing. Remember, Psalm 139 tells us our Bridegroom knows everything about us. He knows when we have tried our best to help people; He knows when we have found ways to bring Him up in our conversations. He knows everything about us, and will reward us for our efforts.

107. Is a Fierce Warrior at Our Side

"*But God*, a most fierce warrior, is at my side. Those who are after me will be sent sprawling—Slapstick buffoons falling all over themselves, a spectacle of humiliation no one will ever forget" (Jeremiah 20:11 MSG, emphasis added).

As we have previously discussed, Jeremiah was in constant conflict about having to deliver "bad news." He knew that people mocked him and waited for him to stumble so they could take revenge on him for all he said (even though it was really what God said). Actually, this is precisely what all the religious leaders did to Jesus. They were always trying to trick Him with their questions, but Jesus was too smart for them. Jeremiah was put in jail because of his prophesies by a priest who was also the chief governor (Jer 20:2). In the New Testament, we read that Jesus' disciples Peter, Paul, and John were also all put in jail at various times because of what they preached.

Jeremiah cursed the day he was born and wished his mother's womb had been his grave (Jer 20:17 KJV). Talk about a bad case of depression! Ultimately, Jeremiah knew that God deserved praise because no matter how much emotional suffering he went through on earth, he knew God would not leave his side.

Like we discussed in BUT GOD #106, the world wants us to tolerate everything—except a Biblical viewpoint, of course. I think people today would persecute and attack Jeremiah just like they did in his time. Jeremiah would have thrown a holy fit if he could see how America has digressed in its morals and values. There are laws that legalize gay relationships and laws that allow a quick divorce at a moment's notice with or without a justified reason. It seems that children in some public schools can go to a special place to worship Allah, but to pray to Yahweh or speak Jesus' name is somehow a violation. My mom has told me that she learned great Bible songs at school, but that is no longer allowed. Even saying the Pledge of Allegiance and keeping God's name in it can cause controversy. Why is it that Bibles are encouraged to be read in jails, but not in schools? Schools will not allow the Ten Commandments to be displayed because the students might willingly read or obey them, but if students do not willingly follow many of them, they may become a menace to society resulting in jail time. Maybe there would be less people in jail if the Bible was seen as an acceptable and positive reinforcement in our schools. Many of our country's founders agreed that the Bible was the best schoolbook in the world. David Barton of Wall Builders Ministry has fascinating evidence of this, along with other quotes and manuscripts from our founding fathers proving that "the Bible is the Rock on which our Republic rests" (President Andrew Jackson).[81]

The Bible's principles on how to live a holy life are being made a mockery of. Our legislators have legalized abominations; laws that clearly go against God's Word are now accepted regularly in society without hesitation. Our nation was built on God's principles, and as the years go by, many leaders have allowed statutes to pass that are against our Christian beliefs. Laws now protect an unborn eagle, but not hundreds of thousands of unborn babies about to be aborted. How have we fallen so far? Kirk Cameron has a movie out called "Monumental," which shows the truths of how our country was founded on biblical principles and how those truths are now inaccurately being rewritten.[82] I would strongly recommend you take a look when you have time.

The way in which Jeremiah wrote this BUT GOD verse reminded me of how David wrote in the Psalms (#72). Just like David recorded that his enemies came after him and that he wanted God's protection and vengeance, so too did Jeremiah. Even though David poured out his problems and what was on his heart, he also gave praises to God about who He was, like Jeremiah did here and elsewhere. Jeremiah knew God's character; he knew what a strong and mighty warrior God is. God is advanced in the way He targets His enemies. This includes any who come after His people who are doing His business.

When people are after us and are making a mockery about what we say and believe, it is hard to not have hurt feelings. You wish those people would just go away, but instead most get louder and meaner as time goes by, especially if you continue to speak truth. The Israelites showed no sign of repentance, otherwise they would not have been so hard to Jeremiah. Their only goal seemed to be to make him feel like an outcast. When you feel alone, it is hard to find friends, but Jeremiah knew he had the ultimate Friend at his side. We too have the ultimate friend in Christ. He will be a warrior for us; He will always stand up for us. He will defend in a way that will make the wise seem foolish. He will stay at our side (just like a perfect Bridegroom would), making sure we know we are not alone. He will not abandon us and said He would be with us always (# 73 and Matt 28:20). We don't need to pray for Him to come into our midst, He is already here! If we don't feel His presence than our feelings are lying. He is fully with us one hundred percent of the time.

108. Sends a Steady Stream of Information

"Not only that *but God* also sent a steady stream of prophets to you who were just as persistent as me, and you never listened. They told you, 'Turn back—right now, each one of you!—from your evil way of life and bad behavior, and live in the land God gave you and your ancestors, the land he intended to give you forever. Don't follow the god-fads of the day, taking up and worshiping these no-gods. Don't make me angry with your god-businesses, making and selling gods—a dangerous business!'" (Jeremiah 25:4-6 MSG, emphasis added).

We see in this BUT GOD a reminder of the numerous times the Lord had sent His people prophets to remind them to do what was right. He sent a steady stream of them, some of which we have read about in the previous BUT GODs. In Jeremiah 25, he is being very specific about what exactly is to come, even to the point of saying how long they will serve the king of Babylon after they have been taken away in captivity—seventy years (Jer 25:11-12)![83]

In Jeremiah 24, we learn about the sign of two baskets of figs and what it meant. One basket had good fruit and one had bad fruit. The Lord said He would acknowledge the captives from Judah who were good and let them know Him, as opposed to those He would deliver into times of trouble. The "bad figs" were the ones who did not listen and stop their bad behavior as this BUT GOD verse discusses.

Daniel and his friends must have been some of the "good figs." The Lord gave Daniel wisdom and favor. He even opened Daniel's eyes to understand the Scriptures so he could encourage his people. Daniel 9:1-2 says it was in the first year of Darius when Daniel's eyes were open to know about the seventy years Jeremiah had foretold. This tells me it was not common knowledge for everyone and the Lord was blessing His faithful servant Daniel with insight. Daniel 9 goes on to say that he prayed and interceded for his nation and reminded God of His covenant. He did this while living in the midst of Babylon.

Beth Moore's Bible study on Daniel discusses that we too live in a society much like Babylon. Everything in our society is how to better our "self"—how to be younger, prettier, and smarter. That is the kind of people King Nebuchadnezzar wanted in his kingdom (Dan 1:2-6). These days our society moves pretty fast. Just think of how quickly information is exchanged via the internet and smart phones. The shipping/trucking/consumer industry replenishes inventory promptly as it is moved off the shelves. Even modern medicine has made swift advances. Getting from place to place, our money spending, gossip spreading, and our days go by so fast. Do you understand what I am saying? When we see something we want, most just go get it, whether it is within the budget or not. When we decide to ride this merry-go-round lifestyle, it is hard to get off. Unfortunately, many of us are on this ride and do not even realize it. Things are so convenient it is imperative we stop and examine what we are filling our days with—things of God or things of this world (remember #92).

As His bride, we have the Holy Spirit to remind us to do what is right. Do not be so quick to dismiss that little voice inside of you giving you a nudge. With practice, you will develop a keen ear to the Holy Spirit's warnings and learn to discern when traps are being set against you by the enemy. His traps are enticing, but will trick you into wrong thinking. Do not be so quick to say "yes" to something when the Holy Spirit is saying "no." Do not get so caught up in your lifestyle that it too becomes a trap.

We need to take an inventory of who is in our lives. Do we have a steady stream of people who are pointing us to Jesus, people who are influencing our lives in a positive way? The Bible reminds us to meet together and encourage one another to do good (Heb 10:24-25). When you meet together regularly in a small group for Bible study or at church, you are reminded to live godly lives, but when you do not, you are putting yourself in a position to be attacked spiritually. Satan likes you to isolate yourself so he can implant lies into your life. Consequently, there is no one around to discuss thoughts or problems with you, pray for you, or hold you accountable for your actions on a consistent basis.

Being intentional in meeting together regularly is different than just hanging out with your friends, because when you go to church or Bible study, there is a constant theme: God. You will not be sidetracked at these meetings and talk about your family, the weather, or your summer plans the whole time. You will all be gathered for the one common purpose of worshipping God and learning more about Him and experiencing Him, which in turn, will influence how you live your life. Our Bridegroom is great at sending people our way to point us to Him. It is up to us as His bride to recognize when it happens and to hear the Holy Spirit's whispers. He is looking for the "good figs" to put in His basket, and you, bride of Christ, should be praying that the basket fills up so much it overflows!

109. Restores

"Again, God's Message: 'Listen to this! Laments coming out of Ramah, wild and bitter weeping. It's Rachel weeping for her children, Rachel refusing all solace. Her children are gone, gone—long gone into exile.' *But God* says, 'Stop your incessant weeping, hold back your tears. Collect wages from your grief work.' God's Decree. 'They'll be coming back home! There's hope for your children.' God's Decree" (Jeremiah 31:15-17 MSG, emphasis added).

One of the most famous verses in the Old Testament is found in Jeremiah 29:11-14. These were words sent to the captives from Jeremiah. It says the Lord knows the thoughts He has toward them of peace and prosperity and has plans to give them a future and a hope. He will bring them back from captivity to the place where they were taken from. This is a picture of restoration just as the above BUT GOD verse is. He is always looking to give us a better future; He corrects in order to bring our thoughts back in accordance with His will. He wants to bring us back to a place that is fully restored. He will bring the captives back to the land and their hearts will be right before Him. He is going to give them a fresh new start.

This BUT GOD verse is also repeated in the New Testament. Remember that we discussed BUT GOD #21, where there was a massacre of death? One of those times is found in Matthew 2:16-18 when King Herod ordered all the male baby boys to be killed in Bethlehem in an attempt to get rid of baby Jesus. That New Testament verse quotes our Old Testament BUT GOD verse, saying prophecy was fulfilled. I cannot even imagine having my baby boy taken from me and murdered. That would be awful! No wonder there was great mourning and moms refusing to be comforted. There is no good found in evil. Satan knew who Jesus was and tried to destroy Him using Herod as his pawn. Thankfully, an angel told Joseph to flee to Egypt for a time until the angel said it was safe for them to return.

I love how the Bible weaves all the verses together so that the theme continues to flow. The verse in the book of Matthew was when Jesus was born. The reason He came the first time was to *restore* our relationship with our heavenly Father and begin to *restore* the kingdom of God! This BUT GOD verse also shows restoration so you can see how both of the verses interrelate and why they are connected together. God's decree is now fulfilled in that we will be "coming back home" to Him. There is hope for us and "hope for our children," who are our future. We know one of our Bridegroom's top priorities for His return is to restore all things back to how they should be on this earth and take His rightful place as King. I cannot wait to see what Earth is going to look like once it is restored and inhabited by our King Jesus.

110. Hides Us / Is Our Deliverer

"Neither the king nor any of his officials showed the slightest twinge of conscience as they listened to the messages read. Elnathan, Delaiah, and Gemariah tried to convince the king not to burn the scroll, but he brushed them off. He just plowed ahead and ordered Prince Jerahameel, Seraiah son of Azriel, and Shelemiah son of Abdeel to arrest Jeremiah the prophet and his secretary Baruch. *But God* had hidden them away" (Jeremiah 36:24-26 MSG, emphasis added).

The Lord told Jeremiah to get a scroll and write all the words that God had told him concerning Israel, Judah, and all the nations. So, Jeremiah dictated all this to his assistant Baruch. The words were read to the people in hopes that they would turn from their evil ways. When word got to the princes, they told Baruch and Jeremiah to hide so no one would know where they were. The scroll was placed in a scribe's chamber. When King Jehoiakim heard of the scroll, he sent for it to be read to him. Each time a part was read, the king would cut it up and throw it into the fire. He did not repent or show fear of the Lord and he tried to seize Baruch and Jeremiah.

God's Word is living and active (Heb 4:12 NIV). It cannot become extinct if someone tries to get rid of it or burn it up; we have it etched in our hearts. The king made a grave mistake not taking this seriously. We should always take God's Word seriously, especially if He continues to warn us. Not only did the king think his deeds were inconsequential, but he thought he could jail the ones providing the truth. I believe this king was having a power trip and allowed an evil spirit to use him to obliterate God's Word. The king did not even listen to people trying to advise him.

When troubles arise, God is our hiding place. We have discussed this before in BUT GOD #89. The Lord has promised to be our shelter when we run to Him for safety, and here is a beautiful example of God following through with this promise. God promised to protect Jeremiah, and He did many times, including this moment. Jeremiah did the job God asked him, knowing full well he would not win any popularity contest. Jeremiah knew involving himself in people's personal business could expose him to peril, but took the gamble anyway, risking his well being, because he was willing to go on this journey with God. Just as the prophet, Elijah, spoke the Word of God and then was threatened to be silenced by Jezebel, so to Jeremiah gave the Word of God and it was followed by a spirit that wanted to destroy that Word. God hid Jeremiah, just like He previously hid Elijah because there was still more work to be done (#52). Also, remember God kept David safe as he hid from Saul. David had friends, like Jonathan, for support, just as Jeremiah and Baruch had each other (#41 and #80). Only God has the power to keep us safe and alive at all times.

There are troubles that we create on our own, troubles the enemy initiates against us, and trials from the Lord to refine us (which at the time might seem like troubles).[84] Jeremiah was facing trouble launched by the enemy and God shielded him from it. Jesus is our Deliverer in times of trouble. We will feel His strength around us and an inexplicable peace if we completely put our trust in Him. Sometimes life does not seem fair, and sometimes it seems as if He is not sheltering us because bad things are still happening. Things may not go the way you planned, and you may never know why until you ask Him face to face, but He cares about you and makes sure your essentials are taken care of. He cares about you by protecting you in ways you will never even know. Maybe your business did not succeed because He was preventing a lawsuit from coming against you that would take away everything you had. Maybe you did not make the team because He has a better position for you. Maybe you got dumped so you could be with the one God originally intended for you. Second Corinthians 1:4 says, "He comforts us in all our troubles so that we can comfort others. When they are troubled, we will be able to give them the same comfort God has given us" (NLT). He protects us as we hide in His shelter, and He may use that time to comfort us so we will be trained to comfort others.

When Jesus taught us how to pray in Matthew 6:5-15, He said to go into a secret place, to hide away. This way we do not draw attention to ourselves and God can meet with us without interruption. He wants us to hide away so His glory can be revealed through us (we die to our old self so He can shine in us). Jesus said to pray for God to "deliver us from evil." Sometimes, like in Jeremiah's case, He hides us away to protect us from evil because He is delivering us. I love Chris Tomlin's song "My Deliverer" from his album *Hello Love*.[85] I think it goes perfect with this BUT GOD verse. Set some time aside to listen to it today and reflect on how God has delivered you.

111. Encourages Us Before He Brings Change

"*But God* says, 'Look around. What I've built I'm about to wreck, and what I've planted I'm about to rip up. And I'm doing it everywhere—all over the whole earth! So forget about making any big plans for yourself. Things are going to get worse before they get better. But don't worry. I'll keep you alive through the whole business'" (Jeremiah 45:4-5 MSG, emphasis added).

Jeremiah 45 does not flow with any particular story; it is random information God decided needed to be placed in the midst of Jeremiah's book, and we are about to see why. This verse has very timely information in it for us today! For some reason, Baruch (Jeremiah's scribe) was feeling down. This is where we see our BUT GOD verse come to play. Jeremiah has been prophesying about God's judgment coming to Israel, and because God is compassionate, he had Jeremiah deliver a personal word to his scribe to uplift his spirit. Even though the Lord told him that things were about to come undone around him, God also encouraged him with the promise that he would maintain his life through it all.

I have said before that when things get dark around us, we need to not fear because we know God's glory is going to come next. If God chooses to show up in the darkest hour, it is only to show us how glorious His holiness is when contrasted against everything that is unholy, unclean, or untrue.

Things are going to get worse before they get better. Many of us have heard this phrase before. How many times have we been involved in such a mess that it took a ridiculous amount of time to sort through all the muck. This can be physically, spiritually, emotionally, professionally, or personally such as basic everyday living. For example, as I am writing this section of the study, I am also in the midst of cleaning out my house. I have huge piles of knick-knacks, clothes, trash, and other miscellaneous items from emptying every drawer from furniture we wanted to move or get rid of. Now that the furniture is moved around where I want it, there is a huge mess to sort through. Thankfully, God has given me a great friend, Deena, who loves to organize and help me out (He surrounds us with help #80). I know when we are done my home will be a better space to live in.

Just as my house needed to be cleaned from the clutter, so our lives do as well. Our bodies are the temple of the Lord where the Holy Spirit resides. God does not want our lives and bodies to be cluttered down with big plans (#92) and unclean thoughts. We have to sort through the mess to filter out the junk. Once we are clean, the Holy Spirit will have a better space to live in and will use us more efficiently. Remember all that we learned in the book of Job (#63-#70). Even though Job was a righteous man, God allowed areas in his life to be refined as Job withstood Satan's horrendous fury against him. God kept him alive throughout it all just as he will do for Baruch.

My friend, Debbie, is an example of Jesus using someone efficiently. Though God intends and desires for us to be healthy, our bodies do not always stay that way for various reasons. Debbie has overcome many obstacles that have proclaimed death and bondage in her life. Her doctors are amazed that she is still living; cancer was expected to have overtaken her by now. She faced the worst before she got physically better. She has endured extensive surgeries—one even lasted fifteen hours! Despite these painful treatments, Debbie gives God the glory with full confidence knowing that the Lord has strategically placed her in situations where divine appointments could take place.

Before one of Debbie's surgeries, the Lord showed me she was like Jonah—she was going into the belly of the whale. However, it was not because she rebelled, but it was because it was how He was going to transport her to a new destination (Jonah 1:17-2:10). God was going to use what the enemy intended as a weapon to destroy her to be flipped around to help heal her and others. Jonah was in the big fish for three days, BUT because of that, the town of Nineveh listened to him all the more. This was because of the way he was *delivered*. You see, a fish was a "god" in Nineveh.[86] That made him credible to them. Through his personal experience, he had the ear and attention of those who would have never listened before. Of course, he also had God's favor on him, as does Debbie. Debbie has the ear of those going through life-threatening diseases that would not have opened their eyes to God's goodness unless she had been there to testify to them. Satan tried to steal her life, BUT GOD has "kept her alive through the whole business" so she could be a comfort to others (#110). Through her testimony, the Holy Spirit speaks and intervenes in lives that are otherwise hopeless and full of despair!

Whether God is about to wreck us or the things around us for His glory, He wants us to be encouraged that He is fully aware of the state of our well being. When Jesus comes back, He will destroy what is unrighteous. This is what God was going to do in the land of Judah and what He was warning through Jeremiah. God does not want anything holding us back from being obedient to His ways. He wants His bride to live in a glorified and holy place where there is no mess to clean up afterward. Jeremiah 18 tells us that God is the Potter making vessels of clay. The New Testament refers to our bodies as these vessels (2 Tim 2:21 KJV). God wants to make sure His vessels rely on Him alone. God's vessels may receive great power and insight, but they need to remember it comes from God. It is about bringing glory to the treasure that is inside, which is Jesus, and not to the vessel itself (1 Cor 1:26-31, 2

Cor 4:7). Jesus wants to be able to trust us to live in the strategic places so we can be a living example of what a pure, holy vessel looks like. Even when there is danger we will be a living example of what Psalm 91 says.

112. Has His Hand on Us

"The Spirit lifted me and took me away. I went bitterly and angrily. I didn't want to go. *But God* had me in his grip. I arrived among the exiles who lived near the Kebar River at Tel Aviv. I came to where they were living and sat there for seven days, appalled" (Ezekiel 3:14-15 MSG, emphasis added).

Well, we get one BUT GOD verse in Ezekiel and here it is. It was the fifth year of King Jehoiachin's exile when the Lord came to Ezekiel in a vision during (Ezekiel 1-2). The Lord appointed Ezekiel to speak to the hard-hearted House of Israel. Ezekiel had literally eaten a scroll with words of lamentations, mournings, and woes that the Lord gave him (Ezekiel 2:10-3:2). Ezekiel was brimming with how the Lord felt—angry about Israel's sin and he mourned over it.

Ezekiel was astonished by his experience; he was in shock. He was filled with wonder after seeing God's incomprehensible glory, overflowing in Technicolor detail. He saw angels with animal faces and moving wheels with eyes—words could not illustrate such an event. Place on top of that, he was then given a book from heaven filled with God's perspective of a nation that He was furious with—the one that is supposed to represent Him! That is a lot to take in. In one moment Ezekiel witnesses how holy God is, and in the next he experiences God's feelings towards a nation that has sinned so greatly against Him. Yet despite this, Ezekiel also feels God's abounding love towards them still. There was some serious righteous indignation going on; no wonder Ezekiel was upset and speechless for a week after encountering all that the vision contained.

When we ask God to use us, we are giving Him permission to tell us where to go and what He wants us to do. Sometimes,

He may ask us to go to places that are personally uncomfortable. Taking that step of faith may be hard, but if we are obedient, He will bless us. The Message Version says Ezekiel "didn't want to go," but other Bible translations say he went in bitterness or in turmoil. I would guess when your people have done such wrong and you have to be the one to tell them, it is not a great feeling. BUT GOD's hand was on Ezekiel. Feeling God's presence and strength helped him get to the exiles he needed to talk to.

This BUT GOD verse was written after Ezekiel encountered God's glory. Ezekiel wrote all the specifics about it for us to read. The Lord's glory was described vividly in the first two chapters, and I would recommend reading them. When Ezekiel saw the Lord, we know He must have fallen to the ground because the Lord told him to stand and the Spirit lifted him up (Ezekiel 2:1-2). In this BUT GOD verse, Ezekiel says "the hand of the Lord was strong upon me" (NKJV). Similarly, John (the beloved disciple) fell to the ground when he encountered God's glory and he also wrote it down for us to read in the book of Revelation. The fascinating part is John wrote a similar phrase regarding the "hand of God" after His vision. Instead of it saying "BUT GOD," it says "BUT HE" and is found in Revelation 1:17. "And when I saw Him, I fell at His feet as dead. *But He laid His right hand on me*, saying to me, 'Do not be afraid; I am the First and the Last'" (NKJV, emphasis added). I love that God's Word is so consistent. God's hand is always there to help, no matter how intimidating His glory can be. In BUT GOD #59, we discussed how God's hand was on David so he could have understanding for the writing of the temple plans. He will touch you, even in His greatness, to help you *stand up* and share His Word or complete the assignments He has for you.

Individually, Hebrew letters can represent pictures, numbers, and words. The word "prophet" is spelled in Hebrew as Nun-Bet-Yod-Alef. One of several ways to interpret this word by using the Hebrew letters are as follows: life-house-hand-leader. So, "it could be said that a true *prophet* is under the right *hand*, or authority, of the *Leader*, Yeshua!" as taught on Passion For Truth Ministries' Facebook page in August 2013. We see this concept again in Nehemiah 2:18. Nehemiah felt God's hand upon him as the Lord commissioned him to rebuild the walls of Jerusalem. Let us be encouraged just as the Jews were to arise and build His kingdom as His hand is upon *us*. Let *us* arise! Let *us* restore and rebuild for His glory!

Isn't it good to know that when our Bridegroom sends us on a job, He will keep His hand on us? He is our partner. We are His mouthpiece and we need to be sure what we are saying comes directly from Him when we are speaking on His behalf. I am certain I could not write any of this BUT GOD study had His hand not been upon me. I am constantly asking Him to help me write this because I do not even know what to say half the time. I have edited this thing a zillion times too because I don't want to misrepresent Him, but only the Bible is perfect, so if you do come upon some mistakes, let them fall to the ground. Ezekiel was blessed with an opening of his spiritual senses. He got to see God's glory, taste a scroll, and hear the noise of the wings and wheels of the living creatures. Ezekiel knew what to share because God told Him. I would love to read about the BUT GODs from a book in heaven so I could copy all the answers! As His bride, we have to rely on faith that what we are hearing is correct as well as discern what is accurate with His Word as our guide. We need to speak boldly once we have digested His Word and/or the visions He has shared with us. We need to pray for favor to speak only truth and that He keeps His hand on us as we represent Him, clothing ourselves with humility as we point to Him the whole entire time.

The Holy Spirit showed me that by using the titles of BUT GODs #106-#111, we can focus on one important message. Listen to this! Jesus is arming us up as He wants us to *share His Word* (#106). As we do, He will remind us that He is *at our side* (#107). We will not be alone in spreading the truth; He will be *sending a steady stream of people:* His bride, your brothers and sisters in Christ (#108). We are to be telling people how *Jesus came to restore* our relationship with God, and that He is coming back (#109). Knowing we will need to have a *hiding place* sometimes for speaking truth (#110), He will be *encouraging us* there (#111) and putting *His hand on us* (#112) so that we will stand up and go in His power. Is this not what sharing the Gospel of the kingdom is all about?

113. Will Have His Way, Which is the Best

"Ephraim, obsessed with god-fantasies, chases ghosts and phantoms. He tells lies nonstop, soul-destroying lies. Both Ephraim and Judah made deals with Assyria and tried to get an inside track with Egypt. God is bringing charges against Israel. Jacob's children are hauled into court to be punished. In the womb, that heel, Jacob, got the best of his brother. When he grew up, he tried to get the best of God. *But God* would not be bested. God bested him. Brought to his knees, Jacob wept and prayed. God found him at Bethel. That's where he spoke with him. God is God-of-the-Angel-Armies, God-Revealed, God-Known" (Hosea 12:1-5 MSG, emphasis added).

Hosea was a prophet used by God in a unique way. God had him live out His message for the people. As we have learned, the Israelites had a tendency to "cheat" on God and worship other idols. God was in a covenant relationship with the Israelites, like marriage, so when they cheated on Him it was as if they were committing adultery. God loved the Israelites and did not like when they strayed from Him. To demonstrate this relationship, He had Hosea live out a physical representation of this for the people to observe. God told Hosea to marry a "wife of harlotry" (Hosea 1:2). He loved her and had children with her, and when she cheated on him, God told Hosea to love her again (Hosea 3:1). God loved the Israelites, even though they were unfaithful. He wanted Hosea's life to demonstrate that love and also demonstrate the reality of what they were doing.

In this BUT GOD, Hosea recounted a story all the Israelites knew well since it concerned one of their forefathers (Gen 25:26, 28:12-19, 32:24-28). I think Hosea was reminding them about some of Jacob's actions. Jacob tried to get his own way, BUT

GOD would not let that happen. God knew what was best for Jacob and "bested" him. Likewise, God knew what was best for the Israelites. They tried to have their own way by *calling* to Him, but not *exalting* Him, because they were "bent on backsliding" (Hosea 11:7 NIV). God is not man and will not come with terror to destroy them (Hosea 11:9), but He will teach them a lesson that will bring them "to their knees," which is where Jacob found himself as we read in this BUT GOD. Jacob "wept and prayed" and God "spoke with him." Hosea told them to be like Jacob. Hosea 12:6 instructed the people not to wait, but to return to the Lord immediately, committing themselves to Him.

Jacob was used to living a life in a way that got him what he wanted. He stole the birthright from his brother and he deceived his father into giving him the firstborn blessing (Gen 25:29-34, Gen 27). He fulfilled the prophecy that God told Rebekah (his mom) would happen: the older would serve the younger (Gen 25:22-23). Despite Jacob's character flaws, we read in the earlier BUT GODs (#9-#15) that he was a very blessed man. Jacob's grandfather was Abraham, so Jacob heard all the stories about God and began having his own "God stories." He soon learned that he could not win a struggle with God, but he knew enough not to let Him go. Hosea did not want the Israelites to "let go" of God either, but they were living life the way they wanted. He knew they were struggling to keep the commandments and he was trying to show them God would have His way. God would follow through with His word and allow punishment to come to them if they did not return to the Lord.

Our Bridegroom will have His way. His way IS the best way and His will *will* be accomplished, whether He utilizes you or someone else. Man is incapable of winning against God or having the upper hand. God always has a better way, a better plan, and a better reward. If you think you can have your way with God, you are fooling yourself. I had a friend once tell me that he and God had "an understanding." Basically, it was a relationship his way, not God's. That is what the Israelites were doing; they were in a relationship with God that was comfortable to them. They were not following His rules, but their own and then fitting God where they *wanted* Him, not where He belonged. Newsflash: God does not really go for that for too long if your heart is in covenant with His. A relationship is a two-way street, but when half of the relationship is also God, the rules change a bit, and at times we need to submit to the fact that it is going to be His way or no way. So, whether God needs to "bring you to your knees" or have you humble yourself before Him, know that is when He will "speak to you." The God of the Angel Armies and the GREAT I AM will speak to you!

114. Is Safe

"The sky turns black, sun and moon go dark, stars burn out. God roars from Zion, shouts from Jerusalem. Earth and sky quake in terror. *But God* is a safe hiding place, a granite safe house for the children of Israel. Then you'll know for sure that I'm your God, Living in Zion, my sacred mountain. Jerusalem will be a sacred city, posted: 'no trespassing.'" (Joel 3:15-17 MSG, emphasis added).

We know God is a safe hiding place (#89 and #110), and that is going to be a really good thing to remember should anyone of us live to see the fulfillment of that first sentence in this BUT GOD verse. It certainly seems that could cause a lot of fear. I know what earthquakes feel like, but not the whole earth and sky quaking at the same time in pitch black with a commanding voice thundering from the most fought after city in the world! A similar description is found in Matthew 24:29, where the Bible talks of Jesus' second coming. In BUT GOD #103, we also read that the earth will shake when God is angry. It sounds very much like what will be happening during the sixth seal being opened in Revelation 6:12. I definitely will want to be with my Bridegroom when that happens (#90)! There will be no other place for people to find comfort.

I wonder what God will shout from Jerusalem. Maybe He will shout that He is God and will reign from Jerusalem with His children, Israel. Maybe He will shout that the end of time has come. Maybe we will hear Him say, "It is done!" as found in

Revelation 16:17. We need to gather as many souls as we can before these dreadful end of days begin; we cannot let a single loved one suffer in this! It will be a nightmare for those who do not believe. All I can say is, "Thank you Jesus for saving me, and thank you God for having mercy on my soul!"

Joel was a prophet of God. He described how the locusts came, causing a famine. He saw it as God's judgment for Judah's disobedience. He prophesied of restoration to the land and of a great outpouring of the Holy Spirit. This was fulfilled on Pentecost, as read in Acts 2. Many believe another outpouring may come again before the day of the Lord's return. This is something to rejoice about instead of being overcome by the frequent saying that things are only going to get worse. Jesus' church may have its greatest moment as it shines bright and assists the angels in bringing in a huge harvest for the Lord (Matt 13:39, Acts 2:17-21).

When I read that God is a safe hiding place, I think of the game Hide and Seek. You find the best place to hide where no one can see you and then you run to the "safe spot" when the coast is clear. Here, God is the "hiding place" and the "safe spot" all at the same time. We do not need to run somewhere else to be safe because we already are. Everything about God is safe, and everything about Jesus is safe. Our secrets are safe, our souls are safe, and His thoughts toward us are safe. Our Bridegroom wants us to trust Him, to feel safe around Him, and to never feel we need to go somewhere else to feel that safety. He is all we ever need.

Since this is our only BUT GOD in the book of Joel, I think it is important to have you look at a few more verses. They should look familiar. The passage is found in Joel 2:10-11 and says, "Before them the earth shakes, the heavens tremble, the sun and moon are darkened, and the stars no longer shine. The LORD thunders at the head of his army . . ." (NIV). This sounds just like the BUT GOD verse above; it is a prophecy about the day of the Lord's return.

There is an event between the years 2014-2015 that should be mentioned, it is known as a "blood moon tetrad". A tetrad is four consecutive total lunar eclipses. The significance is that it is all happening on the Lord's Feast Days. This has happened in the past and they seem to surround important events in Israel's history. The last two times they occurred were in 1949-50 (rebirth of Israel 1948) and 1967-68 (six day war and recapturing of Jerusalem 1967). The next blood moon tetrad occurs on April 15, 2014 (Passover), Oct. 8, 2014 (Tabernacles), April 4, 2015 (Passover), and Sep. 28, 2015 (Tabernacles). There will be solar eclipses on March 20, 2015 (Jewish New Year), and Sep. 13, 2015 (Feast of Trumpets). Genesis 1:14 confirm that the lights in the sky were to be for signs and seasons. God has planned significant events to occur according to His calendar that involve Israel, we don't know which one it is but we do know it is on the horizon.

Therefore, the Lord says ". . . return to me with all your heart, with fasting and weeping and mourning . . . return to the LORD your God, for He is gracious and compassionate, slow to anger and abounding in love . . ." (Joel 2:12-13 NIV). Romans 2:4-5 tells us that God's kindness is intended to lead us to repentance; if it does not then His severity will. He does not want to judge the nations, but He will. Again, we see that familiar phrase listing God's characteristics. Not only are they found in Exodus as stated in the beginning of this study, but also here, in the book of Joel! Jesus' characteristics are the same as God our Father. Our Bridegroom is gracious and slow to anger. We should let others know this about God BEFORE our circumstances here on earth start getting intense. In the midst of end times, He will remain the same—wonderful to us, but not leaving the guilty unpunished.

115. Sends Us a Message / Gives Us a Sign

"But God sent a huge storm at sea, the waves towering. The ship was about to break into pieces. The sailors were terrified. They called out in desperation to their gods. They threw everything they were carrying overboard to lighten the ship. Meanwhile, Jonah had gone down into the hold of the ship to take a nap. He was sound asleep. The captain came to him and said, 'What's this? Sleeping! Get up! Pray to your god! Maybe your god will see we're in trouble and rescue us'" (Jonah 1:4-6 MSG, emphasis added).

If you do not know the story of Jonah, get ready for some entertainment. We talked about it a bit in BUT GOD #111. Jonah was a prophet of God, and God wanted to send him to the town of Nineveh, but Jonah did not want to go. He tried to run away from God and go somewhere else. God knew exactly where Jonah was—on a ship at sea (just like when God remembered Noah on his ship #2). This is where we find our BUT GOD verse. In BUT GOD #113, we learned God will have His way. Well, God wanted Jonah off that ship and so He sent Jonah a message. Jonah knew exactly why that storm hit and told the people to throw him overboard so the storm would go away. Crazy as it sounds, they did not want to. Can you imagine being so heartless as throwing someone overboard in a storm? Finally, they did what he asked and threw him off the ship. The storm stopped and the people on the ship immediately feared the Lord. God had prepared a big fish to swallow Jonah and take him on a first-class trip (in the fish's stomach) to Nineveh (#111). This is all found in just the first chapter alone!

How often do we try to do things our own way and get into trouble? Whatever you run away from will eventually catch up with you. We often create the storms that we face. Had Jonah not run away, God would not have had to send the storm as a sign to Jonah. Did you notice that Jonah was asleep? He was told, "Get up! Pray to your God!" So, too, does the church need to wake up (Eph 5:14-16)! We need to see the signs of the times and the messages being sent and start to pray to our God! There are events happening in the economical and political world that the church needs to make a difference in. Unfortunately, our influence is hindered by the fact that the church is not as united as it should be. The storms are coming and some of us are still asleep! If God is sending us a sign, we need to be alert to discern it is from Him and do something about it. It may not be as drastic as Jonah's was, but we still need to get moving in the right direction. Jonah was only one man, but because he turned back to do God's work, a whole city was saved from devastation. Can you imagine what kind of changes will happen when the bride of Christ unites and works together (Eph 4:13)? Nations and leaders will be changed! I believe it can and will happen someday.

Jonah was a sign to the Ninevites—a sign that would lead to repentance for those who accepted it, and destruction for those who did not. A similar sign would be given from our Bridegroom. People asked to see a sign from Jesus (Matthew 12:38-42). One reason this BUT GOD verse is here is because Jesus said that there would be no sign given, except the sign of Jonah (Luke 11:29-30). Just as Jonah was in the belly of a whale for three days and three nights, so would the Son of Man be in the heart of the earth for three days and three nights. He wants people to know about this story and know about Him. Many verses in Jonah connect to the Messianic Psalms which point to Jesus as our Messiah (Ps 18, 20, 22, 31, 35, 42, 55, 56, 61, 69, 88, 107, and 116).[87]

Jesus went on to say that someone greater than Solomon was there with them. Solomon was known for building the temple (#49 and #57-59). Jesus called His body the temple and said when it was destroyed, it would be raised up again in three days. The people did not understand and thought He was talking of the temple that they worshipped in (John 2:18-22). When the time came, and Jesus died on the cross, the prophesies/signs of Jonah and the temple came true when three days later He rose again in a glorious resurrection (Matthew 28, Mark 16, Luke 24, and John 20).

Our Bridegroom loves sending us signs; He does it in many ways. We will miss them if we are asleep, so church, wake up! Pay attention to what is going on in the world around you. For example, in May 2010, a grey whale was spotted off the coast of Israel. The Israel Marine Mammal Research and Assistance Center identified the creature. The chairman, Dr. Aviad Scheinin, said it was one of the most important whale sightings ever. It baffled scientists because that whale is normally only seen in the Pacific Ocean. The news brought up a comparison to the story of Jonah.[88] Is that a sign? I do not know, but it is definitely worth taking note when the entire world is referencing a Bible story!

116. Uses Creation as a Teaching Tool

"But God prepared a cutworm when the morning dawned the next day, and it smote the gourd so that it withered"

(Jonah 4:7 AMP, emphasis added). *Also found in the NLT and KJV.

After Jonah delivered God's message to Nineveh (the Assyrian's capital city), the people repented. Since they turned from their wickedness, God changed his mind and did not destroy the city as He had said He would. This angered Jonah because he wanted the evil people in Nineveh to perish. He did not want them to repent because he knew God was merciful and would save them. He explains in Jonah 4:2b, "That is why I fled to Tarshish, for I knew that You are a gracious God and merciful, slow to anger and of great kindness, and [when sinners turn to You and meet Your conditions] You revoke the [sentence of] evil against them" (AMP). How interesting! This verse should look familiar since these similar character traits of God were quoted in the beginning of this study and again in the discussion from BUT GOD #114. Now we see it here, in Jonah's story, proving yet again how consistent God's disposition is, even for a city that did not deserve a chance in Jonah's opinion.

Jonah went out to the east and found a perfect spot to watch what would become of the city. The Lord allowed a plant to grow up over him to be a shade over his head and protect him. Jonah was very happy about it until the next day when it was not there anymore. A worm caused it to wither and Jonah lost his extra shade and protection. In BUT GOD #111 I mentioned that the fish was a god in Nineveh. I find it incredibly merciful of God to use their false god as a way to talk to them. God prepared a whale to *transport* Jonah and now God had prepared a plant and a worm to *teach* Jonah a lesson.

The "gourd" was a plant that God mercifully used to ". . . deliver him from his evil situation" (Jonah 4:6 AMP). Jonah needed the Lord's help to work out his issues. He had been defiant towards God and had not listened the first time when told to speak to Nineveh. Now he was burning with anger, pouting it seems, sitting and wanting a whole city to be destroyed. Instead of Jonah rejoicing and seeing that his enemies (the Assyrians) were turning from their ways, he wanted vengeance. He did not want to see them get a second chance, and this was coming from a prophet—a man of God! The Lord had forgiven the people when they repented. God WAS slow to anger and showed great kindness to the people of Nineveh. Jonah needed a change of heart, and God was going to use this plant that grew in one night by God's hand. God killed the plant the next day by a specially appointed worm. God knew this would push Jonah over the edge enough for him to open up in a conversation. God wanted to teach Jonah that even though the Assyrians were not God's anointed nation, He still loves people and forgives anyone who repents. No matter what awful things you have done, he will love you and will forgive you if you repent (2 Chron 7:13-15).

Jonah did not even know how blessed He was that the God of creation was using creation itself to initiate conversation. I love watching the sunrise and sunset. Sometimes it feels like God just wants to show off! The colors exceed all expectations and the clouds take on so many shades it seems everyone must take notice. In Proverbs 30, God has us look to different created things to learn lessons. He will use creation in our everyday situations to teach us new things about Him or about ourselves.

The Lord is coming back for an untainted church, so when we have a mind-set that does not represent Him, He is going to have to confront us in ways that will get a response. Unfortunately, Jonah reacted incorrectly to a few too many situations in a row. He was supposed to be God's prophet, rejoicing for the people's repentance, not harboring resentment! The book of Jonah is an interesting story and is only four chapters long. When our Bridegroom chooses to be creative with His creation, let us bundle those stories up and remember to share them as a tool to initiate conversations, because they can be pretty captivating. The book is read in synagogues everywhere on the Day of Atonement (Yom Kippur) because of its theme of repentance.

117. Has the Right Perspective

> *"But God* said to Jonah, 'Is it right for you to be angry about the plant?' 'It is,' he said. "And I'm so angry I wish I were dead.'" (Jonah 4:9 NIV, emphasis added).

In the whale, Jonah thought he was going to die (Jonah 2:7), BUT GOD saved him. Some say he did die as Jonah 2:3 states he was praying from the belly of Sheol, the land of the dead. After he spoke to Nineveh and heard God was going to spare them, Jonah was so mad that, in the heat of the moment, he wished he would die (Jonah 4:3). Now, in the heat of the sun, Jonah again said he wished he were dead. Jonah had very extreme emotions. God tried to help Jonah self-check his feelings by asking him if it was right for him to be so angry. Jonah had received a moment of happiness with the vine, and then once it was gone, he was mad again. He was so caught up in his own comfortability that he did not see the bigger picture that people could have died in not so comfortable conditions.[89] He was happy about his release from a whale, but not happy about Nineveh's deliverance (Jonah 2:9-10).

Jonah was having severe difficulties. He was allowing bitterness to root in his heart against the people of Nineveh (who were Assyrians) and wanted God to destroy them. Jonah was displacing his anger wrongly, thinking he had a right to be angry at God (Jonah 4:1). The initial root of the matter had still not been dealt with, and so God used the plant to bring the subject up to get some perspective on the issue. There were more than 120,000 people who had needed just one word from Jonah to straighten up. God reminded Jonah that those people being saved, along with livestock, were more important than a plant! Jonah should not have been mad over a plant dying, but the fact that thousands of human beings almost died! Jonah's perspective was all wrong because of his extreme contempt towards the Assyrians.

In our BUT GOD verse, we see that God asked Jonah this question to invoke a self evaluation. It was the same as when God asked Adam, "Where are you?" after Adam and Eve sinned and they hid in the Garden (Gen 3:9). It was not because He did not know where they were. God knows, but asks questions to get us to talk to Him so that we can sort through things together. A different angle on the question as stated by Damon Thompson, could be seen as God asking, "Where are you—spiritually?" because spiritually, Adam had just sinned, and now there was a separation.[90] Spiritually, Jonah had lost sight of the reason for his calling and his anger was not coming from the right perspective. It was not like Ezekiel (#112) who was angry about the nation of Israel sinning and going against God's instructions. Jonah's anger was because God chose to accept Nineveh's repentance and the plant dying just added to his emotional outburst.

God always wants to redeem people (1 Tim 2:3-5) and wants His bride to point to the Redeemer Himself. Who are we to decide who has the right to be saved and who does not? It says in Romans 3:23, "All have sinned and are falling short" (AMP). If you lay aside your old ways and put on a "new self," changing on the inside (Eph 4:22-24 NIV), then you become a "new creation" (2 Cor 5:17 NIV), worthy of being "brought near" to God Himself through the blood of our Bridegroom, Jesus (Eph 2:11-13 NIV)!

Is not Jonah's reaction just like ours today? We get all hot and bothered over various circumstances and say irrational comments that later need to be dealt with. It is not until we remove ourselves from the situation that we start to look at things differently. Perspective is key, and we would be wise not to blow up in anger so quickly because things did not go the way we wanted it to. Reality starts to set in once we actually deal with the "root" of the issue and not blame the "vine."

My friend, Melanie, taught me this quick lesson on perspective. If you put your hand directly in front of your eyeballs, you probably will see some blurry fingers. That is what our perspective is when we are in the thick of a situation. Now, if you move your hand back a couple inches, you probably can see it more clearly. Similarly, if some time passes in our situation, we might see things more clearly. Lastly, if you stretch your arm all the way out and look at your hand in the distance, you will see your whole arm and hand in relationship to the rest of the room around you. That is God's perspective—the whole time. We do not know what the surrounding circumstances are for the situation we are in, but our

Bridegroom does, and we can be certain He sees the whole picture from the right perspective from the very beginning!

118. Is Our Light

"[Spreading Your Wings] Don't, enemy, crow over me. I'm down, but I'm not out. I'm sitting in the dark right now, *but God* is my light. I can take God's punishing rage. I deserve it—I sinned. But it's not forever. He's on my side and is going to get me out of this. He'll turn on the lights and show me his ways. I'll see the whole picture and how right he is. And my enemy will see it, too, and be discredited—yes, disgraced! This enemy who kept taunting, 'So where is this God of yours?' I'm going to see it with these, my own eyes—my enemy disgraced, trash in the gutter" (Micah 7:8-10 MSG, emphasis added).

Before we had started reading the BUT GODs, I quoted the verse where Jesus said that all the prophecies in the Old Testament about Him needed to be fulfilled. The book of Micah contains an important one of those prophecies. It is found in Micah 5:2. It states that the One who would be Ruler in Israel would come from the city of Bethlehem, telling where the Messiah was to be born. Micah's contemporaries were Hosea and Isaiah, whom we have already read from earlier. Isaiah 53 foretold of Jesus' sufferings and were fulfilled on the day of His death.[91]

In a couple previous BUT GODs (#20 and #102), we have discussed how God is our light. Light is needed for life so things can grow, including our insight. In the story of creation, we see that the earth was dark, until God's presence came down and gave it light (Gen 1:1-3). The earth had God's light before He created the sun, moon, and stars (Day 4—Gen 1:14-19). In Revelation 22:5, it says that there will be no more night and no need of lamps or the sun because God will be our light. Psalm 119:105 says God's Word is a lamp for my feet, and a light on my path. God's light directs my personal journey to fulfill God's purposes for me. The verse does not say to shine the light on someone else's path and tell them what to do. We can lead with our light and be an example, but we are not to be mini Holy Spirits. There is a difference between encouraging one another on and bossing others around. Let the Holy Spirit do His job while you focus on where He is leading you.

Micah prophesies about the Lord knowing about Israel's sins (Micah 6:9-16). They were deceitful and violent. They lied and kept idol statues, as well as followed the way of Ahab's counsel (who was married to Jezebel #52). In this BUT GOD verse, Micah knew that when the Lord punished them for these sins, their enemies would be glad they fell, but Micah knew the character of the Lord. He stated that God forgave sins, casting them into the depths of the sea (Micah 7:18-20). God does not remain angry; He delights in mercy and would have compassion on them again. This is why Micah said they would rise again and they would "see the whole picture," because they would be in the light looking from God's perspective (#117)!

I love to be outside in the sun; it makes me feel happier than being inside in the dark. There is a reason for that I am sure. God wants to draw us to the light; He wants us to feel good in the warmth. He wants us to feel safe in the open with ability to see all around us. Light brings clarity, reflecting all the colors. Everything about light can resemble our God. The Bible says in Psalm 112:4 that, "Even in darkness light dawns for the upright for those who are gracious and compassionate and righteous" (NIV). Why would it include these characteristics of God in this verse? It is because His light radiates His character, and His character is reflected on us, His children! Our Bridegroom said in John 8:12, ". . . I am the light of the world. If you follow me, you won't have to walk in darkness, because you will have the light that leads to life" (NLT).

Reinhard Bonnke is considered a general in the army of God in this generation. He has headed up many crusades that have led millions to Christ. As a speaker at the Jesus Culture Conference in Los Angeles in 2013, he shared what the Holy Spirit revealed to him about the Father of Lights (the verse found in James 1:17). In Jesus' days, people used sundials to read the time. As the earth moved, the sun would cast a shadow from the stick placed into the ground, indicating the time. There was only one time there was no shadow—when the sun was at meridian, its peak position. The sun rises and falls, but the verse in James says the Father of Lights has no variation, no shifting shadows. This means that God is always at His peak position. His power does not rise and set like the sun; we are in God's full blast of power and glory all the time. Jesus is the Light of the World always; there is no shadow of turning![92]

119. Is Patient / Does Not Lose His Temper

"God is serious business. He won't be trifled with. He avenges his foes. He stands up against his enemies, fierce and raging. *But God* doesn't lose his temper. He's powerful, but it's a patient power. Still, no one gets by with anything. Sooner or later, everyone pays. Tornadoes and hurricanes are the wake of his passage, Storm clouds are the dust he shakes off his feet. He yells at the sea: It dries up. All the rivers run dry. The Bashan and Carmel mountains shrivel, the Lebanon orchards shrivel. Mountains quake in their roots, hills dissolve into mud flats. Earth shakes in fear of God. The whole world's in a panic. Who can face such towering anger? Who can stand up to this fierce rage? His anger spills out like a river of lava, his fury shatters boulders" (Nahum 1:2-6 MSG, emphasis added).

Remember how Jonah blew up about all the wrong things? That is not what God does, He is able to control His temper because He is all powerful and can do and act how He chooses. His character is patient and kind, but that should not be taken advantage of. He can get angry (#26). Our God proves that He encompasses the ability to restrain Himself and He will not punish unjustly. He will come after His enemies like a fierce warrior (#107), but for justice (#64), not because He wants to see blood.

Nahum was a prophet who wrote on one thing—the fall of Nineveh. We learned about the Assyrian's capital during Jonah's story in BUT GOD #115-#117. Time had now passed (about one hundred and fifty years), and all the people had once again become wicked. Nahum said floods would come to Nineveh, washing away their structures. The people would become captives and would be plundered, fleeing in terror with no strength. The Assyrians were known for being brutal to their enemies, so all who heard the news of them falling would rejoice (Nahum 3:19).

Let us learn from the city of Nineveh and not repeat an offense God has already forgiven us of once before. We want our cities to thrive in God's love, not dive into the pit of Satan's traps. We need to love people enough to teach future generations the truth of God's Word. They can have a chance to be set free and not face irreversible doom like Nineveh. Nahum showed they could not escape the consequences of their actions and Nineveh's efforts to survive were useless (Nah 3:9-15). Similarly, we know from the book of Revelation that people will not be able to get away from God's wrath; even hiding in caves will not help them escape (Rev 6:16; 9:6).

Our Bridegroom is waiting on His Father to tell Him when He can come back to be with us. God is patiently waiting on the bride to be ready. Let us be ready already! It is time to stop "playing church" and be serious about hearing and learning from God. Be the church that is committed, living out His Word, and expecting Him to show up. We are almost hitting that time when all nations will have had a chance to hear about Jesus, especially with the technology and transportation we have today. Our God is slow to anger and great in power. Irreversible doom for the wicked is accompanying our Bridegroom's return when He brings judgment. God is patient, but He will not wait forever (2 Pet 3:9). Our Bridegroom cherishes us and has waited so long to talk to us face to face. The clock is ticking and I have my oil filled to the top (Matt 25:1-13). It is almost midnight, my anticipation is high and my resolve is steadfast. Come Lord Jesus!

120. Is the World's Accountant

"[The Whole World Has Its Eyes on God] War Bulletin: God's Message challenges the country of Hadrach. It will settle on Damascus. The whole world has its eyes on God. Israel isn't the only one. That includes Hamath at the border, and Tyre and Sidon, clever as they think they are. Tyre has put together quite a kingdom for herself; she has stacked up silver like cordwood, piled gold high as haystacks. *But God* will certainly bankrupt her; he will dump all that wealth into the ocean and burn up what's left in a big fire. Ashkelon will see it and panic, Gaza will wring its hands, Ekron will face a dead end. Gaza's king will die. Ashkelon will be emptied out, and a villain will take over in Ashdod" (Zechariah 9:1-6 MSG, emphasis added).

Since this is our last BUT GOD of the Old Testament, it does not surprise me that we are reading about God's judgment on Earth. That is, after all, what will happen at the end of time as we read in the book of Revelation. Zechariah was one of the most quoted prophets found in that last book of the New Testament. In fact, Zechariah was quoted almost as much as Ezekiel in Revelation. Zechariah 14 is all about the second coming of our Lord. Many prophesies about the Messiah are found in chapters 9-14.[93]

History shows that Alexander the Great ravaged the Philistines' country, along with Damascus and Tyre, and some say the "villain" in this verse refers to him, but that is just one opinion. In this BUT GOD verse, it sounds like many of the nations who thought they were financially set were going to be bankrupt. Each nation was described as watching God as He went through their books and threw their wealth into the oceans, burning up everything else in the fire. The next nation in line panicked while the other wrung their hands with worry. Finally, Israel was not the only one who had their eyes on God. When you read this alongside Revelation 20:11-15, you realize that this verse fits as a timely reminder that God is the ultimate accountant. He has several books and they will all be opened. God will sit on His white throne and will be the Judge of all. People whose name is not found in the Book of Life will be cast into the fire.

The countries in this verse learned the same lesson that we need to learn individually. God does not want us to make the riches of this world more important than Him. We see that our worldly goods will be thrown into the fire and burn away. Remember in BUT GOD #77 we discussed the riches of this world should not be trusted because no monetary payment would ever be enough to ransom your soul (Ps 49:6-8). The only things we will be left with are our faith and our works, and whether they glorified Jesus (Matt 6:19-21, Eph 2:8-10). Peter, Jesus' disciple, once said to a lame man who was begging at the temple gate in Acts 3:6, ". . . Silver and gold I do not have, but what I have I give you: In the name of Jesus Christ of Nazareth, rise up and walk" (NKJV). Immediately, the man's ankles and bones received strength and he went away leaping and praising God. All the silver and gold in the world cannot bring healing, only the power of God. Our authority is backed by the healing power of God, and we are to pray for and encourage one another using the gifts of the Holy Spirit.

Demonstrating God's love will bring more people to know Him than scaring people into the kingdom. Since John the Baptist, Jesus, and Peter all told people to repent, I do think it is a message that needs to be shared (Matt 3:1-2, Mark 1:14-15, Acts 2:38). We all sin in some way daily and need to repent and ask forgiveness from God every day. The church body as a whole will need to repent for their lack in letting the fire power of the Holy Spirit demonstrate the power of God. Experiencing the Holy Spirit allows faith to be built and draws others into God's magnificent presence. There are enough churches these days that preach a watered down, feel good message, making people feel comfortable in their sin while they put on a good show for you. BUT GOD does not want any of us to perish! He wants us to hear ALL the truth, not just parts of it.[94] The New Jerusalem that He built is big enough to fit everyone who has lived on this earth and He wants all of us there (2 Peter 3:9, Rev 21)!

Another message of the Gospel is found in this last batch of BUT GOD verses, so take a look. When the lost and wicked turn from their ways, no matter how vile they were toward us, we need to rejoice about their salvation (the lesson from Jonah's story #115-#117). God's character will be revealed when all things are brought to light (#118). We will see how holy and just He is. He patiently waits as long as He can so that all can come to know Him, but eventually those who rejected Him will be lost (#119). God will know who they are because He is an excellent accountant and has records of everyone's deeds and beliefs. Even though all people do not have their eyes on God now, eventually they will, and many will wish they had paid as much attention to Him as He did to them.

In the traditional Jewish book order, 2 Chronicles is listed as the last book. For fun, I took a glance to see what the study would look like if we had ended with those BUT GOD verses instead (#59-#61). Using the titles, we see that Jesus *sets us up for success* and *has a plan,* He has made His bride a kingdom, priests unto God (Rev 1:6) while *Jesus will be KING OF KINGS AND LORD OF LORDS* (Rev 19:16). Though the war described in BUT GOD #61 shows Judah's army losing, the bigger picture is that God *implemented His judgment* as a punishment for those who deserted Him. This is the same picture we are seeing here in Zechariah; this BUT GOD verse states it is a "War Bulletin," those who reject Him will be lost.

Since this BUT GOD used the term "bankrupt," I immediately thought of the banking system and our economy. Since the housing and market crash from 2008, many are hanging on the best they can. Someday the countries will probably form one system of banking for all that will lead to events in the end of days. Many of us need God to come intervene in our finances now. God is the ultimate accountant; He has books on everything and keeps track of who thinks they are ahead and who is going to owe in the end. Once God opens His books up, those who were living the "high life" will only continue living that way depending on how *high* they lifted Him up. If you, like me, are looking forward to some financial freedom, continue to lift God high; this might be the year that He cancels your debts!

No matter how tight things get always try to tithe to your church. Nehemiah 10:35-39 shows how tithes, firstfruits, and contributions were given to the House of the Lord. You cannot out-give God; when these things are done with a happy heart, He will release the fullness of His blessing on you (2 Cor 9:6-15).[95] Sacrificing your money (treasure), your time, and your talent each month is a good way to facilitate growing the kingdom of God. God is a giver (God gave His only Son—John 3:16) and His eyes look to and fro for someone whose heart belongs to Him (2 Chron 16:9). This means trusting Him, even with your finances (Mal 3:10). I am so glad my Bridegroom likes keeping the books straight; it is a chore I will gladly give up!

Conclusion

There are a few books of the Bible that do not have the words BUT GOD, but that does not mean there are not huge BUT GOD lessons in them. There are many books that contain "yet He," "but the Lord," and "but He" that I did not even look up, along with twenty or so "but you" in Psalms alone. I am sure that there are more lessons to learn in those, but first we need to finish this study and move onto the BUT GODs of the New Testament. I already have completed the first draft and am amazed at how much more there is to see. The very first one starts at BUT GOD #121. It is all about forgiveness of sins, which should not be a surprise since Jesus is now on the scene!

Did you see parts of the gospel message exposed in this study? In case you missed it, here is a bit of what I saw. Jesus was revealed (#58) in a hidden rehearsal (#21). Joseph portrayed Jesus' forgiving others (#16) and we learned that God will redeem our souls like He did for Jesus (#77) which gives us hope (#55). Jesus is the Lion of Judah (#99) and a righteous judge (#85) who will overthrow the wicked (#94), but will save (#63) those who have found their identity in Him (#33)! The BUT GODs of the Bible reveal so much and countless lessons can be learned from them.

In February 2012, Pastor Diego Mesa, from Abundant Living Family Church (in Rancho Cucamonga, California), preached a sermon titled "The Buts of the Bible." He said there were four things he noticed people did in the Bible that allowed them to receive a BUT GOD moment. If we need justice, healing, safe keeping, and a BUT GOD in our life, then we should follow their example. Reflect on this Old Testament study and see which people in the Bible followed these four steps.

1. The person had a faithful lifestyle—meaning you have to obey God.
2. The person always kept a good attitude—meaning you do not complain, keep working, be resilient, and expect something better to happen.
3. The person waited on God—meaning you cannot control the clock, you need to be patient.
4. The person kept praising God, no matter how bad things got—meaning you may not know why or how, but you need to stay grateful and keep thanking God.

Some of the BUT GODs we have read in the Old Testament show God's perfect timing in putting people in key positions to be able to thwart the enemies plans. Remember the very first BUT GOD? God always wants to protect us from the enemy. In the book of Esther, we can read how Haman, who had an antichrist spirit, wanted to kill the Jews, BUT GOD placed Esther in a key position "for such a time as this" and was able to spoil Haman's plans. Our Bridegroom does not want us to be deceived by any future antichrists. If we spend time with Jesus and *know His character*, we will be able to discern between our true Christ and the liar.

See if you can find the other BUT GODs hidden in the Bible. Remember, this whole study was to understand our Bridegroom and His characteristics better. As we draw closer to the last days, Jesus is revealing himself more and more as the Bridegroom. His bride needs to know herself better—who she is and to whom she belongs! Mike Bickle, from International House of Prayer in Kansas City, says there are three characteristics of Jesus that will stand out in the end days, and I agree. He describes Jesus as our "Passionate Bridegroom, a Righteous Judge, and a Sovereign King: He burns with desire for us, removes everything that hinders love, and is a God of power!" Continue to seek God and He will continue to reveal Himself to you in so many different ways. Our Father is represented perfectly in Jesus our Bridegroom; their characteristics reflect and complement each other. The Holy Spirit will lead us to Him. "The Spirit and the bride say, 'Come!'" (Rev 22:17a NIV)

I will leave you with two verses and one more song I pray will inspire you. Please listen to Chris Tomlin's song "This Is Our God" from his album *The Noise We Make*.[96] I cannot believe how perfectly it goes with this study! Let each word remind you of what we have already learned. I also will include the devotional poem I wrote that kicked this whole thing into gear. God bless you and thanks for studying with me!

Psalm 105:1-6 *The Message*

Hallelujah! Thank God! Pray to him by name! **Tell everyone you meet what he has done!** Sing him songs, belt out hymns, translate his wonders into music! Honor his holy name with Hallelujahs, you who seek God. Live a happy life! **Keep your eyes open for God, watch for his works; be alert for signs of His presence.** Remember the world of wonders he has made, his miracles, and the verdicts he's rendered—O seed of Abraham, his servant, O child of Jacob, his chosen.

Isaiah 55:6-7 *The Message*

Seek God while he's here to be found, pray to him while he's close at hand. Let the wicked abandon their way of life and the evil their way of thinking. Let them come back to God, who is merciful, come back to our God, who is lavish with forgiveness.

PSALM 119 DEVOTION
Tina Miller on 6/8/08

Choosing, learning, living by your ways

VERSE: 30 I have <u>chosen</u> the way of truth; I have set my heart on your laws. 7 I will praise you with an upright heart as I <u>learn</u> your righteous laws. 9 How can a young man keep his way pure? By <u>living</u> according to your word.

Finding, delighting, giving you praise

VERSE: 35 Direct me in the path of your commands, for there I <u>find delight</u>. 16 I <u>delight</u> in your decrees; I will not neglect your word. 164 Seven times a day I <u>praise</u> you for your righteous laws.

Considering, meditating, seeking your face,

VERSE: 15 I <u>meditate</u> on your precepts and <u>consider</u> your ways. 27 Let me understand the teaching of your precepts; then I will <u>meditate</u> on your wonders. 58 I have <u>sought your face</u> with all my heart

Believing, obeying, rejoicing all my days

VERSE: 66 Teach me knowledge and good judgment, for I <u>believe</u> in your commands. 34 Give me understanding, and I will keep your law and <u>obey</u> it with all my heart. 162 I <u>rejoice</u> in your promise like one who finds great spoil.

Understanding the unfolding of your Word,

VERSE: 130 The <u>unfolding of your words</u> gives light; it gives <u>understanding</u> to the simple.

Lips overflowing, recounting what I've learned.

VERSE: 171 May my <u>lips overflow</u> with praise, for you teach me your decrees. 13 With my lips I <u>recount</u> all the laws that come from your mouth.

**

Loving, walking, singing what I know

VERSE: 127 Because I <u>love</u> your commands more than gold, more than pure gold. 3 They do nothing wrong; they <u>walk</u> in his ways. 172 May my tongue <u>sing</u> of your word, for all your commands are righteous.

The theme of my songs wherever I go

VERSE: 54 Your decrees are the <u>theme of my song wherever I lodge</u>.

I remember your name Lord day and night

VERSE: 97 Oh, how I love your law! I meditate on it all <u>day</u> long! 55 In the <u>night</u> I <u>remember your name, O LORD</u>, and I will keep your law.

You are my portion, in you I delight

VERSE: 57 <u>You are my portion</u>,O LORD; I have promised to obey your words. 35 Direct me in the path of your commands, for there I find <u>delight</u>.

A heritage forever you've given me

VERSE: 111 Your statutes are <u>my heritage forever</u>; they are the joy of my heart.

Great peace for those who love Thee

VERSE: 165 <u>Great peace</u> have they <u>who love your law</u>, and nothing can make them stumble.

**

Accepting, helping, and compassionate

VERSE: 108 Accept, O LORD, the willing praise of my mouth, and teach me your laws. 173 May your hand be ready to help me, for I have chosen your precepts. 77 Let your compassion come to me that I may live, for your law is my delight.

Understanding, knowing, giving discernment

VERSE: 34 Give me understanding, and I will keep your law and obey it with all my heart. 66 Teach me knowledge and good judgment, for I believe in your commands. 125 I am your servant; give me discernment that I may understand your statutes.

Teaching, directing, and strengthening me

VERSE: 135 Make your face shine upon your servant and teach me your decrees. 133 Direct my footsteps according to your word; let no sin rule over me. 28 My soul is weary with sorrow; strengthen me according to your word.

Opening my eyes so I can see

VERSE: 18 Open my eyes that I may see wonderful things in your law.

You've taught me yourself, every word precious and sweet

VERSE: 102 I have not departed from your laws, for you yourself have taught me. 103 How sweet are your words to my taste, sweeter than honey to my mouth!

Faithful, eternal—a lamp unto my feet

VERSE: 90 Your faithfulness continues through all generations; you established the earth, and it endures. 89 Your word, O LORD, is eternal; it stands firm in the heavens. 105 Your word is a lamp to my feet and a light for my path.

**

Unfailing, loving, turning to me

VERSE: 76 May your unfailing love be my comfort. 132 Turn to me and have mercy on me, as you always do to those who love your name.

Always hearing, comforting with tender mercy

VERSE: 76 your unfailing love be my comfort. 132 Turn to me and have mercy on me, as you always do to those who love your name.

Your values wonderful, your promises true

VERSE: 129 Your statutes are wonderful; therefore I obey them. 140 Your promises have been thoroughly tested, and your servant loves them.

Til the end my heart belongs to you

VERSE: 112 My heart is set on keeping your decrees to the very end. 11 I have hidden your word in my heart that I might not sin against you. *(NIV)*

Endnotes

1   The Spirit Himself makes intercession for us (Rom 8:26), and Jesus, our High Priest, lives to make intercession for us as well (Hebrews 7:25).

2   Sid Roth teaches how Jesus is revealed in Scripture by breaking down the meanings of the words and verses in the beginning of his show called, *It's Supernatural!* on July 29-August 4, 2013. http://www.sidroth.org/site/New s2?abbr=tv_&page=NewsArticle&id=13533

3   *The Lamb and the Seven Sealed Scrolls*, Dr. Richard Booker pg.94

4   An interesting point to note is that this may have been where Hagar was given to Sarah as her Egyptian slave.

5   Perry Stone on his program, *Manna Fest*, "The Fullness Factor—God's Sign of the End" www.voe.org

6   *HaYesod* Bible Study by Fruits of Zion Ministry, this info came from the covenant agreements section. www.ffoz.org

7   Jeff Allen trademarked that saying; he is an entertaining Christian comedian www.JeffAllenComedy.com

8   This information is from Joel Richardson's book, *Islamic Antichrist*, pages 33-50. My friends and I met him at a conference and then he came and spoke at our church; He is very knowledgeable. His website is www.joelstrumpet.com

9   I did not read this book, but I did read this article and the book is referenced at this website http://www.jpost.com/LandedPages/PrintArticle. aspx?id=244996

10   There are many places to look up this information, this is just one of them: http://kenraggio.com/KRPN-AntichristStand.htm

11   A couple examples of God changing His mind—Exodus 32:11-14 and Jonah 3:10

12   "The Sign of the Messiah" teaching by Tony Robinson. I met him at a conference, the way he finds connections in the Bible will blow you away, it is so good. His website is www.restorationoftorah.org

13   *The Key to His Heart* by Cindy Powell

14   Chris Tomlin song "I Will Follow You" from the album *And If Our God Is for Us*

15   Dr. Richard Booker's book, *The Lamb and the Seven-Sealed Scroll*, pgs. 148-164

[16] I listened Kim Clement teach on this once. It was an interesting perspective to think that God saw what it would be like. His teachings can be viewed here at www.kimclement.com

[17] Jamie Grace "You Lead" from the album *One Song At A Time*

[18] Matt Redman's song, "Blessed be Your Name" from the album *Blessed Be Your Name the Songs of Matt Redman, Vol. 1*

[19] John Klein and Adam Spears' Volume One Book, *Lost in Translation* pgs.53-75

[20] I heard Brian Howard of Nitzahon Ministries speak at a local church about this subject. Later I was able to talk with him on the phone to get clarification on these words. To get more info about him, you can look up his website at www.nitzahon.com

[21] David Pawson's book, *Come With Me Through Isaiah*, pgs. 65-70

[22] Jeremy Camp "Without You" from his album *Reckless*

[23] I gleaned some of this from Graham Cooke who I heard teach at HRock Church in Pasadena at the 2012 Voice of the Prophets Conference.

[24] An example of this is found in Daniel 1:7. Once conquered by the Babylonians, these Hebrew boys were renamed by the ones that captured them. Their original names had references to the God of Israel and now their names made references to the Babylonian gods.

[25] Joshua said this at a SpiritSpa Retreat I attended in July 2013, Joshua Mills' ministry can be found here: www.newwineinternational.org

[26] Jason Gray "Remind Me Who I Am" from his album *A Way to See in the Dark*

[27] I got this from Cindy Powell's Book, *A Key to His Heart*

[28] Here is an interesting note I thought I would mention since I heard Kim Clement point this out before on one of his internet teachings. God will always honor the sacrifice we bring to Him at the altar. We will reap what we sow. Remember that Gideon offered bread as part of his sacrifice to the Lord. Later we read that it was a dream about bread that encouraged Gideon and showed him that the Lord was going to deliver the Midianites into their hands (Judges 7:13). God is so creative that He can use dreams that seem silly to confirm prophetic events.

[29] David Brickner from Jews for Jesus spoke at our church on 07/07/2013 www.jewsforjesus.org

[30] Check out Obadiah 10—in this verse the word "violence" in Hebrew is *chamac*, and in English is Hamas. This word is #2555 in *Strong's Concordance*. I heard this Hamas definition during a teaching on Israel's timeline taught by Jim Staley of Passion for Truth Ministries, www.passionfortruth.com

[31] Reinhard Bonnke taught on the significance of this symbolism and, since this BUT GOD is talking about the Holy Spirit, I thought I would share his thoughts of the foxes in this story. First he noticed that they were tied two by

two, just as Jesus sent out His disciples two by two (Mark 6:7-13; Luke 10:1-2). Then he noticed they had fire attached to them. Fire had consumed the fields where the foxes had gone. If Samson had not attached fire to them, nothing would have happened to the field. Fire represents the Holy Spirit. Without the fire of the Holy Spirit, nothing is set ablaze. Samson could see the trail that blazed behind the foxes. We are to preach and teach with the fire of the Holy Spirit, or ministries will not be affected and God's glory will not spread. Reinhard Bonnke's ministry is Christ for all Nations (www.cfan.org)

[32] To hear one of the more famous Samson Bible stories, listen to this funny parody by Christian comedian, Tim Hawkins called "Hey There Delilah" http://www.youtube.com/watch?v=2ZUgSrSlYy8&feature=youtube_gdata_player

[33] Though I don't quote directly from it, the One New Man Bible is a good resource of the Hebrew language correctly translated into English from a Hebrew scholar. It was written by William Morford. To make it as accurate as possible, he received help from the Rabbi he had studied under, Rabbi Eliezer Ben-Yehuda, Ph.D. (the grandson of Eliezer Ben-Yehuda, who made Hebrew the modern language in Israel today).

[34] I saw a Facebook post by Bill Johnson on August 7, 2013 that was worth mentioning. He said, "God rewards faith. Yet faith is a gift from Him. He rewards obedience. Yet obedience is made possible by His grace working in us. God rewards righteous acts. Yet it is His righteousness at work in us. Conclusion: God gives us credit for what He does through us."

[35] Barlow Girls "Never Alone" from the album *Our Journey... So Far*

[36] David Pawson wrote this in his book and it stuck with me. He is an amazing teacher and whatever you can learn from him will bless you. www.davidpawson.org

[37] Read the book of Hosea—God had this prophet live out what God felt toward Israel.

[38] Martin Smith's song, "Back to the Start (God's Great Dance Floor)" from the album *God's Great Dance Floor*

[39] "Never Knew Love Like This Before" from the album *The Best of Stephanie Mills*

[40] Jesus was a descendent of David. Jesus' parents were Mary and Joseph. Jesus' genealogy is found in the Gospels of Matthew and Luke, but there are some differences in the names found in those lists. The reason is because one of those genealogies belong to Mary (Luke 3:23-38) and one belongs to Joseph (Matthew 1:1-16). As seen in Matthew, Joseph's biological father was Jacob, whereas, in Luke, Heli was thought to be Joseph's father-in-law.

[41] Kris Vallotton (a pastor at Bethel in Redding, California) taught an interesting perspective concerning Jesus' first miracle that has to do with speaking God's will. He said Mary *expected* Jesus to do something about the shortage of wine in John 2. She *anticipated* that Jesus would bring forth

new wine as she told the servants to do as He said. With faith, prompted by the Holy Spirit, she *spoke into existence* new wine to be released which was the Father's will for Jesus. I believe God is releasing new wineskins (new strategies, new ways of doing things) in this day; let us speak them into existence according to His will! Regarding wineskins—Matthew 9:17 talks about them. Though Jesus said it was not His time, He was released by God to perform a miracle.

[42] There are many teachings on the Jezebel spirit, here is just one: http://jonhamilton.org/jezebel.htm

[43] Some oral Hebrew traditions claim this boy was Habakkuk, http://bible.org/article/introduction-book-habakkuk

[44] Chris Tomlin's song, "Our God" from the album *And If Our God Is for Us*

[45] Joseph Seiss' book, *The Gospel in the Stars*. The whole book is interesting, but I got this info from pg. 149

[46] For a great, quick teaching that mentions a quick history of the temples, I recommend listening to Jon Courson Radio Teaching on Revelation 11, http://m.joncourson.com/teachings/radioprogramsplay.asp?airdate=122112

[47] David Stewart, *Healing Oils of the Bible*, pgs. 135-136

[48] James Maloney, *Ladies of Gold*, pgs. 15-16

[49] For more information on the Jehu Anointing, contact Dr. Patricia Venegas from Without Spot or Wrinkle Ministry www.wosow.org

[50] I heard Graham Cooke call nonbelievers "pre-Christians" and I liked it. www.grahamcooke.com

[51] Jeremy Camp's song, "I'm Alive" from his album *Speaking Louder Than Before*.

[52] Ayaan Hirsi Ali, "The War on Christians" *Newsweek*, 2/13/12

[53] Cindy Powell's book, *The Key to His Heart*

[54] Beth Moore is an amazing Bible study teacher; she has several entertaining and educational materials. She has said "There ain't no high like the Most High!" a few times on her DVDs. Her website is: www.lproof.org

[55] Dr. Richard Booker, *The Lamb and the Seven-Sealed Scrolls*, pgs. 57-58

[56] Martha Lawley's bible study book, *Attending the Bride of Christ*, was an amazing study I did with my friends.

[57] Casting Crowns' "Praise You in This Storm" from the album *Lifesong*

[58] The only time I heard Damon speak was on TBN, and I agreed with all of his teaching. I hope to hear more from him, you can too at: www.damonthompsonministries.net

[59] From Matthew West's album, *The Story of Your Life*

[60] Pastor Henry Wright's book, *A More Excellent Way to Be in Health*, has an extreme amount of valuable info in it relating Bible verses to specific diseases. He discusses how repentance along with retraining your mind to be obedient to God's Word helps prevent and solve various issues. He holds free seminars throughout the year (www.beinhealth.com). Doctor Caroline

Leaf explains in her book *Who Switched off my Brain* how our body is negatively affected when we think unhealthy, toxic thoughts. I met and went to Dr. Aiko Hormann's seminars; she is a very educated woman who shares a wealth of knowledge about the connection between the mind, heart, and gut. She was the first person I heard talk about God administering creative miracles. www.aikohormann.org

[61] This information was gained from the book, *Healing Oils of the Bible* by David Stewart. As a distributer for Young Living Essential Oils, I also must add that there is much information to be gained on that website as well (www.youngliving.com) Feel free to contact me about purchasing oils or becoming a distributer to get a discount.

[62] Psalm 45:7-8 suggests that oils which promoted gladness could be myrrh, aloes (sandalwood), and cassia. There is also a blend of oils sold by Young Living Essential Oils that has uplifting aromatic qualities and is named Joy.

[63] Martha Lawley's study book *Attending the Bride of Christ*

[64] "Strong Tower" by Kutless from the album *Strong Tower*

[65] You can view some Bethel Church services here: www.ibethel.tv/home

[66] Glenn Clark's book, *The Man Who Talks with the Flowers*

[67] This was found in the glossary section of the One New Man Bible under the word Anokhi. Another good reference is Ann Spangler's book, *Praying the Names of God*.

[68] Phil Wickham's song, "At Your Name (Yahweh, Yahweh)" from the album *Singalong 2*

[69] The Azusa Street Revival was the origin of the Pentecostal movement where William Seymour preached and the baptism of the Holy Spirit fell. Amazing miracles accompanied this move of God which stirred the whole city and surrounding areas. People came from all over to experience this revival.

[70] There is also another well-known sign God gave in this story. In the Old Testament, there were some prophecies that had a double fulfillment, one immediately for that time and one for the future. God may have given King Ahaz that kind of prophecy. It is found in Isaiah 7:14, "Therefore the Lord Himself will give you a sign; Behold, a virgin shall conceive, and bear a Son, and shall call His name Immanuel" (KJV). We know this is a prophecy about our Messiah, Jesus, but this is also a prophecy that may have been fulfilled in King Ahaz's day. One explanation is given by David Pawson where he states he is giving his "best educated guess" on this verse. He explains the Hebrew word for virgin used here is *almah*, which means virgin or woman of marriageable age. He goes on to say that usually in those days the man would name the son, but this verse says "she" would name him. Many kings had concubines and they, apparently, were the only women who were known to name their sons. David Pawson goes on to say that this could mean this woman may have been a concubine. This is how Ahaz would have had

proof that God was the one who made Damascus and Samaria come to ruin although he refused to ask for a sign. There is no Bible verse confirming that this statement happened in Ahaz's day, but since we know God fulfills His Word (Is 46:11 KJV), I think it did! By 722 B.C., both of those capital cities had become rubble, and I would venture a guess there was a little baby boy named Immanuel around at the time. This information came from David Pawson's book, *Come With Me Through Isaiah*, Chapter 4

[71] Sunrise Church in Rialto, California www.sunrisechurch.org/rialto

[72] Michael W. Smith's song "I'll Stand" from the album *Stand*

[73] An amazing teaching on this can be heard by Pastor John Courson on 9/26/12 called "Ruth: Prophetic Addendum" http://m.joncourson.com/teachings/teachingsplay.asp?teaching=S7028

[74] I had just finished this particular devotion on 11/10/11, the day before I was to attend a prayer conference at the Rose Bowl in Pasadena, Calif. I remember the next morning meeting my friends and reading them this particular BUT GOD verse because I was so excited about it. Jesus' title as the Lion of Judah stood out to me. In the afternoon of 11/11/11, my husband and I noticed a painting that had been completed during a time of worship so full of brilliant colors and unlike any artistic creation we had ever seen before. It was a majestic lion. We were unable to buy it, but never forgot it. Now, years later, I realized the picture and the devotion both had the lion theme, and both were created at the same time. The cover picture on this book is one of many lion paintings created by the same artist that drew that lion at the conference, Janet Hyun. Finding her was a miracle and having her painting on my book is a true answer to prayer.

[75] Zoe Girl's song, "Even If" from the album *Life* is a great addition to listen to if you have time.

[76] This was resourced from the book, *Restoration of the Tabernacle of David, Preparing the way for the King of Glory*, sold here: www.jhopfan.org

[77] I went to a conference held at Kansas City International House of Prayer (www.IHOPKC.org), and this info is resourced from Mike Bickle's notes on *The Battle for Jerusalem* from www.mikebickle.org/resources/resource/3063?return_url=http%3A%2F%2Fmikebickle.org%2Fresources%2Fsearch%2F%3Fsearch_terms%3DThe%2BBattle%2Bfor%2BJerusalem%2B%2B%26x%3D20%26y%3D24

[78] David Crowder Band's song, "No One Like You" from the album *Illuminate*

[79] evil spirits/demons have existed longer than we have, therefore, they existed in the past and know or took part in past events

[80] "Secretary Clinton Delivers Powerful Religion Speech After Middle East Embassy Attacks" by Dana Hughes on September 13, 2012 resourced from this site: http://abcnews.go.com/blogs/politics/2012/09/secretary-clinton-delivers-powerful-religion-speech-after-middle-east-embassy-attacks/

[81] David Barton of Wall Builders Ministry spoke at my church 7/14/13—what a wealth of interesting information! His website is www.wallbuilders.com

[82] I grew up watching *Growing Pains*, I loved Kirk Cameron and am so happy he is a Christian! You can find his movie at the site: http://kirkcameron.com/monumental

[83] I thought it was interesting to note that Jeremiah 25:1 and Daniel 1:1-2 both refer to the same king, King Jehoiakim of Judah, so you know it is the same timeframe.

[84] Lance Wallnau posted a great teaching on this on his Facebook page on July 28, 2013

[85] Chris Tomlin's song, "My Deliverer" from his album *Hello Love*.

[86] Sean Smith's video, "I am your sign" was done for a conference in 2012 and told interesting information about Jonah, you can access it here www.vimeo.com/31638679 along with Sean's information at: www.seansmithministries.com

[87] As taught by Tony Robinson on Hebraic Roots Network "Messianic Psalms, part 7" http://www.ondemand.hebraicrootstelevision.com

[88] *Scientists stunned as grey whale sighted off Israel* by AFP on 5/13/10 www.ynetnews.com/articles/0,7340,L-3888813,00.html

[89] For more in-depth study, you could research this symbolism. In John 15:5, Jesus says He is the vine and we are the branches. Since this verse uses the word "vine" as the object Jonah was mad about, the imagery points to a deeper issue. Remember, the problem was that Jonah was still mad at God for His decision to save the city, not just the plant dying.

[90] Damon Thompson was a guest on Trinity Broadcast Network's show "PTL," which aired on 1/24/12.

[91] A good book explaining this is by Mitch Glaser, *Isaiah 53 Explained*

[92] Reinhard Bonnke's ministry is Christ for all Nations (www.cfan.org)

[93] Jack Hayford's NKJV *New Spirit Filled Life Bible* is an excellent resource with good commentary.

[94] Alistair Begg is an amazing Bible teacher; his ministry is Truth For Life. He gave a sermon on 11/26/12 called, "A Day in the Life of Jesus" Part One A and B, message #2677 It is an example of a non-watered down message. You can access it from his website www.truthforlife.org/broadcasts/2012/11/26/a-day-in-the-life-of-jesus-part-one-a/

[95] Chuck Pierce's book, *A Time to Advance*, is very informative about the revelation of God's calendar and the tribes of Israel. I found this particular reference on pgs. 86-87

[96] Conclusion: Please make sure to listen to this song. Every line is a perfect description of our Bridegroom in Chris Tomlin's song, "This Is Our God" from his album *The Noise We Make*.

Bibliography

Abundant Living Family Church. N.p., n.d. Web. <http://www. abundantfamily.org/>.

AFP. "Scientists Stunned as Grey Whale Sighted off Israel." *Health and Science.* YNETNews, 13 May 2010. Web. 05 Nov. 2011.

Ali, Ayaan H. "Christophobia." *Newsweek* (2012): 28-35. Print.

Barton, David. *WallBuilders | Presenting America's Forgotten History and Heroes, with an Emphasis on Our Moral, Religious, and Constitutional Heritage.* N.p., n.d. Web. 14 July 2013. <http:// www.wallbuilders.com/>.

Begg, Alistair. "A Day in the Life of Jesus, Part One, A." *Truth For Life.* N.p., n.d. Web. 26 Nov. 2012. <http://www.truthforlife.org/ broadcasts/2012/11/26/a-day-in-the-life-of-jesus-part-one-a/>.

BibleGateway.com: A Searchable Online Bible in over 100 Versions and 50 Languages. N.p., n.d. Web. 2008.

Bickle, Mike. "The Battle for Jerusalem." *Http://mikebickle. org/resources/.* Www.ihopkc.org, n.d. Web. 2011. <http://mikebickle.org/resources/resource/3063?return_ url=http%3A%2F%2Fmikebickle.org%2Fresources%2Fsearch %2F%3Fsearch_terms%3DThe%2BBattle%2Bfor%2BJerusale m%2B%2B%26x%3D20%26y%3D24>.

Booker, Richard. *The Lamb and the Seven-Sealed Scroll.* Shippensburg, PA: Destiny Image, 2012. Print. Pages 57-58, 94, and 148-164

Clark, Glenn. *The Man Who Talks with the Flowers; the Intimate Life Story of Dr. George Washington Carver.* Saint Paul, MN: Macalester Park Pub., 1939. Print.

Courson, Jon. "Jon Courson Radio Programs-Revelation 11 Part 1." *Jon Courson Radio Programs.* N.p., n.d. Web. 21 Dec. 2012. <http://m.joncourson.com/teachings/radioprogramsplay. asp?airdate=122112>.

Courson, Jon. "Searchlight with Jon Courson—Ruth: Prophetic Addendum." *Searchlight with Jon Courson—Teachings.* N.p., n.d. Web. 26 Sept. 2012. <http://m.joncourson.com/teachings/teachingsplay.asp?teaching=S7028>.

Glaser, Mitch. *Isaiah 53 Explained.* [New York]: Chosen People Productions, 2010. Print.

Gold, Dore. *The Rise of Nuclear Iran: How Tehran Defies the West.* Washington, D.C.: Regnery Pub., 2009. Print.

Heidler, Robert. "Rosh Chodesh—The Blessing of Firstfruits." *A Time To Advance.* By Chuck Pierce. Denton, TX: Glory of Zion International, 2011. 86-87. Print.

Hess, Tom. "Restoration of the Tabernacle of David." *Restoration of the Tabernacle of David.* Jerusalem, Israel: Progressive Vision, 2005. 11. Print.

Hughes, Dana. "Secretary Clinton Delivers Powerful Religion Speech After Middle East Embassy Attacks." *ABC News.* ABC News Network, n.d. Web. 13 Sept. 2012. <http://abcnews.go.com/blogs/politics/2012/09/secretary-clinton-delivers-powerful-religion-speech-after-middle-east-embassy-attacks/>.

I Am Your Sign. By Sean Smith. Perf. Sean Smith. N.p., 2012. Web. <http://vimeo.com/31638679>.

""Jeff Allen Is One of the Funniest, Most Inspirational, Corporate Comedians Working Today"" *Corporate Comedian Jeff Allen.* N.p., n.d. Web. 12 June 2013. <http://www.JeffAllenComedy.com/>.

Johnson, Bill, and Kris Vallotton. *Bethel Church.* N.p., n.d. Web. 2012. <http://www.ibethel.org/>.

Kasnett, Israel. "A View from Israel: Deterrence Is Irrelevant." *The Jerusalem Post.* The Jerusalem Post, 11 Nov. 2011. Web. 12 June 2012. <http://www.jpost.com/LandedPages/PrintArticle.aspx?id=244996>.

"Ken Raggio: Will The Real Antichrist Please Stand?" *Ken Raggio: Will The Real Antichrist Please Stand?* N.p., n.d. Web. 12 June 2013. <http://kenraggio.com/KRPN-AntichristStand.htm>.

Kim Clement. N.p., n.d. Web. 20 Nov. 2012. <www.kimclement.tv>.

Klein, John, Adam Spears, and MIchael Christopher. *The Book of Revelation Through Hebrew Eyes.* Vol. 2. Bend, OR: Covenant Research Institute, 2009. Print. Lost in Translation. Chapters 1-3

Lawley, Martha. *Attending the Bride of Christ: Preparing for His Return*. Nashville, TN: LifeWay, 2005. Print.

Leaf, Caroline. *Who Switched off My Brain?: Controlling Toxic Thoughts and Emotions*. [S.l.]: Inprov, 2009. Print.

Malick, David. "An Introduction to the Book of Habakkuk." *Bible. org—Worlds Largest Bible Study Site | NET Bible, Bible Studies, Bible, Free,*. N.p., n.d. Web. 01 June 2013. <http://bible.org/article/introduction-book-habakkuk>.

Maloney, James. "Who Were The Golden Candlestick." *Ladies of Gold. the Remarkable Ministry of the Golden Candlestick*. Bloomington, IN: WestBow, 2011. 15+. Print.

Michael, Boaz, comp. *HaYesod*. Marshfield, MO: First Fruits of Zion, 2010. Print.

Moore, Beth. "Living Proof Ministries." *Living Proof Ministries*. N.p., n.d. Web. 2008. <http://www.lproof.org/>.

Morford, William J. *The One New Man Bible: Revealing Jewish Roots and Power*. Travelers Rest, US: True Potential, 2011. Print.

Pawson, David. *Come with Me through Isaiah*. N.p.: Terra Nova Publications, 2010. Print.

Powell, Cindy. *The Key to His Heart*. Redlands, CA: Simple Faith, 2012. Print.

Restoration of Torah Ministries. N.p., n.d. Web. 12 Nov. 2010. <http://www.restorationoftorah.org/>.

Richardson, Joel. *The Islamic Antichrist: The Shocking Truth about the Real Nature of the Beast*. Los Angeles, CA: WND, 2009. Print.

"Sean Smith Ministries." *Sean Smith Ministries*. N.p., n.d. Web. 12 June 2013. <http://www.seansmithministries.com/>.

Seiss, Joseph A. "Primeval Man." *The Gospel in the Stars*. Grand Rapids, MI: Kregel Publications, 1972. 149. Print.

Spangler, Ann. *PRAYING THE NAMES OF GOD*. N.p.: Thorndike, 2005. Print.

Stewart, David. *Healing Oils of the Bible*. Marble Hill, MO: Care Publications, 2012. Print.

Stone, Perry.*—Voice of Evangelism*. N.p., n.d. Web. 2012. <http://www.voe.org/>.

Strong, James. *The New Strong's Exhaustive Concordance of the Bible*. Nashville, Tn.: Thomas Nelson, 1990. Print.

Sunrise Church. N.p., n.d. Web. <http://www.sunrisechurch.org/rialto>.

"The Tony Robinson Show | HRN On-Demand." *Hebrew Roots Network*. N.p., n.d. Web. 4 July 2012. <http://ondemand. hebraicrootstelevision.com/index.php/browse/teachings/tony-robinson>.

Tucker, Kent. *In The Red Zone*. Rancho Cucamonga: Share Your Faith Ministries, 2013. Print.

Water of Life Community Church. N.p., n.d. Web. <http://www. wateroflifecc.org/>.

Welcome | Brilliant Perspectives. N.p., n.d. Web. 12 June 2013. <http://grahamcooke.com/>.

Welcome to Aiko Hormann Ministries! N.p., n.d. Web. <http:// aikohormann.org/>.

Without Spot or Wrinkle Ministries International—Welcome. N.p., n.d. Web. 02 Oct. 2011. <http://www.wosow.org/>.

Wright, Henry, and Henry Wright. *A More Excellent Way to Be in Health*. New Kensington, PA: Whitaker House, 2009. Print.

Zechariah. New Spirit Filled Life Bible. Nashville, TN: Thomas Nelson Bibles, 2002. Print.